Regional Competitiveness and Smart Specialization in Europe

NEW HORIZONS IN REGIONAL SCIENCE

Series Editor: Philip McCann, *Professor of Economic Geography, University of Groningen, the Netherlands and Professor of Economics, University of Waikato, New Zealand*

Regional science analyses important issues surrounding the growth and development of urban and regional systems and is emerging as a major social science discipline. This series provides an invaluable forum for the publication of high quality scholarly work on urban and regional studies, industrial location economics, transport systems, economic geography and networks.

New Horizons in Regional Science aims to publish the best work by economists, geographers, urban and regional planners and other researchers from throughout the world. It is intended to serve a wide readership including academics, students and policymakers.

Titles in the series include:

Media Clusters
Spatial Agglomeration and Content Capabilities
Edited by Charlie Karlsson and Robert G. Picard

Spatial Scenarios in a Global Perspective
Europe and the Latin Arc Countries
Edited by Roberto Camagni and Roberta Capello

Creative Knowledge Cities
Myths, Visions and Realities
Edited by Marina van Geenhuizen and Peter Nijkamp

Societies in Motion
Innovation, Migration and Regional Transformation
Edited by Amnon Frenkel, Peter Nijkamp and Philip McCann

Innovation, Global Change and Territorial Resilience
Edited by Philip Cooke, Mario Davide Parrilli and José Luis Curbelo

The Regional Economics of Knowledge and Talent
Local Advantage in a Global Context
Edited by Charlie Karlsson, Börje Johansson and Roger R. Stough

Entrepreneurship, Social Capital and Governance
Directions for the Sustainable Development and Competitiveness of Regions
Edited by Charlie Karlsson, Börje Johansson and Roger R. Stough

The Geography of the Internet
Cities, Regions and Internet Infrastructure in Europe
Emmanouil Tranos

Social Capital and Rural Development in the Knowledge Society
Edited by Hans Westlund and Kiyoshi Kobayashi

Regional Competitiveness and Smart Specialization in Europe
Place-based Development in International Economic Networks
Mark Thissen, Frank van Oort, Dario Diodato and Arjan Ruijs

Regional Competitiveness and Smart Specialization in Europe

Place-based Development in International Economic Networks

Mark Thissen

PBL Netherlands Environmental Assessment Agency, The Netherlands

Frank van Oort

Utrecht University, The Netherlands

Dario Diodato

PBL Netherlands Environmental Assessment Agency and Utrecht University, The Netherlands

Arjan Ruijs

PBL Netherlands Environmental Assessment Agency, The Netherlands

With a contribution by Philip McCann and Raquel Ortega-Argilés

NEW HORIZONS IN REGIONAL SCIENCE

Edward Elgar

Cheltenham, UK • Northampton, MA, USA

Published by
Edward Elgar Publishing Limited
The Lypiatts
15 Lansdown Road
Cheltenham
Glos GL50 2JA
UK

Edward Elgar Publishing, Inc.
William Pratt House
9 Dewey Court
Northampton
Massachusetts 01060
USA

A catalogue record for this book
is available from the British Library

Library of Congress Control Number: 2013942240

This book is available electronically in the ElgarOnline.com
Economics Subject Collection, E-ISBN 978 1 78254 516 3

ISBN 978 1 78254 515 6

Typeset by Servis Filmsetting Ltd, Stockport, Cheshire
Printed and bound in Great Britain by T.J. International Ltd, Padstow

Contents

Acknowledgements

This book is based on more than four years of research at the PBL Netherlands Environmental Assessment Agency. We are grateful for the help we received from a large number of individuals in writing this book. Special thanks are due to Stephaan DeClerck for his assistance in programming, and Sofie de Groot, Pieter Wijngaarden and Martijn van den Berge for their work on data collection. We thank Martijn Burger, Guillaume Burghouwt, Jan Franke, Henri de Groot, Jan Oosterhaven, Otto Raspe, Bas Turpijn, Wouter Vermeulen, Paul Veenendaal, Eugene Verkade and Anet Weterings and many colleagues at PBL Netherlands Environmental Assessment Agency and JRC-IPTS for critical and useful comments. Mark Thissen has worked on this book during a part of his stay as a guest researcher at the JRC-IPTS in Seville. However, the views expressed in this book do not necessarily reflect the position of the European Commission. Finally we thank Philip McCann and Raquel Ortega-Argilés for complementing this book with their excellent chapter on smart specialization.

1. Introduction

Regions differ from each other economically. They compete in different products and geographical spaces, they exhibit different strengths and weaknesses, and they provide different possibilities for growth and development. What fosters growth in one region, hampers it in another. Regional economic development policy should therefore be based on a 'one-size-fits-one' approach and is not particularly helped by a 'one-size-fits-all' strategy propagated by economists in favour of a place-neutral strategy. Such place-based policies should be tailored to the specific regional context for firms and people to accomplish economic growth and higher welfare. This book confirms that the often presumed contradiction of place-based and place-neutral development strategies (see, for example, Barca et al., 2012) should be nuanced in a European context: place-based smart specialization and regional development can reinforce both place-neutral as well as place-specific economic processes. The simultaneous importance of location and network relations in regional economic development is emphasized by the wealth of heterogeneity in the specific trade relations of every region, the resulting region-specific geographical markets on which firms from different regions compete, and the various dynamic competitive relations that are analysed in this book.

In this book a novel methodology is introduced and used to develop smart specialization strategies that are central in the place-based policy initiatives of the new European cohesion policy. The approach provides a solid framework for identifying the key priorities and strengths on which policy actions are able to build, as well as the weaknesses, bottlenecks or missing links which need to be rectified, in the very real context of global competition. As such, the approach gives a foundation for building a place-based smart specialization policy-prioritization logic that integrates the regional profiling element of smart specialization with the implementation of a regional development strategy where policy is targeted at specific actions and interventions that are amenable to measurement, monitoring and evaluation.

In line with earlier theoretical contributions on smart specialization and place-based development (for example, McCann and Ortega-Argilés, 2011), the analysis in this book shows empirically that crucial inputs in public–private partnership processes of discovery and learning ('differentiated knowledge base') on the part of both entrepreneurs and policy-makers regarding the most likely avenues for entrepreneurial opportunities, are subject to international network embeddedness ('connectedness'), locally unique competitive forces and local institutional circumstances. It clearly shows that a smart specialization strategy is not about becoming increasingly specialized, but is rather about deepening the linkages within the region and between regions ('relatedness') with the greater potential for long-lasting scale effects, while at the same time helping regions to diversify and link up in high-potential competitive networks. The pattern and distribution of the intended recipients of policy interventions emerge from an explicit policy-prioritization logic based around regions' assets, capabilities and weaknesses.

1.1 SCOPE, AIMS AND MAIN CONTRIBUTIONS OF THIS BOOK

Since the early 1990s, the concept of regional competitiveness has become part of a hegemonic discourse within public policy circles in developed countries (Sheppard, 2000; Bristow, 2005). The concept has been enthusiastically adopted as a policy goal by the European Commission and by national governments across Europe. Most policy documents present the concept as a clear beneficial attribute of a local or regional economy (Martin, 2005). Competitiveness is especially portrayed as inducing economic growth, regional export orientations, sources of increasing returns and network and hub-positions of regions in a globalizing world (Porter, 2000; Martin, 2005). Strong economic growth and associated welfare gains are expected if a region outperforms its competitors on relevant conditions. The strategic imperative is to take the required steps to attract and retain innovative firms, skilled labour and knowledge workers and mobile investment, with particular emphasis being placed on the relevant conditions in the microeconomic environment (including offering high-end working and living environments) within which productive firms can prosper.

In the geographical and political discourses on competitiveness, the concept has mostly progressed in measurable and benchmark directions. The emergence of regional competitiveness as a discrete and important policy goal has spawned the development of indicators by which policy-makers and practitioners can measure, analyse and compare competitive performance, and find out who is 'winning'. Benchmarking exercises have become increasingly popular within the sphere of regional economic policy-making in recent years (Huggins, 2010; Huggins and Izushi, 2012).

The international literature has predominantly been very critical about the limited ability of regional competitiveness circumstances to be copied elsewhere, as a kind of 'one-size-fits-all' policy (Bristow, 2005).

The trouble with many (if not all) performance rankings is that they tend to combine disparate industries and indicators into aggregates that obscure important differences (Cortright and Mayer, 2004). They also compare regions that may initially not be competing with each other on the same markets. The discussion of territorial competitiveness awaits an applied analytical framework that moves beyond the critical and problematizing stand that (actually too easily) is applied in the literature recently (Kitson et al., 2004). An applied analytic framework is needed that takes into account economically valued network relations between places of (mobile) production factors and traded goods. This book provides such a framework. In this publication we argue that for the concept to be valued correctly, regional competitiveness should not be solely identified by structural asset characteristics of cities and regions (summarized in benchmarks or listings), but additionally and alternatively by a theoretically informed analytical framework that uses actual networks of competing and economically valued relations between regions. Conceptually, we therefore introduce *revealed competition* as an indicator for measuring interregional competitiveness, determining which region competes with whom, on what and where. On *individual* markets, benchmarks of the *relevant* competitors can be determined, providing more useful information on competitive advantageous circumstances for every region and sector. We empirically underpin our analytical framework by using a newly created dataset on trade relations between European regions in goods and services (fully introduced in the Appendix).

Our scale of analysis is European, and the book's main discussion is on the possible policy trajectories on international regional competitiveness that was propagated since the introduction of the Lisbon Agenda in 2000, and accumulated into the current (smart, sustainable and inclusive) growth objectives of the Europe 2020 policy programme that are also central in the envisioned cohesion policy reform after 2013. The European Commission (2004, p. viii) envisions a common future for competitiveness and cohesion policies, stating that 'strengthening regional competitiveness throughout the Union and helping people fulfil their capabilities will boost the growth potential of the EU economy as a whole to the common benefit of all'. Currently, place-based development policies are proposed for future cohesion policy (Barca, 2009), but actually little is known about the relevant competitive circumstances of specialized industries in European regions. This book helps to identify the relevant circumstances and competitors for European NUTS-2 regions. It also fills a gap in identifying the place-specific local and network circumstances necessary for identifying relevant development strategies in Europe. The approach proposed in this book aims to contribute to place-based development strategies (Barca, 2009) that have recently been extended into smart specialization concepts in European regional development. This policy initiative of the European Union tries to build on a systems way of thinking about innovation and growth, emphasizing the complexity of regional systems and economic networks (McCann and Ortega-Argilés, 2011). Our revealed competition indicator introduced in Chapter 5 provides information to develop a place-based sophisticated benchmark tool that underpins smart specialization strategies for European regions.

Compared to other monographs, this book unites a novel methodology that is not difficult to understand, a thorough conceptual discussion of regional competitiveness, and an up-to-date discussion on regional development policies in Europe in the past and the near future. The book aims to contribute to the current academic discussion on regional competitiveness and the policy debate on smart specialization, place-based development and cohesion policy in the European Union. It introduces a new dataset on interregional trade in Europe and gives tools and examples to address the local discussions on smart specialization strategies proposed by the European Commission. This chapter further introduces the various analytical and conceptual steps taken in our research that will be dealt with in the respective chapters. We will first introduce the types of regions we distinguish in our study. Our study regions are chosen to represent a complete cross-section of European regions, distinguished by size, development stage and sectoral specialization. In the subsequent sections we follow the outline of the book and introduce an up-to-date discussion on place-based development and smart specialization in European regions, the theoretical backgrounds of the regional competitiveness debate, the current European regional economic structure and development paths, measured revealed competition, dynamics in revealed competition, and smart specialization-based revealed competition benchmarking.

1.2 A REPRESENTATIVE CROSS-SECTION OF EUROPEAN REGIONS

In this book we focus on representative region and sector combinations to illustrate the applicability of our data and conceptualization for potential place-based development and smart specialization strategies. These region–sector combinations are presented in Table 1.1. The regions are chosen with respect to their location in Europe, their size, and their sector

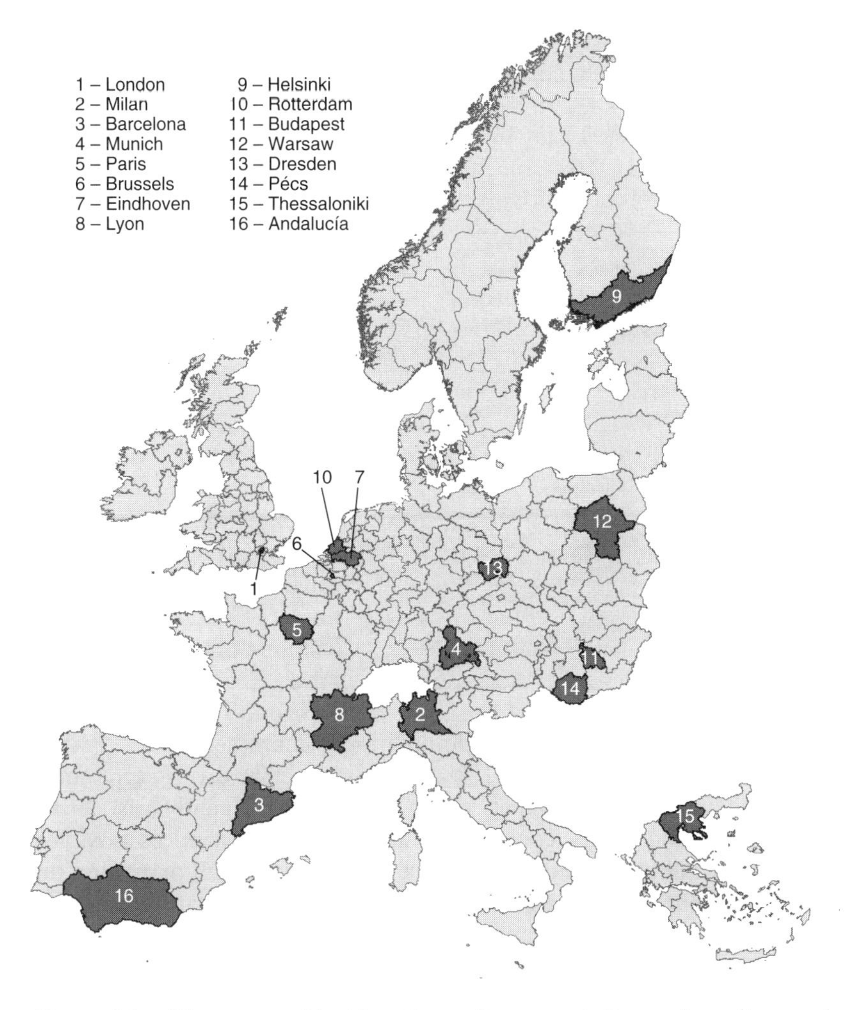

Figure 1.1 The geographical locations of representative regions discussed in this book

orientation. Figure 1.1 shows that the geographical locations of the chosen regions cover the whole of Europe. The group of region–sector combinations presented in grey in Table 1.1 covers a complete scope of type of regions in Europe and is therefore representative of the European Union. We describe the regions using the name of their major city because we think that most readers are more familiar with the city names. In Table A.3 in the Appendix we give all official NUTS-2 region names and the associated NUTS-2 region code.

Table 1.1 Region–sector combinations analysed in this book

	Total production	Agriculture	Financial & business services	Manufacturing		
				Low-tech	Medium-tech	High-tech
London			■			
Milan	■				■	
Barcelona	■					
Munich						■
Paris	■		■			
Brussels			■			
Eindhoven					■	
Lyon						■
Helsinki						■
Rotterdam		■				
Budapest					■	
Warsaw	■		■			
Dresden	■			■		
Pécs		■		■		
Thessaloniki	■					
Andalucía		■				

We distinguish the large agglomerations (inner-) London, Milan, Barcelona, Munich and Paris. These regions are large diverse economies embedded within world city networks (Taylor, 2004; Ni and Kresl, 2010). We therefore analyse the complex of all industries and services in Milan, Barcelona and Paris. London and Paris are both dominant players on the market for financial and business services and are therefore discussed from this perspective, while we discuss the medium technological industries in the region of Milan, and the high technological production in the region of Munich. The implication of the place-based development strategy discussion is that European medium-sized city-regions have not declined in importance compared to larger urban ones, which has been indicated in monitoring publications by the OECD (2009b, 2011d, 2012a, 2012b), but there was until now little empirical support for this by explanations based in economic network studies (compare Bontje et al., 2011). We therefore study Brussels, Eindhoven, Lyon, Helsinki and Rotterdam–The Hague as examples of this group of medium-sized regions. Helsinki and Lyon are typical centres for high technological producers while Eindhoven hosts a large number of medium technological firms. In Brussels we focus on the financial and business services. The city of Rotterdam is mainly known for its harbour, but the NUTS-2 region of South-Holland in which it is embedded also hosts one of the largest horticulture sectors in Europe (Westland area). We therefore focus on the agricultural sector in the region of Rotterdam–The Hague.

The peripheral regions and (Eastern European) emerging market economies are often considered as problematic regions from an economic perspective, as they are characterized by relatively low levels of income. These regions do have economic potential and have higher growth rates (especially in productivity, and more so in capital cities) than the Western regions (Marrocu et al., 2012; Dogaru et al., 2011). We have selected Budapest and Warsaw as typical large agglomerations in these emerging markets with specializations in the medium technological industry and the financial and business services, respectively. Warsaw is also analysed from the perspective of a large and diverse economy. Dresden and Pécs are analysed as medium to small-sized emerging markets. We analyse the Pécs economy with respect to agriculture and low-technological industries, while we focus on the total economy and the low-technological industries in Dresden. Thessaloniki and Andalucía are both large and typically peripheral regions. The total complex of production is central in our discussion of Thessaloniki's economy. Andalucía is analysed especially with respect to the large agricultural sector in this region.

1.3 PLACE-BASED DEVELOPMENT STRATEGIES AND SMART SPECIALIZATION OF EUROPEAN REGIONS

In Chapter 2, European spatial development trajectories are placed in the current policy discussion of smart specialization and place-based development. Regional competitiveness is introduced as an essential element in smart specialization policies of regional development in a networked competitive setting and not a purely local-assets setting. The origins of the smart specialization concept are thoroughly discussed to clarify the different elements of place-based smart specialization policies. Place-based smart specialization strategies integrate regional profiling with the implementation of a regional development smart specialization strategy where policy is targeted at the key priorities and strengths on which policy actions are able to build, as well as the weaknesses, bottlenecks or missing links which need to be rectified, in a network of economic relations. Any specific policy action and intervention should also be amenable to measurement, monitoring and evaluation, taking the specific regional network position into account.

The approach of network connectedness proposed in this book intends to contribute to precisely this recent policy discussion on place-based or place-neutral development strategies in the European Union. This debate is highlighted in the context of a series of recent major policy reports: the place-neutral policies in the 2009 World Bank report (World Bank, 2009) and the European place-based development strategies in Barca (2009) and Barca et al. (2012). Place-neutral strategies rely on the agglomerative forces of the largest cities and metropolitan regions to attract talent, trade and growth potential. Based on current economic geographical theories of innovation and density of skills and human capital in cities and globalization, spatially blind approaches argue that intervention, regardless of the context, is the best way to resolve the old dilemma of whether development should be about 'places' or about 'people' (Barca et al., 2012, p. 140). It is argued that agglomeration in combination with encouraging people's mobility not only allows individuals to live where they expect to be better off but also increases individual incomes, productivity, knowledge and aggregate growth (World Bank, 2009). Consequently, development intervention should be space-neutral, and factors should be encouraged to move (people and production) to where they are most productive. In reality, this is equivalent to a movement of people and capital to the large agglomerations in Europe. Following this line of reasoning the short-term underutilization of the factors of production are push factors stimulating movement towards booming economic centres of activity. However, as was argued in Barca (2009), short-term underutilization of factors of production also implies the costs of 'missed' production. These short-term costs can hardly be ignored or labelled 'short term' in the situation of the 2010s where European country unemployment levels have risen to more than 20 per cent of the labour force, and regional unemployment levels are even higher. Clearly, a regional hands-off policy may not be appropriate in these extreme cases.

Place-based development strategists on the other hand claim that the polycentric nature of a set of smaller and medium-sized city-regions in Europe, each with their own peculiar characteristics and specializing in the activities to which they are best suited, creates fruitful urban variety, which enhances optimal economic development. The interactions between institutions and geography are critical for development, and many of the clues for development policy lie in these interactions. To understand the likely impacts of a policy, the interactions between institutions and geography, therefore requires explicit consideration of the specifics of the local and wider regional economic context (Barca et al., 2012, p. 140). Following up on this debate, the discussion of place-based development strategies in the European Union has recently been extended into smart specialization concepts that built on a systems way of thinking about innovation, entrepreneurship and growth (Foray et al., 2012). It emphasizes issues of economic potential, allowing for the complexity of regional systems and economic networks (McCann and Ortega-Argilés, 2011). A smart specialization strategy identifies regional factors and endowments related to location factors and clusters (Martin, 2005), but should simultaneously assess a region's position in international value chains and networks of trade, knowledge and foreign direct investment (FDI) that co-determine regional potentials (McCann and Ortega-Argilés, 2011). Smart policy-making then should build explicitly on insights from local and network data to make the most appropriate choices given the challenges that a region faces. Although much smart specialization strategy documentation stresses the international network orientation of regions, there is little to no international comparable data available for economic networks between European regions. Our revealed competition indicator introduced in this book provides the opportunity to develop a place-based sophisticated benchmark tool that underpins smart specialization strategies for European regions.

The differences between place-neutral and place-based policies are less pronounced than it seems. In place-neutral development strategies, insights in interregional economic networks are equally valuable as for place-based development strategies. Moreover, place-based policies are often place-neutral policies targeted at locations where economic problems exist. Place-based policies try to improve the capabilities of firms and people in locations characterized by economic problems. They involve them in the economic process and, if necessary, stimulate them to move to regions where they can reach their full economic potential. Place-based policies also imply facilitating firms and people in the economically most successful regions to build on their success. The *relation* of regional economic endowments with economic network positions is central in place-based policies. This gives the possibility to include those regional policies that may prove economically successful for a region, and especially preclude those policies that support only regional vested interests and have no regional economic potential. Proper place-based policies therefore reinforce place-neutral processes and prevent precisely those policies that proponents of place-neutral policies are so vehemently against.

1.4 THEORETICAL FRAMEWORKS ON REGIONAL COMPETITIVENESS AND BENCHMARK STUDIES

In Chapter 3 the debate on competitiveness and regional development is introduced, including a discussion on its conceptual usefulness and definitions. The competitive position of regions and different conditions generally used in benchmarks studies related to regional economic development are thoroughly discussed from a regional economic theoretical perspective. The practice of regional and urban benchmarking is questioned, and the relation between regional comparative advantage (leading to specialization) and revealed competitive advantage (based on market overlap) is introduced and discussed.

Martin (2005), in an eclectic approach, distinguishes six macroeconomic theoretical approaches that contribute to the competitiveness debate (see Figure 1.2): classical theory; neoclassical theory; Keynesian economic theory; development economics; new (endogenous) growth theory; and new trade theory. Each of these major schools of economic theory carries implications – explicit or implicit – for the notion of 'competitiveness' as it relates to nations and in some cases firms, and which therefore are of direct relevance to any discussion of 'regional competitiveness'. In addition to macroeconomic perspectives, Martin (2005) argues that the understanding of regional competitiveness also requires some insights in some complementary perspectives that can be derived from microeconomy as well as sociology. Of the many theories and concepts that exist, four schools are discussed with a clear relevance for a better understanding of regional competitiveness (Figure 1.2): urban growth theory, 'new' institutional economics, business strategy economics and Schumpeterian or evolutionary economics. Although all of these theories have relevance to the understanding of competitiveness, they often lack a territorial dimension that is so crucial for understanding regional competitiveness (Martin, 2005, p. 13).

The obvious source for such theories is the field of economic geography, which may be taken to include three streams of literature: economic geography proper; regional economics; and the so-called 'new economic geography' within economics. Yet, although economic geographers have long been concerned with regional development and with the factors that make for regional economic success, traditionally they have not cast their analyses explicitly in terms of regional 'competitiveness' or 'competitive advantage', or even 'productivity'. Therefore, the field of economic geography has drawn heavily on neighbouring disciplines (see Figure 1.2). In discussing regional competitiveness, Martin (2005) distinguishes three basic conceptions of regional competitiveness that cut through all theoretical disciplines. The first sees regions as sites of export specialization. This notion is closely related to factor endowment and export-based economics. The second view understands regions as a source of increasing returns. This notion belongs to the heart of economic geography proper, but has also been adopted by the 'new economic geography'. The

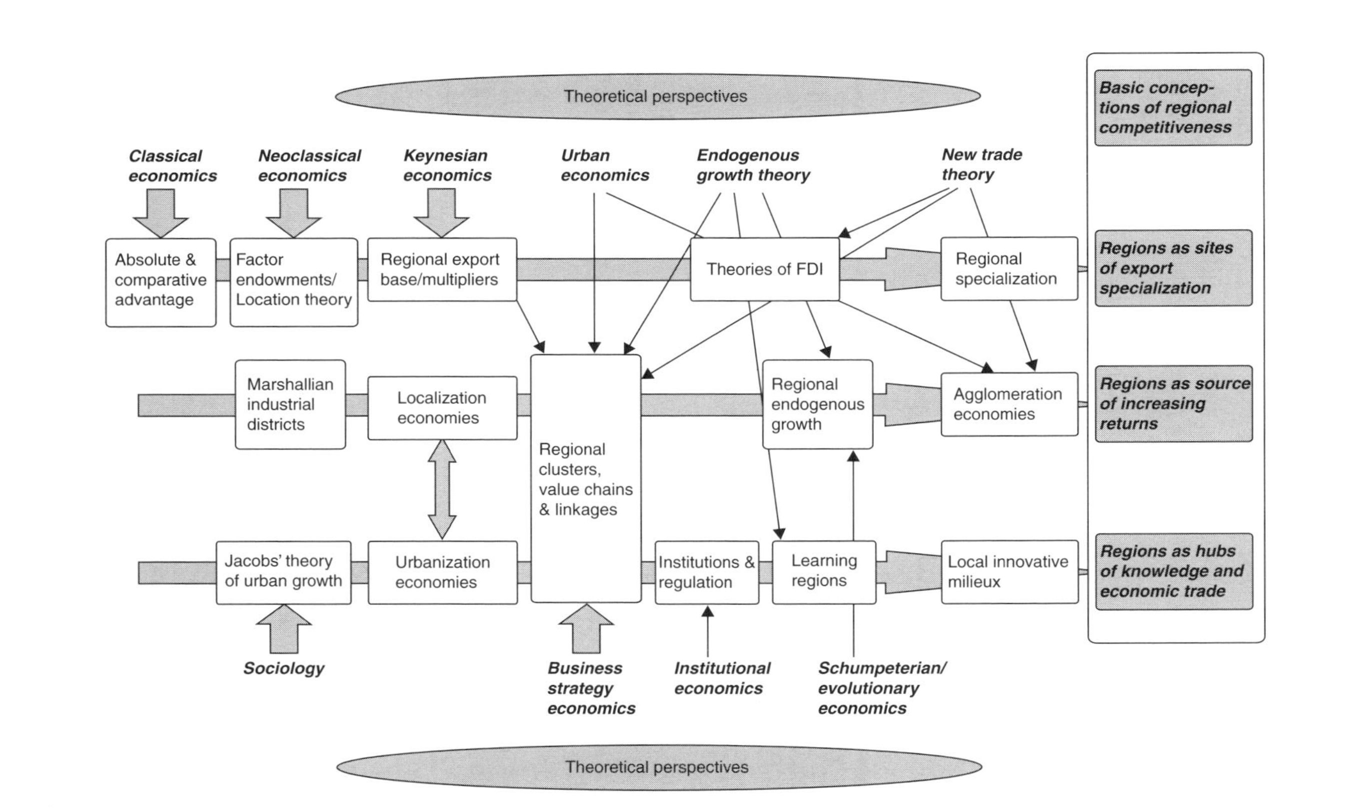

Source: Adapted from Martin (2005), p. 14.

Figure 1.2 Conceptions of regional competitiveness in theoretical disciplines

third view regards regions as hubs of knowledge and economic trade. This notion extends the above concept both to 'softer' factors, including sociological and institutional elements (Boschma, 2005), and has also been labelled 'new industrial geography', but also to harder factors related to trade and FDI relations (Gardiner et al., 2004). Essential for all theoretical disciplines is the notion of who actually competes with whom, on what and where. Besides locational attributes, network attributes are needed for understanding this basic question, but until recently data limitations prohibited a thorough analysis of network dynamics in trade and knowledge. We conclude that our newly introduced approach (focused on international competitiveness of European regions) potentially contributes to many theoretical research fields, and also that simple benchmark studies that only compare locational attributes of regions and cities are generally inaccurate, opportunistic and only partially informed in nature.

1.5 SETTING THE STAGE: EUROPEAN REGIONAL DEVELOPMENT PATHS AND ECONOMIC STRUCTURE

There is a burgeoning body of literature on the possible additive influence of network proximities in relation to regional physical proximity, but until now these are predominantly focused on networks of knowledge relations (Basile et al., 2012; Moreno et al., 2005; Ponds et al., 2010; Varga et al., 2012; Vinciguerra et al., 2011). The relation between development paths and economic structure should be conceptualized on the regional level since trade relations are important networks for the identification of regional and interregional economic supply and demand opportunities, as well as knowledge related to this trade (pecuniary externalities; see Cresenzi and Rodriguez-Pose, 2012). The different types of regions in Table 1.1 are chosen because we expect that they have different development opportunities depending on their location and position in the network of trade in specific products, in combination with their locational geographic, economic and institutional strengths and weaknesses. Chapter 4 presents the economic structure and positions in interregional trade networks of European regions – important predetermined aspects that influence the course of economic development of regions considerably. An analysis of European sectoral specializations and clustering is provided. Specialization is measured on the regional level and the sectoral level (with the Theil indicator based on location quotients). This chapter provides detailed empirical insights in clusters that are defined in terms of sectors in relation to their regional suppliers (backward linkages describing subcontracting and intermediate deliveries). Openness is introduced as a new indicator that describes the quality of an industry's inputs network related to an optimal network derived from the Krugman–Venables–Fujita model on geographical economics (new economic geography). European regions are presented in a typology on the clustering and specialization dimensions, ranging from specialized to diversified economies on the one hand, and from autarkic to interregional open economies on the other.

We distinguish, based on these two dimensions, four different types of regional characterizations (revealed economic strategies) based on regional openness (network) and cluster orientations in combination with specialization versus diversification strategies:

1. Product specialization: a region specializes in a limited number of sectors obtaining intermediate products from suppliers in other regions.
2. Supply chain specialization: a region specializes in the complete supply chain of a limited number of sectors. Thus also the intermediate products used in the production come from the same region (industrial districts; Porter, 1990).
3. Self-sufficiency: a region follows a diversification strategy producing all sorts of goods and services, including the intermediate inputs required for the final product.
4. Trade dependent diversification: a region follows a diversification strategy producing all sorts of goods and services but obtains its inputs by importing intermediates from a vast array of different regions.

We find in Chapter 4 that preconditions and network orientations of regions are of crucial importance for their potential development path. In our conceptualization, the open network approach and the cluster approach fundamentally differ from each other. If in the former, agglomeration advantages are shared among a group of different regions; in the latter a region tries to capture and appropriate the agglomeration benefits by itself. We find that large and small regions in the core of Europe are generally characterized as diversified and open. Small regions appear to be more specialized than large regions in the core of Europe but they are far more diversified than peripheral regions. The size of the large regions allows them to engage in a diverse range of activities while the small regions may be able to 'borrow this size' from their neighbours. The central position of both types of regions fosters trade of inputs with many neighbouring regions and they can therefore be classified as 'trade dependent diversified'. Large regions in the periphery show relatively high rates of diversification and clustering. Internal mass is an important driver of diversification (Farole et al., 2009). A location outside the core, though, seems to be a crucial determinant of the self-sufficiency development path of some regions (Frenken and Hoekman, 2006). Small, peripheral regions on the other hand are typically supply chain specialized regions. They appear to make use of the full extent of localization economies, with specialization on a limited range of products and all relevant intermediate inputs (Gardiner et al., 2004).

In Chapter 4 we argue that place-based policies have much to gain from taking into account their location in Europe and their specific economic structure. Regions in the core of Europe may benefit from a thick network of interactions with their neighbours while this is barely possible for the peripheral regions. The awareness of the level of specialization/diversification and clustering/openness, together with the comparison with other similar regions, can be of help in the design of smart specialization and place-based regional policies. For instance for a small, peripheral region, it may prove convenient to focus its resources and policies to a limited number of sectors (specialization and cluster strategies). It will, however, be difficult to get a sufficient economic return to cluster-promoting investments if these sectors have a natural tendency to spread (for example construction, low-tech manufacturing, and many services) and there is little economic benefit of specialization or clusters. On the other hand, if a region has the right preconditions, investment in sectors that have a tendency to concentrate (high-tech manufacturing, tourism, financial and business services) may be repaid with the appropriation of localization economies. It is important to keep in mind that once a sector has already concentrated in some specific regions, it is very hard to move such an agglomeration elsewhere. This makes a focus on cluster or specialization policy more appropriate for these small regions.

1.6 REVEALED COMPETITION (2000)

A well designed specialization policy should take into account regional interactions and regional complementarities. In Chapter 5 therefore our measurement of revealed competition of European regions by market overlap is introduced. Competition is traditionally related to the contest between firms for consumer or inter-industry demand and a firm is considered to have a good competitive position if it has a large market share and succeeds in improving or maintaining this share. In this chapter, we apply a newly developed trade network approach to determine in which regions in Europe firms are the most successful in gathering a share of the European market. By investigating market overlap, we learn which markets are most important for firms, and from which regions they obtain strongest competition. These important markets and the regions with competing firms differ with respect to the location of the firm and the type of product traded. We illustrate the method by typical case studies for different types of European regions.

From the analyses in the chapter, it becomes clear that the competitiveness of a region is to a large extent determined by its trade connections with other regions. These trade connections show with which regions a city competes, on what, and where. The major European agglomerations of Paris, Milan and Dublin are seen as important competitors by almost all regions (based on our trade network measured for the year 2000). The case studies show the many different competitors with whom specialized regions compete, on what, and where. These specialized regions may not face competition from as many regions as suggested by common specializations only. Eindhoven, Milan and Budapest are all specialized in medium-tech manufacturing, but do not face mutual competition in the same degree. Eindhoven faces a lot of competition from Milan, but Milan does not face the same magnitude of competition from Eindhoven. They also compete (more) with firms from other regions. Although specialized firms in the Budapest region may show a lot of similarities in magnitude and reach of their export orientation in comparison with Dutch regions, for instance, they focus on different regions and markets altogether. Geographical proximity for manufacturing goods and hierarchical functional proximity for (high-end) services coincide in practically all regional trade patterns analysed. A general conclusion may be that the technologically more advanced production is more concentrated, more internationally traded and receives the most international competition.

1.7 DYNAMICS IN REGIONAL COMPETITIVENESS (2000–10)

In Chapter 6 the dynamics in revealed competition are analysed and the mathematical properties of the proposed methodology are more thoroughly discussed. The development in revealed competition is measured for the period 2000–10. We show that geographical clusters of regions in Europe strengthened their competitive position in industrial and agricultural trade, while the largest urban regions are particularly important for growing export positions of business and financial services. We show that improving competitive positions of regions is related to different segments (sectors) of the economy for different regions. We also find evidence for Central and Eastern European countries' growing integration into the European competitive economy. This again emphasizes the importance of place-based development strategies.

1.8 REVEALED COMPETITION BENCHMARKING

In Chapter 7 we discuss revealed competition benchmarking. Knowing the 'real' competitors for industries means that more focused and targeted benchmarks can be constructed in which regions are only compared with their *actual* competing regions. Locational or network characteristics of these other regions may provide clues for improvement of one's own region (note that this reasoning involves intuitive learning opportunities and does not imply a formal test of causality). Chapter 7 shows variances in importance of locational attributes in competitors compared to individual scores. The locational factors used for benchmarking are the cluster, openness and specialization indicators introduced in Chapter 4 together with (available) indicators generally used in benchmarking studies. The cluster and openness indicators are sector specific and only relevant within their own sector. The regional specialization indicator is relevant across sectors. The more commonly used indicators are grouped in the following factors: public knowledge, private knowledge, agglomeration size, and accessibility by road and rail, accessibility by air, access to the internet, labour market, and foreign direct investments.

The trade network-based applications and descriptions in this book show the wealth of heterogeneity present in relative competitiveness linkages between regions in Europe. As argued, the major competitors differ per region and within each region even per sector. This is caused by the differences in market overlap per region and per sector. This calls for a careful addressing and evaluating of place-based policies of regional, national and European governments. The debate on regional development and regional competition has inspired a number of policies aimed at attracting and retaining mobile resources, such as physical and human capital (Martin, 2005). Among many, we recall fiscal incentives for Foreign Direct Investment or the creation of an optimal environment for business to flourish. Next, local governments have been attempting to increase the level of amenities their regions offer, since mobile, highly educated workers are sensitive to this (Florida, 2002). In addition, some policies have been aimed at the creation or fostering of clusters (real estate projects, incentives for firms to group together, collaborations with local universities), while some others have been incentivizing networking (collaborations with international actors in business and academia; Huggins and Izushi, 2012). The European Commission has had a strong regional development policy via its cohesion policy that is now to be reshaped, preferably in place-based and smart specialization local policies. Knowing the 'right' competitors for industries, means that more focused and targeted benchmarks can be constructed and used in these policies. In Tables 1.2 to 1.4 we summarize the result of the benchmark analyses (comparing 'real' competitors only) for the case study regions in this book. The tables are a concise representation of the benchmarks presented in Chapter 7 and they can be interpreted visually, suggesting a possible investment agenda related to smart specializations. Dark fields indicate that a sector in a region underperforms on that indicator and that investment may tend to improve the sector's competitive position vis-à-vis its competitors. More specifically, the length of the bars signifies the importance of an indicator for its competitors while the shading of the bar indicates the score relative to its competitors. A long bar shows that the sector- and region-specific competitors are strong with respect to this indicator. A white bar means that a region has a higher score than the average of its competitors, while a darker colour implies that the sector in that region underperforms if compared to the average of its competitors. The higher the degree of underperformance, the darker is the colour. A black bar signifies that the region has a normalized score less than 30 per cent of the average of its competitors. The bar of agglomeration size is thinner in Table 1.2. This indicates that we are mainly interested in the reasons why agglomeration size is important. Underlying factors that may induce agglomeration economies are specialization, concentration and cluster strength. These are analysed by separate indicators in the revealed competition benchmark.

Table 1.2 shows that the large agglomerations in Europe in general have a strong position relative to their competitors. This is an expected result because their performance has made them strong and large agglomerations in the past. However, it is striking that even the best regions underperform on certain indicators if compared to their actual competitors. Milan clearly underperforms on its knowledge creation while Munich even underperforms on its concentration of high-tech manufacturing. In the case of Paris and Milan we also observe that different factors may be important for different sectors. Thus while in Paris private knowledge is important (has a long bar) for total production, it is not important (has a smaller bar) for the financial and business services. We can also see that in Milan a concentration of financial and business services is important for total production, but apparently not for medium-tech manufacturing. Finally, we observe that the score on an indicator of a region relative to its competitors may change according to the sector. This is because firms

Table 1.2 The revealed competition benchmark of large agglomeration regions in Europe

	Inner London	Milan		Barcelona	Munich	Paris	
	Financial and business services	Regional production	Medium-tech manufacturing	Regional production	High-tech manufacturing	Regional production	Financial and business services
Private knowledge Public knowledge							
Connectivity by road and rail Connectivity by air Connectivity internet							
Foreign owned companies							
Cluster orientation Network orientation Concentration of medium-tech manufacturing Concentration of high-tech manufacturing Concentration of financial and business services Concentration of agriculture Agglomeration size							

Table 1.3 The revealed competition benchmark of strong medium-sized regions in Europe

	Brussels Financial and business services	Eindhoven Medium-tech manufacturing	Lyon High-tech manufacturing	Helsinki High-tech manufacturing	Rotterdam–The Hague Agriculture
Private knowledge Public knowledge					
Connectivity by road and rail Connectivity by air Connectivity internet					
Foreign owned companies					
Cluster orientation Network orientation Concentration of medium-tech manufacturing Concentration of high-tech manufacturing Concentration of financial and business services Concentration of agriculture Agglomeration size					

Table 1.4 The revealed competition benchmark of peripheral regions and emerging economies in Europe

	Budapest	Warsaw		Dresden		Pécs		Thessaloniki	Andalucía
	Medium-tech manufacturing	Regional production	Financial and business services	Regional production	Low-tech manufacturing	Agriculture	Low-tech manufacturing	Regional production	Agriculture
Private knowledge Public knowledge									
Connectivity by road and rail Connectivity by air Connectivity internet									
Foreign owned companies									
Cluster orientation Network orientation Concentration of medium-tech manufacturing Concentration of high-tech manufacturing Concentration of financial and business services Concentration of agriculture Agglomeration size									

from different sectors operate on different geographical markets and therefore have different competitors.

In Table 1.3 we see the benchmark results for the strong and medium-sized regions in Europe for different sector specifications. Here we see that competitors are often larger (the regions underperform on agglomeration size) and the underlying factors that are related to this compared to their competitors are identified. Helsinki, for instance, is clearly smaller than its competitors but seems to compensate for this by a strong cluster orientation and a concentration of high-tech manufacturing. The medium-tech manufacturing sector in Eindhoven underperforms on precisely these cluster and concentration indicators, which may therefore be important aspects to improve in future policies, contributing to a better agglomeration position.

Table 1.4 shows the benchmark for our selected peripheral and emerging market economies. This gives a very different and, in terms of development possibilities, much more problematic picture than the results for the large and medium-sized regions. We see a lot of dark shaded and long bars, signifying underperformance on many important indicators. The region of Warsaw, for instance, seems to be mainly strong in attracting foreign capital but still underperforms on many of the other distinguished indicators when compared to its competitors. The Dresden region sticks out as performing exceptionally well on knowledge creation when compared to its direct competitors. The underperformance of Dresden appears relatively small. The Pécs region is clearly specialized in agriculture: its present strengths lie in the structure of the agricultural economy, with a strong cluster and concentration. The Thessaloniki region seems to underperform on almost all indicators, suggesting that large investments in many factors would be needed to make its economy competitive.

1.9 POLICY CONCLUSIONS

The book concludes in Chapter 8 with a discussion of the introduced methodology and its link with place-based and place-neutral policies. The main conclusion derived from this book is that regional economic development policy should be based on a 'one-size-fits-one' approach. This is in line with the OECD (2011d) which argues that 'the supposed conflict between place-based, as opposed to place-neutral policies, is overblown'. The place-based policy question that remains and to which this book gives a partial answer is what policy mixes work in what circumstances. Place-based policies are 'people and firm based policies in places' targeted at the improvement of conditions such as regional education levels and accessibility to improve the needs of firms and people to enhance welfare and stimulate growth given the specific regional context. Proper place-based policies reinforce place-neutral processes and preclude those policies that support only regional vested interests and have no regional economic potential. In this way place-based smart specialization and regional development can reinforce both place-neutral as well as place-specific economic processes in order to accomplish economic growth and a higher welfare. This calls for a careful addressing and evaluating of place-based policies on different governance levels, ranging from the region itself to the country and the European Union.

2. Smart specialization, regional innovation systems and EU cohesion policy

Philip McCann and Raquel Ortega-Argilés

2.1 THE ORIGINS OF THE SMART SPECIALIZATION CONCEPT: THE TRANSATLANTIC PRODUCTIVITY GAP AND THE EUROPEAN RESEARCH AREA

The smart specialization concept originated in the literature that was analysing the productivity gap between the US and Europe, a gap which had become evident since 1995 (Van Ark et al., 2008). The transatlantic productivity differences appeared to be paradoxical, in that they became most evident precisely when they were least expected. On the eve of the establishment of the EU Single Market in 1991/92, productivity levels on both sides of the North Atlantic had more or less completely converged, after adjusting for differences in the number of working hours, following a long period of European catching up. Deeper European integration and falling cross-border institutional and trade barriers were widely expected to enhance the EU's growth performance. Moreover, this growth-enhancing integration process would also be bolstered by the new information and communications technologies which by then were coming on stream and which were assumed to reduce the costs of distance. From the early 1990s, the observed emergence of a rapidly-growing productivity gap in favour of North America therefore appeared to be something of a paradox, and a large amount of literature then developed seeking to understand the reasons why this had occurred (Ortega-Argilés, 2012) and what, if anything, could be done to help rectify the situation.

2.1.1 The Reasons for the Emergence of the Transatlantic Productivity Gap

In terms of identifying the reasons why the gap had occurred, part of the explanation was argued to be related to transatlantic differences in labour market performance including differences in the quality of human capital (Gu et al., 2002), the rigidity of the European labour markets (Gordon and Dew-Becker, 2005; Gomez-Salvador et al., 2006), differences in the adoption of new managerial practices and organizational investments (Gu and Wang, 2004; Bloom et al., 2005b; Crespi et al., 2007), or differences in the availability of venture capital. Yet, even allowing for differences in the hours worked, the reasons why differences in the performance of human capital and labour markets should have emerged since 1995, which was precisely a period when EU labour markets were increasingly deregulating, cannot be related to labour markets alone. Instead, it became apparent that clues must also be sought from observations of industrial performance, and here the resulting industrial explanations fall into two broad themes (Ortega-Argilés, 2012).

The first explanation, which was referred to as the 'structural effect', emphasizes transatlantic differences in industrial structure. In particular, the EU industrial structure is disproportionally characterized by traditional, middle- and low-tech sectors, and this implies a lower capacity to translate R&D into productivity gains (Mathieu and Van Pottelsberghe de la Potterie, 2008). The second explanation, known as the 'intrinsic effect', argues that even within the same sectors, European firms exhibit a lower ability to translate R&D into productivity gains or other types of investments (Erken and Van Es, 2007). Yet, whichever approach is adopted, one common theme which clearly emerged was the critical role which information and communications technologies (ICTs) play in explanations of this productivity gap. Part of this appears to be an ICT-related structural effect, in that ICT-producing sectors have been a key component of US productivity performance over the last two decades (Jorgenson, 2001; Jorgenson et al., 2005, 2008; Stiroh, 2002a, 2002b; Timmer and Van Ark, 2005). This has sometimes been called the 'Silicon Valley effect', whereby US firms in particular stole a clear march on EU firms in terms of the global competition for new ICT products and services. The US surged ahead of Europe in terms of the performance of these high-technology sectors (Ortega-Argilés, 2012).

As well as the ICT-related structural effect, there also appeared to be an ICT-related intrinsic effect in that there have also emerged differences in the scale and impacts of ICT adoption, adaptation and diffusion in ICT-using sectors (O'Mahony and Van Ark, 2003; Gordon, 2004; Draca et al., 2006; Wilson, 2009). These ICT-using sectors are sectors which adopt and embody ICTs, but also adapt these new general-purpose technologies (GPTs) to the needs and possibilities of their particular activities. This effect has sometimes been called the 'Walmart effect', and reflects the productivity-enhancing effects which firms in entirely different sectors experience from rapidly adopting and adapting new general-purpose technologies to their specific requirements (Ortega-Argilés, 2012).

Although the estimates of the actual contributions of these ICT-related structural and intrinsic effects to the transatlantic productivity gap vary, most evidence suggests that they both play a significant role (Oliner and Sichel, 2000). In addition, the relative importance of these effects appears to have changed over time. Jorgenson et al. (2008) argued that the US productivity growth after 1995 and up to 2000 was driven by productivity growth in ICT-producing sectors and ICT-capital-deepening effects, whereas after 2000, productivity growth was driven primarily by productivity growth in ICT-using industries. Non-ICT-producing sectors were less able in Europe to embody the outputs of the ICT-producing sectors. In other words, ICT-using sectors in Europe were weaker than in North America to such an extent that the 'European productivity slowdown is attributable to the slower emergence of the knowledge economy in Europe compared to the United States' (Van Ark et al., 2008).

These ICT-related explanations of the transatlantic productivity gap imply that the revealed technological disadvantage of the EU relative to the US, which is best proxied by ICT-based R&D investment, is what ultimately constrains the demand for human capital, the diffusion of ICTs, the diffusion of innovative organizational and management practices, and the diffusion of innovation through embodied technology in new capital formation. In spite of the Single Market, which was designed precisely to foster economic scale and integration, Europe still appeared to be much weaker in translating new knowledge, ideas and applications throughout its economy. The transmission linkages between sectors, places and institutions were much more limited in speed and strength, thereby reducing the scale and availability of knowledge spillovers and diffusion effects. The reasons for this appear to be related to the heterogeneity of the integration process. While there has been much progress for example in goods markets, energy markets, transportation markets and some financial markets, in many service industries in particular, the EU markets are still highly fragmented, and this fragmentation limits the flow of knowledge, ideas, new techniques and systems.

2.1.2 The Response to the Productivity Gap: The Non-spatial Smart Specialization Concept

As a direct response to this issue the European Research Area (ERA) was established as a mechanism for engendering EU-wide integration and scale advantages in activities generating and disseminating knowledge. The policy was aimed at promoting European R&D and EU-wide knowledge spillovers via the development of knowledge-intensive agglomerations and cross-border network systems of researchers, universities, entrepreneurs and innovators. As such, the ERA was aimed both at promoting knowledge-integration and also maximizing dissemination in many of the very sectors that currently lack EU-wide integration. At the same time, a high-level think-tank known as the 'Knowledge for Growth' expert group (K4G) was set up in order to advise the then European Commissioner for Research, Janez Potocnik, as to the most promising policy approaches available to bolster the aims of the European Research Area.

This group of specialists developed a policy-prioritization logic which they termed 'smart specialization', and the concept was designed to help overcome the weaknesses in the European knowledge-dissemination frameworks (Foray et al., 2009, 2011). Smart specialization emphasizes economic potential and the mechanisms whereby such potential is most likely be realized, and provides a method by which policy-makers were enabled to best identify the types of priorities most appropriate for their context. The original concept is abstract and non-spatial and increasingly became more concrete and applied in an explicitly regional context.

In terms of the original non-spatial abstract concept, the smart specialization process is understood to operate within a domain, and assumes that entrepreneurs will search out the smart specialization opportunities within their domain. These entrepreneurial search processes play the role of identifying and exploiting the potential advantages of general-purpose technologies (GPTs) to regenerate the targeted economic domain (production or services) through the co-invention of applications (Foray et al., 2009, 2011; David et al., 2009). However, the relationship between the domain and other dimensions of the economy is also important. The relevant size of the domain concerns the size of those sectors which could potentially most benefit from the knowledge spillovers generated by the initial development of the applications (Foray et al., 2009, 2011; David et al., 2009), and the greater is the connectedness of the domain with other domains, the greater will be the possibilities for knowledge flows and learning. Within the particular domain, the entrepreneurial search process leads to the identification of the distribution of potential opportunities for (ICT) technological improvements to be embodied in a range of activities and occupations; the relevant size issue relates to the potential magnitude of the innovation outcomes associated with these opportunities; and the connectedness issue relates to the potential for learning about both these opportunities and magnitudes.

Because the original smart specialization concept arose out of the literature on the transatlantic productivity gap, it initially emphasized the importance of R&D, and in particular in high-technology sectors.

However, as we move through the nine policy briefs produced by the Knowledge for Growth expert group between 2006 and 2009, it is possible to discern a marked shift away from the early emphasis on R&D, and in particular on multinational R&D, through to institutional and governance issues relating to knowledge dissemination, and finally towards technological specialization based on the adoption, dissemination and adaptation of GPTs, primarily understood as ICTs, across a wide range of sectors. The theoretical approach is entirely systemic and emphasizes the need for overcoming any weakness in the regional innovation systems which inhibit people from taking advantage of entrepreneurial opportunities and turning new ideas into innovations.

The smart specialization concept was not intended to encourage 'picking winners' on a sectoral basis or for imposing sectoral specialization by means of top-down government planning. Rather, it was always seen as a public–private partnership process of discovery and learning on the part of both entrepreneurs and policy-makers regarding the most likely avenues for entrepreneurial opportunities and innovation breakthroughs. In particular, the concept emphasizes the role which policy experiments may play in helping to foster entrepreneurial behaviour.

2.2 TRANSLATING THE SMART SPECIALIZATION CONCEPT TO THE CASE OF REGIONS: MOVING FROM ASPATIAL TO SPATIAL ISSUES

The shift from a non-spatial and rather abstract logic to an explicitly spatial smart specialization logic was facilitated by assuming that the region was the appropriate domain. Applying the smart specialization logic in this manner, David et al. (2009) argued that one of the features of many European regions is a weak correlation between regional R&D, regional training specializations and the structure of local and regional activities. Such weak relationships would inhibit the local flows of new ideas and limit the application and embodying of new technologies and techniques within local industry. A regional policy recommendation from the smart specialization proponents is therefore that the government should foster human capital formation for the new 'knowledge needs' of the region's *traditional* industries which are starting to adapt and apply these new GPTs. The interventions could relate, for example, to network-building schemes. However, the aim of such a policy would be to promote a local skill base which can facilitate widespread local incremental improvements as well as develop specialized application technologies in the region.

This was a profound twist on much of the prevailing thinking around innovation, which at the time tended to heavily emphasize the importance of high technology activities, whereas the smart specialization approach emphasized the system-wide role played by many activities and the need to find ways to disseminate new knowledge and technologies as widely as possible throughout the economy. The smart specialization logic followed on naturally from the insights of the literature on the transatlantic productivity gap, and reflected the implicit assumptions behind the creation of the ERA, namely that different countries and regions would tend to specialize in different knowledge-related sectors, depending on their capabilities (Von Tunzelmann, 2009). If the outcome of the ERA was that a small number of countries or regions increased their domination of all knowledge-related activities, then the ERA will not have served the EU in a manner which is consistent with the territorial and social cohesion principles of the Lisbon Treaty. As such, in terms of the Lisbon growth agenda, smart specialization was conceived of as a realistic and appropriate way to reconcile unrestricted agglomeration processes with a relatively balanced distribution of research capacities and capabilities across Europe.

In order to translate the smart specialization concept fully to the regional context we can employ three ideas which are familiar in economic geography terminology, namely embeddedness, relatedness, and connectivity. Smart specialization when applied to regions implies increasing both the embeddedness and related variety (Frenken et al., 2007; Frenken and Boschma, 2007; Boschma and Frenken, 2011; Boschma and Iammarino, 2009; Neffke et al., 2011; Boschma et al., 2012) properties of the region. In other words, smart specialization is not about becoming increasingly specialized, but it is rather about deepening the linkages within the region with the greater potential for long-lasting scale effects, while at the same time helping them to diversify. As such, embeddedness combined with related variety allows for emphasis of the importance of strategic specialized diversification and translates exactly to the relevant domain element of the original smart specialization concept.

Finally, the third element of the aspatial-sectoral smart specialization concept which we must translate into spatial-regional terms is the issue of connectedness. The original connectedness idea emerged from a sectoral way of thinking, whereby the national innovation system is comprised of a set of sectoral innovation systems and inter-sectoral linkages and knowledge spillovers (McCann and Ortega-Argilés, 2013). In economic geography, however, the idea of connectedness is defined in terms of connectivity, which is a concept widely employed in the global cities literature (Sassen, 2002) and which was originally borrowed from sociology. Connectivity relates to all of the interactions associated with trade, transportation, passenger movements, information flows, knowledge exchanges, flows of finance, and cross-border decision-making capabilities, which are situated at a particular location. The smart specialization logic suggests that it is essential to build on a region's most connected activities, so that the local regional economic base is best positioned to learn from the more advanced regions. At the same time, the development of such interregional networks will only be effective in promoting local and regional knowledge development if parallel actions are aimed at maximizing local knowledge spillovers and learning linkages within regions. In other words, connectivity and embeddedness are closely related.

2.3 INNOVATION SYSTEMS ISSUES: APPROPRIABILITY, SPILLOVERS, BOTTLENECKS, MISSING LINKS AND OPPORTUNISM

There is already a large body of literature on the difficult issues faced by all regional innovation discussions, namely issues of appropriability, spillovers, bottlenecks, missing links and opportunism. Issues of appropriability relate to the problem that firms will only invest in R&D, engage in entrepreneurial actions, or undertake other innovation-related activities, as long as they feel that they will reap the rewards of those investments, if and when they are successful. The expectation of free-rider problems, unintended outward knowledge spillovers, or opportunism on the part of local actors, will all reduce the extent to which firms will undertake innovation-related investments, and insufficient local innovation-related investments will limit the innovation potential of the region. In order to overcome these market failures, traditional policies such as SME-credit subsidies and R&D grants have been widely used in order to boost the innovation potential of regions. However, there is always the problem of which firms or sectors should be the object of the policy actions. The smart specialization agenda does not seek to replace these types of actions. Rather, it aims to situate the use of these interventions in a broader context, in which the pattern and distribution of the intended recipients of these interventions emerges from an explicit policy-prioritization logic based around the region's assets, capabilities and weaknesses. The promotion of entrepreneurship is seen as the key priority, but this must also be contingent on those regional assets – activities, technologies, sectors or institutions – which offer relevant scale and the opportunities to help diversify and upgrade the economy around its existing core and traditional industries. Moreover, the smart specialization logic also emphasizes the importance of understanding the positioning of the region in the context of the emerging global value-chains. Understanding relevant scale implies not only considering the local regional context, but also how this fits within the broader national and international context.

Because it is based on a systems way of thinking, the smart specialization logic turns the traditional policy-prioritization argument around. Rather than automatically emphasizing the need for SMEs or high-technology sectors to be prioritized, the smart specialization logic also gives real latitude for the upgrading of traditional sectors by linking them to high-technology sectors and newly-emerging activities. In order to achieve these aims, the smart specialization logic emphasizes the importance of finding ways to build greater linkages and synergies between firms and across sectors. The role of any publicly-funded actions and interventions is to facilitate the building of such linkages in order to overcome any missing links or bottlenecks associated with problems of appropriability, spillovers or opportunism. Such actions are likely to be somewhat experimental in nature and to involve a certain amount of trial and error, as is always the case with innovation issues, and the policy framework must be sufficiently flexible to allow for demonstration effects. As such, smart specialization shares many common elements with the regional innovations systems literature (OECD, 2012a), while at the same time emphasizing the policy-prioritization logic and the need for experimentalism in policy design and actions.

The types of actions or interventions employed in smart specialization initiatives vary greatly. Some regions employ innovation voucher schemes, designed for example to help firms seek partnerships with research institutions. Revolving and recyclable financial schemes, rather than direct grants, are becoming increasingly popular, as are schemes providing the finance to underwrite network-building activities. Subsidies to SMEs for R&D, or schemes designed to accelerate SME patenting activities are commonplace, as are schemes fostering linkages between large firms, small firms and universities. Other cluster-type programmes are also possible, as are skills-related schemes, and public–private partnerships in research ventures. Yet, whatever approach is used and whichever policy tools are adopted, the smart specialization approach emphasizes that the policy prioritization must be built on an explicit assessment of the region's assets and capabilities and aimed at solving coordination problems inhibiting the generation and dissemination of new ideas and knowledge.

2.4 SMART SPECIALIZATION IN PRACTICE: INNOVATION UNION AND EU COHESION POLICY

The principles embodied in the smart specialization concept are central to the Europe 2020 agenda, which aims at fostering smart growth that is both sustainable and inclusive. In particular, these principles are enshrined with the place-based regional development objectives inherent in the new reforms to EU Cohesion Policy (Foray et al., 2012). The imperative for regions and countries to develop a smart specialization strategic framework is demonstrated by the fact that this is now one of the conditionalities which must be met in order for regions and countries to receive European development funding. Regions will be required to develop such policies, and then to engage in ongoing monitoring and evaluation of the progress of their policies.

At the same time, the smart specialization concept is now also a major driving force behind the new Innovation Union flagship programme of the European Commission, the successor to the European Research Area, the aim of which is not only to foster EU-wide economies of scale in high-technology and knowledge-intensive sectors, but also to accelerate the dissemination of smart technologies throughout the EU economy. As we have already seen, it was from this agenda that the concept of smart specialization originally emerged, and in order to build greater synergies between this agenda and the regional development agenda, new programmes are currently being developed to allow a funding stream allied with both the Innovation Union agenda and the Cohesion Policy agenda to be dovetailed. Explicitly, this approach assumes that all regions can play a part in promoting European economic growth, and not just the core regions or the high-technology centres, and recent evidence (OECD, 2009a, 2009b, 2011a, 2011b, 2012a) increasingly points to exactly this conclusion. The important point here is to ensure that policy design is appropriate for the regional context, and that it is aimed explicitly at promoting the development and dissemination of new ideas, knowledge, techniques and technologies. Any regional smart specialization strategy necessarily involves a consideration of all matters relating to local intangible capital, including capabilities and competences, and institutional issues (Foray, 2008), exactly as argued by Barca (2009). The smart specialization approach is very consistent with the place-based logic in that it explicitly argues for policy frameworks which are tailored to the local context on the basis of the best data available, the most detailed knowledge, and an explicit consideration of the realistic potential of the region.

2.5 REGIONAL COMPETITION, STRUCTURE AND SMART SPECIALIZATION

The following chapters in this book develop a novel methodology which is completely in line with the smart specialization framework. The approach developed here allows for the identification of a region's characteristics and the benchmarking of its performance in terms of all of its relevant scale and connectivity dimensions, and the way in which it does this is to position the region in terms of its competitors. Traditional methods of identifying regional characteristics and strengths tend to focus on issues of structure and then proceed to benchmark comparator regions on the basis of similar industrial and geographical characteristics. In contrast, the approach developed here identifies those regions which are most closely related to each other in terms of both product space and geographical space, as determined by the patterns of their trading relationships as well as their structural features. Regions are then benchmarked against those other regions which are most closely competing in these same multidimensional spaces, as well identifying those regions that are the major trading partners. This approach integrates the profiling element of smart specialization with the value-chain positioning element of smart specialization. Such an approach provides a framework for identifying the key priorities and strengths on which policy actions are able to build, as well as the weaknesses, bottlenecks or missing links which need to be rectified, in the very real context of global competition. This approach also offers the possibility of designing targeted actions and interventions which ought to be amenable to measurement, monitoring and evaluation. The use of indicators, monitoring and evaluation are all central both to smart specialization and also to the place-based approach (McCann and Ortega-Argilés, 2013), and the framework developed here provides an explicit basis for this. Regions are different; they compete in different product and geographical spaces, they exhibit different strengths and weaknesses, and they provide different possibilities. Policies must be tailored to the context in order to be effective, and the methodology developed here provides a solid foundation for building a place-based smart specialization policy-prioritization logic.

3. Regional economic development and competitiveness

The development of important regions is increasingly considered as one of the main contributors to the economic growth of nations (World Bank, 2009). These important regions are generally large agglomerations and important players in the global economy. Countries may follow different regional economic development strategies in an attempt to create these strong regions and stimulate development in lagging regions. Direct policy interventions seem, however, to have only a limited effect and the transformation of lagging into leading regions appears to be largely beyond the control of policy-makers. As a consequence, national policy-makers may follow a laissez-faire approach and leave regional development to regional administrators. Differences in regional economic development, however, affect the regional distribution of income which may trigger national redistribution policies. These redistribution policies interfere with the laissez-faire approach and are problematic when allocating scarce national resources over different regions in combination with soft regional budget constraints. Moreover, the laissez-faire approach does not seem to solve the short-term problems that are the main justification for the place-based development policies that are leading in future cohesion policy (Barca, 2009).

The place-based policies evolved directly from the Lisbon Agenda in 2000, and accumulated into the current (smart, sustainable and inclusive) growth objectives of the Europe 2020 policy programme that are central in the envisioned cohesion policy reform after 2013. The policies take the form of a smart specialization development perspective based on a systems way of thinking about innovation and growth. It emphasizes the economic potential of a region given its place within a complex regional system (McCann and Ortega-Argilés, 2011). Smart policy-making explicitly builds on network data available for the specific regional context. In this section we therefore discuss modern theories of regional economic development. We especially address how different characteristics of regions that can be influenced by different policies, such as clustering, specialization, size and accessibility, may affect regional economic development. We discuss different factors that are often associated with regional economic development and how they are analysed in benchmarking studies to derive policy conclusions on regional economic development.

3.1 REGIONAL ECONOMIC DEVELOPMENT

Regional economic development has its roots in classical regional economic growth theory and geographic theories of development. The economic growth differences between nations were the main research interest of the classical economists. The underlying questions which are still relevant today were related to the drivers of the economic growth of regions with a central role for the difference between the growth of a region and the growth of a firm. Recently, regional economic development theory became dominated by the New Economic Geography (NEG) and associated agglomeration-based theories of economic development. These recent regional development theories are, contrary to earlier theories, primarily based on endogenous growth theory and characterized by mathematical rigour and empirical testing. The new theoretical insights from NEG are in line with the empirical observation that interregional disparities, especially within countries, have grown since the 1980s (Puga, 2002; Combes and Overman, 2004; Brülhart and Traeger, 2005) and urbanization has increased on a global scale (World Bank, 2009).

Classical economic growth theory is based on Solow (1956) where economic growth is determined only by consumers' and producers' preferences, the distribution and availability of resources, and the accumulation of capital. Central in the classical argument of regional economic development is the theory of comparative advantage developed by Ricardo (1821). It was shown by Ricardo that regions that are better in the production of all goods (absolute advantage) should still specialize in the production of goods they are *relatively* better in (comparative advantage). The goods whose production they are relatively worse in should be obtained via trade with other regions. This specialization is automatically realized in a free trade economy. Heckscher (1919) and Ohlin (1933) extended this theoretical framework and showed that not only does this lead to a beneficial situation for both trading nations, but also to equal wages among the trading regions in the long run. According to the Heckscher–Ohlin international trade theory, regional specialization in the production of a typical type of products will only occur in the presence of regional physical differences such as the availability of specific natural resources. Efficient firms may go bankrupt because other firms from the same region perform better, and not because they perform more poorly than their competitors from other regions. This is a result of the economic processes involved in free trade where all firms from the same region compete for the same pool of employees and capital (external finance), thereby driving up costs for all firms and resulting in the bankruptcy of the least efficient firms and specialization in the production of goods that firms in a specific region are relatively good in. The recent relocation of labour-intensive production from Europe and the US towards Asia is a typical example of a regional relocation of industries due to a shift in the comparative advantage between regions.

The observation that economic activities are not spread homogeneously in space, but clustered in concentrations of different sizes, is an important element in economic geography. Theories on agglomeration advantages as an explanation for this observed spatial concentration of economic activities have been widely used in economic geography and regional economics since the work of Von Thünen (1842), Marshall (1890) and Weber (1909). In traditional economic geography the focus was on explaining the choice of location of firms and the 'hierarchy of cities' (Christaller, 1933). Martin and Sunley (1996) in this respect summarize differences in the weights of the factor levels of spatial scale and the acceptance of heterogeneous actors and non-economic (for example psychological and socio-political) factors. The empirical literature on the comparative advantage of nations or regions is commonly based on the Balassa (1965) index. The Balassa index ranks the industries with respect to their export orientation, thereby indicating in which industries a country (or region) has a comparative advantage. In this interpretation regions create a mix of products and compete with other regions. This interpretation is problematic for regions in a currency area. As was argued by Camagni (2002), quantity adjustment, not price, occurs at the regional level, and competition between regions concerns absolute, not relative, advantage. Moreover, competition occurs at the firm level, and not at the regional level and has little to do with the export structure of regions (cf. Storper, 1997).

In this book we focus on the underlying structural factors that determine the comparative advantage of regions. These factors are exogenous properties of the regions, such as the availability of natural resources, or endogenous factors related to human capital and institutions. We especially focus on the spatial factors related to agglomeration economies and networks although we also address most other factors. Agglomeration economies describe the advantages of concentration of economic activity in space leading to lower costs and a higher productivity. The reasons for these advantages are related to internal and external economies of the firm introduced by Marshall and the quality and size of the network. Physical and non-physical networks affect transport and commuting costs which, besides facilitating trade, determine the size of an agglomeration and the possibility of agglomeration economies.

In discussing the cost and productivity of the firm, Marshall (1890) introduced the notion of external and internal economies of the firm, that is processes that increase the productivity of the firm. Internal economies are inherent to the firm and incorporate elements such as the division of labour, the improved use of machinery and economies of scale. External economies are external to the firm but internal to the industry, implying that the productivity of the industry will increase with the number of firms in the same region. The external economies of agglomeration occur due to better information, availability of skilled labour and economies in the use of specialized machinery (shared facilities). This started a new line of research discussing the importance of the clustering of firms in the same industry, which was later extended by Jane Jacobs (1969) to the importance of clustering of different type of firms due to knowledge spillovers over different industries.

Agglomeration economies build on the concept of externalities or spillovers. Externalities or spillovers occur if the behaviour of a firm or person increases the performance or welfare of another firm or person without the latter having to pay compensation or the first having had the intention of generating this effect. Spatially bounded externalities are related to location decisions of firms or persons and their network context. All discussions of spatial externalities link to a threefold classification as made by Hoover (1948) and Isard (1960) in which the sources of agglomeration advantages are grouped together as:

- *Internal increasing returns to scale*. These may occur to a single firm due to production cost efficiencies realized by serving large markets. There is nothing inherently spatial in this concept.
- *External economies* within the group of local firms in a sector due to firm size or a large number of local firms: *localization economies*. These may occur due to labour pooling, specialized suppliers or knowledge spillovers (Marshallian externalities).
- *External economies* available to all local firms irrespective of sector: *urbanization economies*. Urbanization economies are often seen as being interchangeable with variety- or Jacobs' externalities. It is argued that, apart from spillovers occurring between firms within a sector, spillovers also occur between sectors (Jacobs, 1969; Glaeser et al., 1992; Van Oort, 2004).

The size of a region can be affected by infrastructure and networks. Infrastructure and networks shorten the (time) distances among firms and between firms and customers or employees, and are therefore an alternative for the concentration of firms in a specific geographical area. Next to infrastructure the organization of the economy may also be a source of agglomeration economies. This depends on the type of externalities causing the agglomeration economies. Localization economies are related to the size of the industry. In other words, specialization of a regional economy having a concentration of firms producing the same type of products will lead to overall higher productivity. Urbanization economies, however, are related to inter-industry relationships. They emphasize the importance of linkages between firms. In this case regional industrial complexes including the suppliers in the supply chain of the firm would result in higher productivity and not in the specialization in the production of only one product.

These so-called clusters, describing regional (industrial) complexes of trade relations in the supply chain of the firm, form the foundation of urbanization economies. Complemented with competitiveness as a driving force for economic development, Porter (1998) stressed the role of localization economies in clusters. Storper and Venables (2004) argue that face-to-face contacts in clusters are important: when contacts can be codified, there is inherently less need for firms to cluster in space. Although the cluster concept is popular among (regional) policymakers and in planning, the concept is, like competitiveness, quite multifaceted and ambiguous in character (Asheim et al., 2006; Krugman, 1996b).

3.1.1 Regional Development Paths

This difference in localization economies and urbanization economies which can be partly translated into product specialization and clustering gives us a framework with which to analyse regional development paths from these two possible sources of agglomeration economies and economic growth. The framework is graphically depicted in Figure 3.1. On the horizontal axis we see the degree of clustering versus network orientation in European regions. When a region has a high degree of clustering it implies that it is specialized in producing not only certain final products, but also the intermediate products needed in the region's production processes. For example, a region has a strong cluster in shoe production if it makes not only shoes, but also shoe laces, leather and rubber soles, and has a strong livestock sector (to make the leather). At the opposite end of the spectrum, a region can be network oriented in production. This implies that the region is getting the material needed in the production of a typical product (like shoes) from an optimal network of suppliers chosen from all possible regions. On the vertical access we have the degree of regional specialization versus diversification. A region

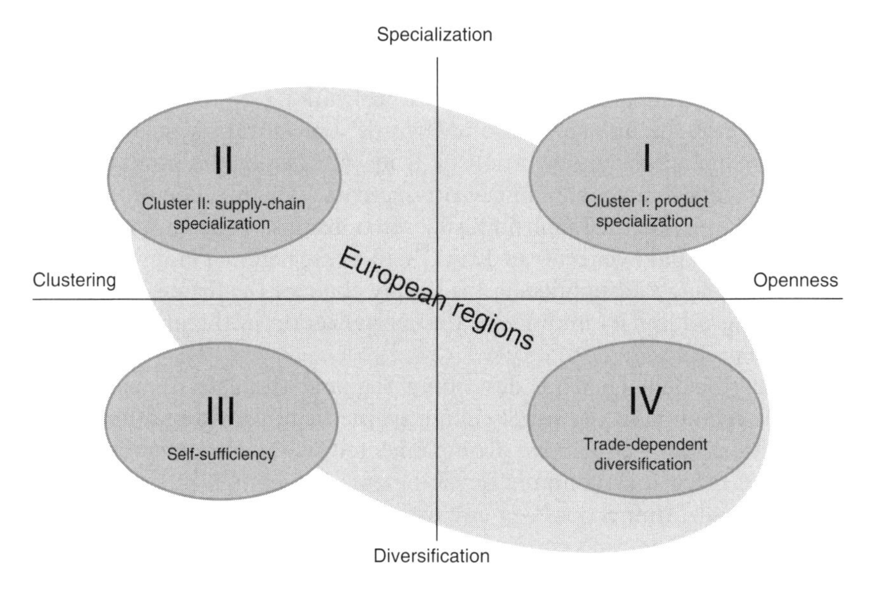

Figure 3.1 A framework to analyse regional development paths

that is specialized produces more of certain products than other regions. A region being diversified means that the region has a very 'average' production structure.

The shaded ellipse in Figure 3.1 describes the present location where most of the European regions are positioned within this conceptual framework (see Chapter 4). The quadrant in which a region is located tells us something about its economic profile. We distinguish the following four quadrants and associated economic profiles:

1. *Product specialization*: in the first quadrant regions have specialized in the production of certain products but not in the complete supply chain (geographic concentration of production). In other words, they get the intermediate products needed in the region's production processes from all over Europe.
2. *Clustering*: in the second quadrant regions are specialized in one or several strong clusters who depend on suppliers from the own region. This is an implementation of Porter's definition of clusters.
3. *Self-sufficiency*: in the third quadrant the regions seem to be relatively self-sufficient. These regions produce many products and are therefore diversified. At the same time they obtain most of their intermediate products needed for production from the own region.

4. *Trade-dependent diversification*: in the fourth quadrant we find a diverse region producing many different products using the optimal inputs irrespective of where they are produced.

In the next chapter we show that only a few regions can be classified as product specialized, some of the very large regions are self-sufficient, and most European regions can either be classified as having strong clusters or as relying on trade-dependent diversification. In Chapter 4 we will apply this conceptual framework not only to the regional level, but also to the sectoral level. This gives us important insights into the differences among industries with respect to clustering and specialization. We find that the position of a region in this conceptual framework depends on both its sector structure and its location in Europe. In other words, depending on the location of a region and its comparative advantage, it may have a different optimal economic trade network and economic structure. This is in line with different types of externalities that may operate in different sectors of the economy.

The specialization in the production of a type of product (like shoes) is closely linked to the concept of geographical concentration. This can be confusing because concentration is often reserved in economics to describe the degree of competition by measuring the number of firms operating in a market. When we use the term 'concentration' in this study we never refer to the number of firms in a market but always to geographical concentration.

3.1.2 Recent Developments in the Theories of Regional Economic Development

The recent developments in the context of the new economic geography (Krugman, Fujita, Venables) attempt to combine classical international economic growth theory with economic geography in a conceptional economics framework where external economies may take place in different regions connected via trade networks.[1] Contrary to classical international trade theory, the NEG disputes that regional inequalities can be explained by differences in available resources only, and argues that regional inequalities will not automatically disappear over time. The general equilibrium framework is still based on trade driven by the comparative advantage of regions. Thus, firms survive at the regional level not only by outperforming firms from other regions, but especially by outperforming firms from the same region that compete for the same labour and resources. Moreover, increased productivity and growth in 'competing' regions are not at the cost of the own region but to the benefit of the own region because products become relatively cheaper. This implies some differences for policy targeted at firms or at national or regional economic growth *where the support of productive firms with a comparative disadvantage is not to the benefit of a nation.*

The main difference between the NEG proper and related economic geography theories is that the first is based on a distribution of economic activity and population resulting in different *welfare* effects and the second is based on the implications of different spatial distributions of people and activity for productivity and GDP levels or growth. Recently both approaches became intertwined, and increased productivity effects in agglomerations also occurred in NEG models.[2] Both theories share the recently observed trend towards increased urbanization as an outcome.

The New Economic Geography literature proper based on the seminal paper by Krugman (1991b) discusses the distribution of economic activity and population over space and its welfare implications. Moreover, it discusses agglomeration forces leading towards a dynamic and self-enforcing process of increased agglomeration and higher welfare of the population in these agglomerations. These welfare effects were generated by a love of variety for consumers and a supply of varieties that increased with the economic size of a region. This love of variety is based on small differences between products that fit to the specific needs of different customers. A higher supply of varieties will therefore lead to a higher level of welfare. Thus, the original NEG model is about the welfare implications of the distribution of people and industries over space and the dynamic process that results in large agglomeration, and *not* about productivity growth.

With the introduction of variety effects in production (Venables, 1996; Bröcker, 1998) where the availability of more (varieties of) intermediate goods leads to higher productivity, technological development and economic growth is incorporated in the NEG literature and explained in its regional context. This love of variety in production is based on small differences in intermediate products fitting to the special needs of different firms. An increase in the variety of available intermediate inputs will therefore lead to an increase in the productivity of the firm. This increased productivity is driven by differences in the regional size of economies, which may be affected by changes in physical infrastructure. In these theories, location matters for both technological development and economic growth. More specifically, the NEG investigates the relationship between 'economic mass' and productivity. Economic mass is defined as the size of the economy at locations. The theory proposes that an increased size of an economy results in a larger variety of goods supplied, which is good for consumers (base model) as well as producers (vertical linkages model, Venables, 1996) and therefore increases welfare, productivity levels and thus economic growth. This theoretical model emphasizes the combination of urbanization and localization economies in regional clusters.

Infrastructure networks and infrastructure investment occupy a special place in the NEG literature. Infrastructure may be used to lower trade cost or to create bigger agglomerations without migration by reducing the time-distance between regions. This may result in different effects. Creating bigger agglomerations in the periphery via infrastructure investment may seem good policy from an equity point of view, but it is not efficient (overall growth will be lower) and it may induce a larger income inequality within regions between capital owners and wage earners (see Baldwin et al., 2003, chapter 17). Interregional infrastructure that reduces trade costs between regions may also have different effects. It may reduce income inequality between regions when trade costs are already low but it will increase income inequality between regions when the trade costs are high. This increased income inequality is caused by large positive effects from additional migration to the bigger agglomeration in relation to the small effect of lower transport costs (Baldwin et al., 2003). This effect was also shown in empirical NEG models with respect to opening up peripheral regions in Europe (Bröcker et al., 2004; Bröcker and Schneekloth, 2006; Bröcker et al., 2009).

Finally, it may be shown that in the presence of congestion costs better infrastructure may even result in lower overall economic growth, high spatial concentration and high income inequality (Baldwin et al., 2003). Trade costs between regions, however, are also affected by the logistics sector and non-physical networks (see below) of business contacts. The limited availability of regional trade data in Europe at the present time prevents the analysis of these effects and their possible influence on economic growth.

3.2 MEANS TO INFLUENCE REGIONAL GROWTH: THE FUNDAMENTALS

Policy intervention targeted at changing available resources, the internal or the external economies of the firm are a means of influencing the economic development of regions and the specialization in types of production. The classical factors that determine regional specialization in types of industries, the availability of natural resources, are generally assumed to be given and cannot be influenced. The quality of the available resources, however, can be affected by means of, for instance, education of the labour force. Other examples of policies affecting available resources are investment in public resources supplying firms with a good working judicial system, or facilitating trade via a well functioning infrastructure network. The internal economies of the firm are largely a matter for the firm. The government may try to stimulate product and organizational innovation by subsidies or education, but mainly it is the task of the firm to improve upon its internal economies. In this study we therefore focus on the external economies, and not on the internal economies of the firm.

The external economies are much debated in the recent literature. Many different types of external economies have been distinguished. We will discuss below the most important elements that are used in this study.

3.2.1 Available Resources and Education

The classical literature[3] focuses on the availability of natural resources such as oil, or abundant supply of land, which will lead to regional economic specialization based on a comparative advantage of firms in different regions. This specialization in different sectors and regions results, however, not in a difference in wealth over the regions as income levels, wages and interest rates will equalize in the long run. Policy intervention is limited since the specialization of different regions is completely driven by the available natural resources. Education may be an option with which to influence the specialization of regions as education may have an effect on the quality of human resources available to a region.

3.2.2 Education, Innovation and Creativity

The role of knowledge and human capital as a determinant of economic growth has acquired greater importance after their incorporation in economic growth models by Romer (1986) and Lucas (1988). In these models, knowledge spillovers between economic agents play a crucial role in the growth and innovation process leading to external economies of scale in production. At the core of the new economic growth theory that builds on this framework lies the concept of technological change as a non-rival and partially excludable good (as opposed to the neoclassical view of knowledge as a public good). New technological knowledge is here tacit, meaning that its accessibility, as well as its growth spillovers, are bounded by geographic proximity of high-tech firms or knowledge institutions, and by the nature and extent of the interactions among these actors in an innovation system (Acs, 2002). A large and growing empirical literature has grown around testing this idea using data from cities (Glaeser et al., 1992; Henderson et al., 1995; Dumais et al., 2002; Van Oort, 2004). The proposition is that if knowledge spillovers are important to growth and firm dynamics, they should be more easily identified in cities where many people are concentrated into a relatively small and confined space and where knowledge is transmitted more easily. A more recent, additional explanation is provided by Florida (2002) claiming that creativity can be additionally important for productivity, next to education and innovation.

3.2.3 Agglomeration Economies

The driving mechanism in agglomeration economies is that increased size of agglomerations leads to increased productivity (and/or welfare), which will attract more people to migrate to larger agglomerations. This in turn will cumulatively cause higher productivity levels and higher economic growth. Naturally there are also dispersion forces at work, but after a certain threshold of transport cost and freeness of trade has been reached, the strength of agglomeration economies will outweigh the dispersion forces. Depending on the actual amount of the transport costs this results in a certain number of agglomerations that may differ in size.[4] The presence of diseconomies of scale also leads to a discussion on the optimal size of cities (see Box 3.1). Agglomeration economies can be based on efficiency effects in intermediate products (1), available varieties in production (2), regional knowledge spillovers (3), shared intermediate (4) and labour markets (5), and urbanization and density advantages of services (6) and infrastructure (7). The empirical evidence for the existence of agglomeration economies is strong, and in an overview paper by Rosenthal and Strange (2004) it is shown that a doubling in the size of an agglomeration leads to an increase in productivity of somewhere between 3 and 11 per cent.[5]

3.2.4 Specialization, Clusters and Concentration

The concentration of economic activity in space may lead to lower costs and higher productivity due to external economies of the firm, but the policy options to affect the physical size of an agglomeration are limited. However, policies may affect agglomeration economies depending on the cause of the agglomeration effect. For example, investment in physical or non-physical networks can be used to affect the distances between firms and thereby the actual economic size of an agglomeration (see below). Other examples are the organization of economic activity within the region where economic mass is created for a subset of the economy. Specialization of a region in a typical industry may be important if external economies are due to economies of scale in production or spillovers between the same types of industries (localization economies). However, clusters of different industries in an industrial complex producing typical products may be important if the external economies to agglomeration

BOX 3.1 THE OPTIMAL SIZE OF CITIES

In this book we focus on the competitive position of firms and abstract from the wider welfare effects related to the environment or social interactions. These wider welfare effects may be induced by growth in transport volumes and possible associated increase in greenhouse gases, or via other increasing diseconomies of urban scale due to agglomeration economies. A sustainable regional development strategy (see also Thissen and van Oort, 2010) requires that diseconomies of urban scale that may involve congestion costs, housing costs and environmental degradation (Duranton and Puga, 2005) should also be taken into account. The dynamic process in agglomeration economies does not, however, necessarily result in a (social) welfare optimal situation. The reason that the result might not be optimal is that people or firms do not take into account the effect of their action on others. Thus, when people migrate from a small city to a large agglomeration they do not take into account that other people in the big agglomeration benefit from the increase in size of the agglomeration and those who stay behind in the small city lose. Although these effects are small for individuals migrating, they become large if many people migrate. This may result in too much migration to big agglomerations (Ottaviano and Thisse, 2002 and Baldwin et al., 2003). Little research has been done on the optimal size of cities. The OECD (2006) estimates this optimal size for productivity effects in the short run to be about 6 million people, given all local capital such as infrastructure and factories, and analysed in a static framework. Henderson (2009) arrives at a much higher estimate for the optimal size of cities in China.

are due to spillovers between different types of industries (urbanization economies) or the interaction between firms in the complete production process. The importance of clusters or specialization may differ among industries.

3.2.5 Networks and Transport Costs

Physical and non-physical networks play an important role in several of the more recent regional economic development theories. These networks determine the shape of space in which agglomerations develop, and thereby determine the size of agglomerations and the size of agglomeration externalities at a specific location. The traditional NEG models are based on trade relations which are often supposed to be related to travel times and road infrastructure, which determines the cost of trade between different agglomerations and regions. These models have often been used to analyse the welfare impacts of a change in infrastructure and a consequent redistribution of population and economic activity over space (Bröcker et al., 2004; Bröcker and Schneekloth, 2006; Bröcker et al., 2009; Thissen, 2005). More direct policies such as road pricing that affect commuting and transport costs have also been analysed in this framework (Thissen et al., 2009, 2011).

Non-physical networks are potentially important as channels for knowledge spillovers and their possible effect on innovation. Innovation is central in the Lisbon Strategy of the European Commission. It is argued that the spatial diffusion of knowledge and its effect on innovation is of major importance to ensure productivity growth and to improve the welfare of nations. As knowledge is hard to appropriate, it generates benefits to other agents through several spillover mechanisms. Understanding the geographical structures that underlie these spillover benefits is necessary for any evidence-based innovation policy to stimulate Europe's transformation towards a knowledge-based society (Fritsch and Slavtchev, 2007). In contrast to geographically localized channels of knowledge spillovers such as labour mobility (Almeida and Kogut, 1999), spinoff dynamics (Klepper, 2007) and informal networking (Lissoni, 2001), research collaborations are increasingly taking place over long distances. Non-physical research collaboration networks therefore typically bridge large distances and are not well approximated by physical distances. This implies that both geographically localized knowledge spillovers from regions nearby, and knowledge spillovers from research collaborations over long distances via network connections are important to knowledge production and the innovative performance of regions. Frenken et al. (2007) find that both localized knowledge spillovers and the knowledge spillovers stemming from collaboration in a network affect the innovative performance of NUTS-3 regions within the European Union. These results provide support for EU policies aimed at creating European collaboration networks (a European Research area). The importance of non-physical networks for regional economic growth is at the least suggested by the existence of so-called convergence clubs (Quah, 1996); regions that are not related by proximity seem to follow a comparable growth pattern.[6]

3.3 COMPETITIVENESS AND REGIONAL ECONOMIC DEVELOPMENT

Since the early 1990s, the concept of regional competitiveness has become a hegemonic discourse within public policy circles in developed countries (Bristow, 2005, 2010a, 2010b). The concept has been enthusiastically adopted as a policy goal by the European Commission and by national governments across Europe (Baldwin and Wyplosz, 2009, pp. 381–415). Most policy documents present the concept as an unambiguously beneficial attribute of a local or regional economy. Competitiveness is especially portrayed as the means by which regional economies are externally validated in an era of globalization. The strategic imperative is to take the required steps to attract and retain innovative firms, skilled labour and knowledge workers, mobile investment and central and supranational government subsidies and funds, with particular emphasis being placed on the relevant conditions in the microeconomic environment (including offering high-end working and living environments) within which productive firms can prosper (Bristow, 2010b). Firms will prosper if a region offers better conditions than its competitors and welfare gains are expected. The European Commission (2004, p. viii) for instance states that 'strengthening regional competitiveness throughout the Union and helping people fulfil their capabilities will boost the growth potential of the EU economy as a whole to the common benefit of all'. In general, reference to economic geographical and regional economic theory is made to justify competitive policy and planning strategies of regional policy-makers related to endogenous regional development potential (Dühr et al., 2010). But actually, the literature is not unambiguously positive about the concept; it can be even quite hostile in its conceptualization. Good insight into the competitiveness of European regions is therefore more important than ever, as many believe that Europe is losing momentum compared to the United States, Japan or China (De la Dehesa, 2006).

3.3.1 Welfare Gains and Benchmarks

Economists by tradition argue that competition is good, as it brings out the best in firms and regions and will ensure an efficient distribution of investments (Glaeser, 2001). But there are also cautionary remarks in the literature that point to potential welfare losses if budgets for attracting investments are high and only a few regions will be 'winners' (Peters and Fischer, 2004; Bartik, 2005). Prisoner's dilemmas may also induce too much competition over scarce investments where cooperation may be more beneficial from a welfare point of view (Geerdink, 2010). In the more geographical and political discourses on competitiveness, the concept has progressed into measurable and benchmark directions. The emergence of regional competitiveness as an important policy goal has spawned the development of indicators by which policy-makers and practitioners can measure, analyse and compare competitive performance. In recent years especially benchmarking exercises have become increasingly popular within the sphere of regional economic policy-making (Huggins, 2010). The international literature has predominantly been very critical on the limited ability of regional competitiveness circumstances to be copied elsewhere, as a kind of 'one-size-fits-all' policy (Bristow, 2005). But rankings do have value as regional benchmarking, undertaken carefully and meaningfully, is an essential prerequisite for informed and strategic policy-making (Malecki, 2007; Camagni, 2002). Benchmarking is linked to notions concerning the means by which regions or regional governments are able to learn, particularly through methods based on comparison or monitoring (Sabel, 1996; Rose, 1993). It is argued that benchmarking does not aim to strive for the most perfect situation, but functions as a means to progress by learning and bettering from comparing: 'Even if one is interested only in one's own society, which is one's prerogative, one can understand that society much better by comparing it with others' (Boxwell, 1994 in Huggins, 2010). This comparison can be applied to three fields of expertise. Performance benchmarks compare regions on the basis of quantitative material. This results in a 'winner', and regions can learn from knowing how success was achieved. Process benchmarks are based on qualitative data on structures and processes in regions. This often focuses on institutional best practices that can be applied in one's own region. Policy benchmarks are based on qualitative data, and compare policies between regions (Lundvall and Tomlinson, 2002; Borras and Tsagdis, 2008). Regions can learn from successful policy initiatives elsewhere.

3.3.2 An Applied Analytical Framework: Revealed Competition and Trade Networks

The trouble with many (if not all) performance rankings is, though, that they tend to combine unlike industries and indicators into aggregates that obscure important differences. And even provided that rankings compare like with like, they are still pernicious because they distract attention from the next important and necessary step to be taken: applied analytic frameworks that take into account economically valued network relations between places of (mobile) production factors and traded goods. The discussion of territorial competitiveness awaits an applied analytical framework that moves beyond the critical and problematizing stand that (actually too easily) is applied in recent literature (Kitson et al., 2004). In this publication we argue that for the concept's potential to be valued correctly, regional competitiveness should not be solely identified by structural characteristics (summarized in benchmarks or listings) of cities and regions, but alternatively by a theoretically informed analytical framework that uses actual networks of competing and economically valued relations between regions. Conceptually, we therefore introduce *revealed competition* as an important indicator for measuring interregional competitiveness. Measuring revealed competition between regions is an attempt to unambiguously determine which region competes with whom, on what and where. We will do so on a European scale, embedded in the discussion of regional competitiveness that has been boosted since the introduction of the Lisbon Agenda in 2000, and accumulated into the current (smart, sustainable and inclusive) growth objectives of the Europe 2020 policy programme that are also central in the envisioned cohesion policy reform after 2013.[7] Our analysis of revealed competition uses interaction data between regions in Europe – interaction by way of the mutual trade in goods and services – to pinpoint market overlap in internationally mobile and traded products, goods and services, and hence to measure competition on these markets.

3.3.3 The Discourses of Regional Competitiveness

Competitiveness usually refers to firm performance (Bristow, 2005). The concept is generally regarded as a somewhat abstract quality conferred upon successful firms by the markets within which they operate. Thus, 'the market is impartial and ultimate arbiter of right behaviour in the economy and competitiveness simply describes the result of responding correctly to market signals' (Schoenberger, 1998, p. 3). The fusion of economics with evolutionary theory has imbued the concept with the notion of 'survival of the fittest'. Firms, like living organisms, are seen as living on the edge, with survivors being those who are able to survive or 'win' in a dynamic world of economic competition (Sheppard, 2000). Competitiveness is also central in the discourse of the business community where it represents the fundamental external validation of a firm's ability to survive, compete and grow in markets subject to *international* competition (Schoenberger, 1998).

3.3.3.1 From micro- to meso-level conceptualization

Thus, at the micro (firm) level, competitiveness has a relatively clear meaning. Relative firm performance hence can be measured on a common scale – in terms of input–output relations. According to Michael Porter (1990) firm competitiveness is a proxy for productivity. A firm is able to produce more output with fewer units of input than their rivals, and this generates a competitive advantage. A firm's productivity thus depends on its entrepreneurialism, which enables process innovation, enables access to new markets and targets actual and new consumer demands (Spender, 1998). Porter has extended and applied his model of the competitive advantage of firms to the competitive advantage of regions, nations, cities, places and locations (see Porter, 1995, 2000). He made a strong case in arguing that places are equivalent to corporations, competing for market share within an increasingly interconnected and fiercely competitive global economy. Porter argues that whilst it is firms that compete, it is governments that create the market conditions to allow firms to exploit each economy's inherent competitive advantage (Bristow, 2005). Porter played an important role in propounding a microeconomic, productivity and output-related conceptualization of regional competitiveness. As with firms, Porter states that regional competitiveness and productivity are equivalent terms: 'A region's standard of living (wealth) is determined by the productivity with which it uses its human, capital and natural resources. The appropriate definition of competitiveness is productivity' (cited in Bristow, 2005). According to Porter, regional productivity is dependent on two interrelated sets of variables. The first concerns both the value of goods and services and the efficiency with which they are produced by firms and traded – their competitive advantage. Second, region-specific contexts determine this firm productivity: more sophisticated company strategies require more highly skilled people, better information, improved infrastructure and accessibility, better suppliers, more advanced research institutions and stronger competitive pressures. Both the spatial concentration of firms and the degree of integration between firms and their territory (via networked linkages) determine international competitiveness. Porter has successfully branded, transformed and exported his diagnosis of how regions may improve their competitiveness in localized clusters to development agencies and governments all over the world. This also fuelled the so-called theory of 'New Regionalism' that always starts from the concept of competitiveness and from the belief that the region should be the prime focus of economic policy (Lovering, 1999).

3.3.3.2 Macroeconomic competitiveness

According to Bristow (2005), a broader – yet overlapping – definition of regional competitiveness has emerged within the regional development literature, which has macroeconomic connotations. Michael Storper (1997, p. 264) is a principal proponent of this definition, which states that 'competitiveness is the capability of a region to attract and keep firms with stable or increasing market shares in an activity, while maintaining stable or increasing standards of living for those who participate in it'. This definition has gained widespread academic acceptance and use. Whilst this definition differs from that used by Porter, it derives from the same discourse of firm-based, output-related competition. This definition is in fact a direct application of a definition of (inter)national competitiveness adopted by the OECD (1992). Deliberately, the focus is not on firm-level productivity (only), but on regional economic development in general (Bristow, 2005). Microeconomic productivity is considered a necessary condition, but not a sufficient one for financial returns, market share and improved macroeconomic and welfare performance. A region is competitive when it has the conditions to enable it to raise the standard of living of its inhabitants. These conditions include a mixture of Porterian competitive advantage for firms and the attractiveness of the regional environment for business and human capital in an international context. Figure 3.2 shows the pyramid model of regional development and competitiveness adapted from Jensen-Butler (1996), Begg (1999), Lengyel (2003) and Gardiner et al. (2004). This figure suggests that productivity in regions may differ for a host of different reasons based on the discussed theoretical concepts. It is this pyramid model that gains most attention in academic

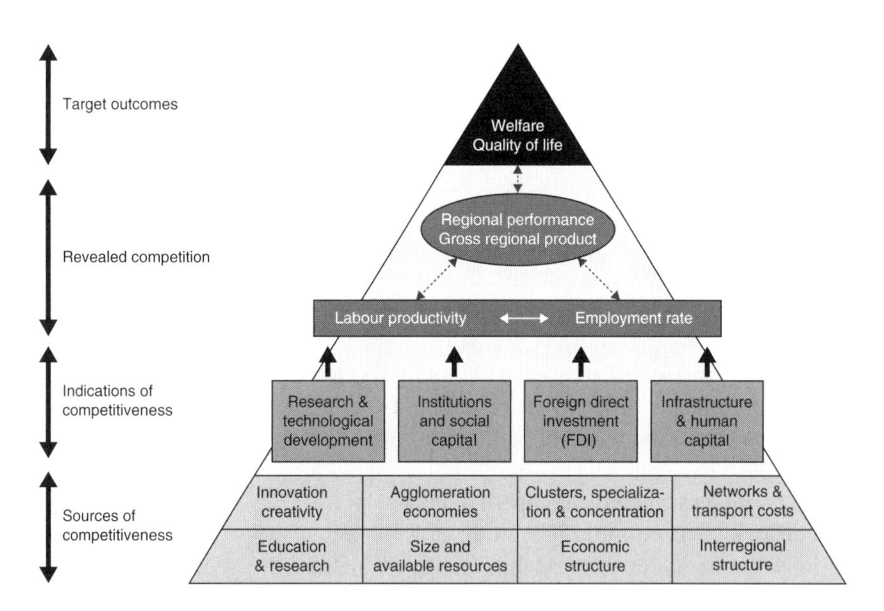

Figure 3.2 Building blocks of regional competitiveness

and policy circles, and offers most opportunities for a (diverse) research agenda. Gardiner et al. (2004) link this to an eclectic approach to (spatial) economic theories, ranging from neo-classical growth models, endogenous growth models to New Economic Geography models.

What also becomes clear from the figure is that regional competitiveness and regional prosperity are an interdependent notion, if not directly equivalent (Gardiner et al. 2004).

3.3.3.3 The policy discourse of regional competitiveness: economic valuation and networks

Bristow (2005) takes the richness of the above discussion to conclude that regional competitiveness lacks a clear, unequivocal and agreed meaning within the academic literature. Hence it is not surprising that the policy discourse around regional competitiveness is confused. She argues that policy-makers have tended to favour the macroeconomic definition of competitiveness which equates it with regional prosperity. She quotes a UK example, which states that regional competitiveness describes the ability of regions to generate high income and employment levels while remaining exposed to domestic and international competition – a definition actually also utilized by the European Commission (Annoni and Kozovska, 2010). The critique Bristow expresses profoundly, is that regional competitiveness seems to be more and more related to good governance, regional capacity for innovation, entrepreneurship and skills development and the creation of good business environments, clustering and knowledge density – all in relation to productivity – but shying away from identifying explicit causal relationships between productivity and attributes related to regional living standards. Instead, she argues, policy publishes series of indicators of all kinds of regional development (for example, those mentioned in Figure 3.2), and generally no explanation is provided as to how or to what extent these indicators relate to the overall definition of regional competitiveness (p. 290). Benchmarks and composite indexes, using inputs, outputs and outcomes of competitive processes are presented, without much discussion on causality and weighing. This then turns into a chaotic discourse, exemplifying a wider tendency towards 'theory led by policy' (Lovering, 1999). In that case, its content is thin and by definition ill-defined. She argues that the region-based theories might overlook that in some instances, the competitiveness of firms in a region might be altogether disconnected from the region. Much evidence presented in the literature is anecdotal, takes firm-level evidence wrongly for regional development (Markusen, 1994), and ignores the constitutive outside influences of social relations and international networks shaping regions and their development processes. Concerning regional development, Malecki (2002) and Tracey and Clark (2003) have drawn attention to the potential importance of global networks as sources of goods and knowledge in shaping firm competitiveness in an area. This international relatedness in terms of trade and relations is exactly what is missing from empirical studies of competitiveness. Krugman (1996b) suggests that, although sounding cynical, the competitiveness debate should actually deal with several time-honoured fallacies about international trade and productive relations that by now are dressed up in new and (too) pretentious rhetoric (p. 24). The international network dimension should be brought into the analyses of international and regional competitiveness – and that is what this study is about to do on a European regional scale. We want to add to the academic and policy discussion exactly to overcome that – in the words of Bristow (2005, p. 296):

> all composite measures of regional competitiveness, particularly those which develop composite rankings, fall into the trap of trying to make comparisons across very different regional entities, without exploring the extent to which these places are indeed competing with one another in tradable and commensurable markets in a manner measurable on a common scale.

This does not mean that composite measures and benchmarks are useless – but not taking the economic (valuation) and network dimensions into account leaves the competitiveness debate orphaned.

In this book we take the notion of smart specialization to explicitly incorporate economic networks in the concept of competitiveness embedded in theories of regional development.

NOTES

1. Excellent and extensive overviews are available in scientific papers (Puga, 2002; Combes and Overman, 2004), books (Brakman et al., 2009; Baldwin et al., 2003; Fujita and Thisse, 2002) and policy documents (World Bank, 2009; Barca, 2009; Farole et al., 2009).
2. The vertical linkages model of Venables (1996) is one of the first examples where productivity effects are integrated in the NEG model.
3. Classical international regional economic development is derived from the Heckscher–Ohlin model. See Ohlin (1933) or a more recent discussion in Krugman and Obstfeld (2000).
4. See Fujita et al. (1999) for an analysis of multiple agglomerations in the base model with neutral space. See Stelder (2005) for a simulation analysis using the model to reproduce an approximation of the actual size distribution of European cities given the presence of locally bounded physical capital such as road infrastructure.
5. Melo et al. (2009) report an interval which is even larger. With a sample of 34 studies on agglomeration economies, for 729 estimated values of elasticity, the authors find a variation of up to 29 per cent. Melo et al. (2009) in a meta-analysis find that the differences depend significantly on the inclusion of human capital, on the time of analysis,

on the industrial sectors included and on the geographical area considered. In another meta-analysis which considers 31 studies, De Groot et al. (2007) conclude that the theory provides 'strong indications for sectoral, temporal and spatial heterogeneity'.

6. Although it should be noted that this may also be caused by other common factors in these regions.
7. The most recent EU policy documents on competitiveness in relation to cohesion policy are: *Europe 2020: A European Strategy for Smart, Sustainable and Inclusive Growth* [COM (2010) 2020 3.3.2010]; *Fifth Cohesion Report on Economic, Social and Territorial Cohesion: Investing in Europe's Future*, European Commission, Brussels, November 2010; *Europe 2020 Flagship Initiative Innovation Union* [COM(2010)546]; *Regional Policy Contributing to Smart Growth in Europe* [COM(2010)553] and *The EU Budget Review* [COM(2010)700]. In the Europe 2020 programme, competitiveness is a central element in the 'smart growth' pillar, but also in cohesion policy – traditionally designed for redistributing wealth from stronger to weaker nations and regions – it is argued that over the years 'softer' investments in human resources and R&D prevail and there is a more heard critique that 'cohesion has become detached from its redistributive origins and incorporated in a discourse of competitiveness and growth' (Dühr et al., 2010). For an extensive discussion on this, see Barca (2009).

4. Clustering and specialization in European regions

4.1 INTRODUCTION

It would prove hard to discuss regional development without exploring the role of agglomeration economies. According to this idea, regions with a large urban population have a tangible advantage compared to less populous areas. A number of reasons have been put forward to back up this theory. In agglomerated areas, for instance, it is easier to have a good match between workers and employers, because of the wider range of possibilities provided by a larger labour market. It is also easier for a firm to purchase its inputs, as in a large populated region it would have better access to specialized suppliers (Marshall, 1890; Porter, 1990). Next, a number of authors noticed that agglomerated areas are ideal places to create, attract, accumulate and retain knowledge (Jacobs, 1969; Florida and Gates, 2001). Moreover, an enterprise can benefit from the access to a large local market. If the production technology of a sector exhibits increasing returns to scale, selling to a consistent base of local consumers may help firms to reach an efficient output size, which enables firms to compete successfully with firms in other regions (Krugman, 1991; Venables, 1996).

All in all, the theoretical debate (as well as a convincing body of empirical exercises[1]) concluded that the size of the agglomeration has a fundamental role in enhancing the capacity of local firms to emerge as successful players in international markets. Although there are indications that agglomeration also enhances congestion costs (for example traffic, pollution, housing prices), theory suggests that – on average – urban areas display features of increasing returns to scale.

In neoclassical theory of trade,[2] it does not constitute a big issue if a region is more agglomerated than another one. The advantage that the urban agglomeration has on the less populous area is, in fact, only comparative. When a region has a relative abundance of labour, it is directly implied that this region has a relative disadvantage in some other factors of production. In the long term, given homogeneous technology, this model expects the convergence of wages and all other prices of production factors.

Theories of agglomeration economies have questioned these conclusions. For instance, in New Economic Geography (NEG) models, wage convergence of different regions does not always occur. It is shown in these models that the agglomerated region often provides higher real wages (Puga, 1999). This is because NEG models incorporate a mechanism of increasing returns to city scale, which means either that workers in the larger region become more productive or that they benefit from a higher level of welfare. Additionally, many NEG models allow for interregional migration: some workers abandon the small region in favour of the agglomerated one, which offers better living conditions. This move makes the large region even more productive, which in turn makes it more attractive for those workers that are still in the less populated area. In the most extreme case, all mobile workers abandon the smaller region.

We observe that integrating trade models with labour mobility and increasing returns to city scale leads to a pretty hard conclusion. In many scenarios imagined by NEG theories, larger regions will experience persistently higher real wages. In these models, the abundance of labour in the agglomerated region is not to be measured in relation to the endowment of other factors of productions (the Ricardian comparative advantage), but it directly translates into productivity or welfare gain, hence into an absolute advantage (see also Camagni, 2002).

These theories have pushed many observers, both in universities and among policy-makers, to move part of the discussion on competition from nations to regions. The region that is able to attract and maintain mobile production factors, such as human and physical capital, is expected to make better use of increasing returns to urban scale and raise the welfare of its citizens. Naturally, regional competition is, to a large extent, a competition among firms in different regions. Nonetheless, firms compete for mobile resources whose agglomeration in a region will result in benefits for its residents. From a certain perspective, then, it is fair to say also that regions themselves compete for mobile resources, as their attraction is not only advantageous for the firms, but it will eventually have spillover effects on every actor in the region.

From regional competition to competitiveness is a short step. Regional competitiveness is seen as the capacity of a region to attract innovative firms, skilled labour, financial resources and government funds, while providing a suitable microeconomic environment in which firms can prosper and workers can experience high standards of living (Storper, 1997; Bristow, 2010b).

4.1.1 The Prospects for Small Regions

The cumulative effect between spatial agglomeration of resources and regional welfare has raised questions on the role of small regions with low population density. Is the disadvantage in size effectively turning into an absolute disadvantage? Are these regions destined to decline? Will the entire population eventually abandon the region, as in the most extreme cases of NEG models?

Theoretical reasoning combined with empirical observation indicates that this is not necessarily the case. First of all, there exist a large number of counter forces that are likely to prevent full agglomeration to occur. Traffic congestion, pollution and cost of housing are straightforward examples.

Other less obvious mechanisms are unveiled by NEG theory itself. Regional immobility, for instance, keeps an incentive for firms to locate in peripheral regions. In NEG models, the long-term equilibrium depends on the percentage of mobile workers against the percentage of immobile ones. In Europe the percentage of people who relocate each year is around 2 per cent (Combes et al., 2009, p.166). This number shows that a significant portion of the population is, as a matter of fact, immobile.

Transport costs also contribute to prevent full agglomeration. Counterintuitively, high transport costs are shown to give an incentive for economic activities to spread over the territory. In fact, high transport costs incentivize certain goods or services to be supplied locally. Low transport costs, instead, push activities to agglomerate in space in a small number of locations. Firms in agglomerated areas can produce more efficiently and then ship their products cheaply to peripheral areas. The progress of technology, together with that of logistics, has certainly contributed to the fall of transportation costs. However, as noted by Anderson and van Wincoop (2004), transport costs are far from being irrelevant in today's world. Rephrasing Mark Twain, the two authors write: 'The death of distance is exaggerated. Trade costs are large, even aside from trade-policy barriers and even between apparently highly integrated economies.' And if this is true for manufacturing (the focus of Anderson and van Wincoop, 2004), it is even more so in the case of services. For instance, restaurant services must have a very steep distance decay, as few people are willing to travel hundreds (or thousands) of kilometres for a dinner.

Product differentiation is another driver of agglomeration. Once more against intuition, the more products are differentiated, the higher the incentive for agglomeration. In NEG models, this happens because differentiation decreases the price sensitivity of consumers. With differentiated products consumers are more willing to buy products from other regions, even if they cost more, making it possible to initiate that cumulative causation which leads to agglomeration. With undifferentiated products, transport costs weigh more in consumers' decisions, giving local firms an advantage that other firms cannot outperform.

All these spreading forces suggest that small regions won't disappear any time soon. But there is another, perhaps more important, reason why these regions are not condemned to decline: even small and peripheral regions may take advantage of agglomeration economies. To understand the argument we need to think about the sectoral and geographical scope of agglomeration economies.

- *Sectoral scope of agglomeration economies.* Agglomeration economies are believed to work in two ways: intra-sector and inter-sectors. Localization economies are the spillovers or externalities that arise where there is co-location of activities of the same kind. So if an industry, let us say manufacturing of medical equipment, has features of localization economies, a firm in this business can only experience agglomeration advantages by locating close to other firms supplying medical equipment. In the literature, these types of agglomeration economies are also known as Marshall–Arrow–Romer externalities. Since they do not require the agglomeration of all kinds of activities to ensure a regional advantage, small regions can successfully emerge by specializing in a limited number of sectors.

  Urbanization economies, by contrast, are those agglomeration externalities that emerge in a large and diverse environment. In this case, it is more difficult to imagine a small region that can offer both a large and diversified economic environment. Urbanization economies (at times called Jacobs' externalities) are thus associated with leading agglomerated urban regions.
- *Geographical scope of agglomeration economies.* The geographical scope of agglomeration economies opens another discussion on growth opportunities of small regions. The concept of agglomeration economies is based on the idea that the benefits of the externalities attenuate with distance. But how is distance measured and until what distance are agglomeration economies important?

  Recent theoretical developments suggest that at least a part of urban externalities (for instance knowledge spillovers) are not simply 'in the air', but are channelled and transmitted through a network of relevant economic relations. Among these relations we can think of labour mobility, intermediate supply contracts, co-patenting and so on (Breschi and Lissoni, 2009; Neffke and Henning, 2012). Small

> regions can compensate for the lack of internal economic mass by establishing relevant connections with larger regions. To a certain extent, small regions can 'borrow size' from large regions (Alonso, 1973). For this reason it may prove convenient to a small region to open the economy and widen the geographical range of its economic interactions.
>
> In conclusion, small regions can survive not only because a set of congestion and spreading forces keeps them alive. Through specialization and/or through openness they may achieve productivity and welfare levels, comparable to those of agglomerated regions.

Some empirical evidence comes in support of these arguments. If it is true that agglomeration often coincides with wealth, there are many examples suggesting that this is not necessarily implied. Combes and Overman (2004), who focus on the EU15 in 1996, show that the wealthiest regions are not the only agglomerated ones. In this research we focus on 25 European nations (EU25, plus Norway, minus Cyprus) and we reach the same conclusions. The maps in Figure 4.1 depict population density and output per capita in the 256 regions we analyse in this book.

European population is distributed across the continent rather unevenly. A significant part of human activities in Europe are concentrated in the central part of the continent, along the area that came to be known as the blue banana. It roughly goes from England to the north of Italy, passing through Belgium, the Netherlands and West Germany. Outside this central agglomeration, other regions are fairly populous. The region of Paris in France, the regions of Madrid, Valencia and Barcelona in Spain, the regions of Rome and Naples in Italy are some examples. Also Poland, the Czech Republic and Hungary display some relatively dense areas. By comparing the distribution of population in Europe with their wealth (measured as GDP per capita), we see that the most densely populated areas are often those with the greatest GDP per capita. However, as noted by Combes and Overman (2004), this is not always the case. We observe that Eastern Europe, despite the presence of densely inhabited regions, still lags behind in comparison to the West. Other peripheral areas in southern Italy, Portugal, Greece and Spain are rather densely populated. The agglomeration of activities, nonetheless, does not always correspond to high levels of GDP per capita. In contrast, a number of central regions in Austria, Germany and France are scarcely populated and yet show above-average earnings. This evidence gives an indication that agglomeration economies might spill over to core regions. Small central regions may be taking advantage of the vicinity of the leading agglomerations in Europe, while peripheral regions, even when they are populous, may be

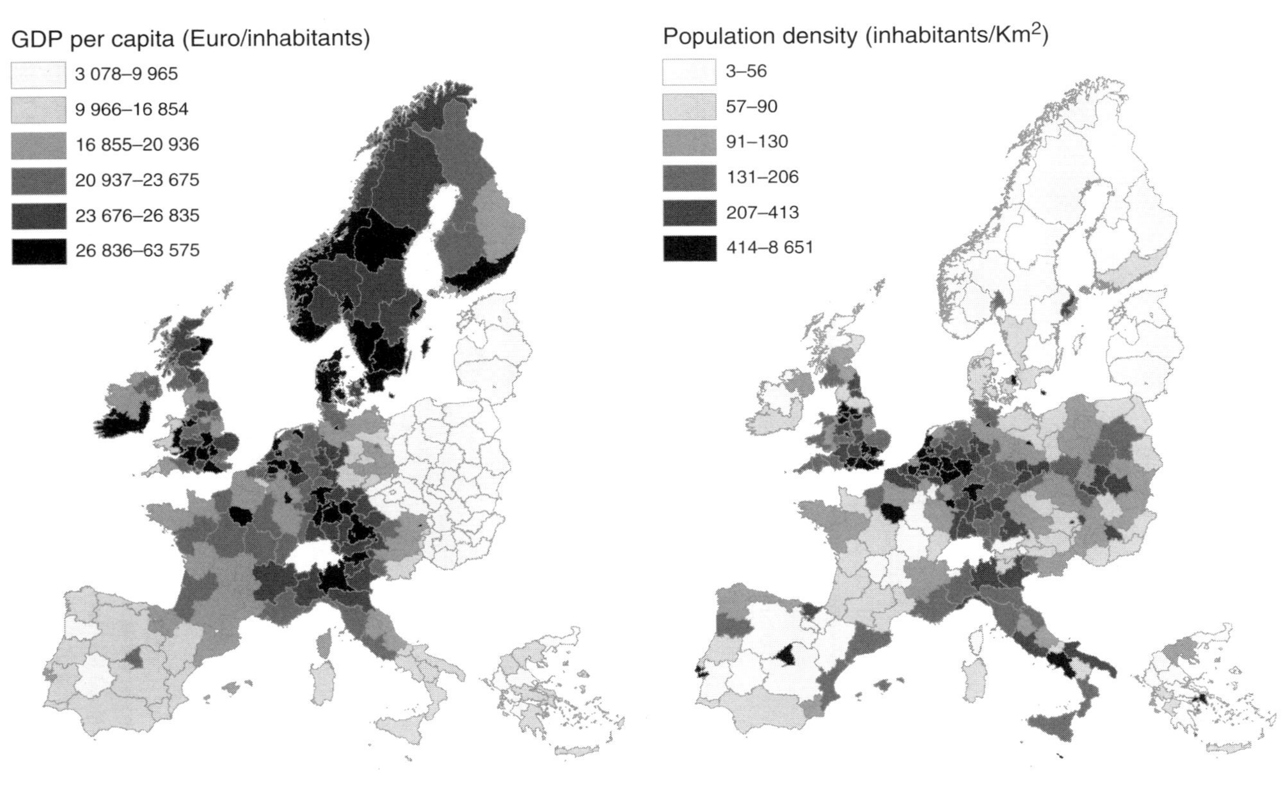

Figure 4.1 GDP per capita and population density of European regions

penalized by the less convenient position. The case of Northern Europe (Denmark, Norway, Sweden and Finland) provides a counter-example of peripheral low density areas with high per capita GDP. This shows that a low-density peripheral region is not necessarily sentenced to decline.

In addition to this static evidence, reports that focus on growth reach similar conclusions. In a study by the OECD (2009b) analysing regional economy in the period 1995–2005, it is noticed that a large contribution to growth comes from 'unexpected' places: lagging regions. The study observes that in half of OECD countries, more than half of the growth comes from below-average regions (50-50-50).

4.1.2 The Aim of this Chapter

The arguments presented are suggestive of substantial differences between regions of different size. Large, highly populated urban areas are thought to prosper in a diversified environment. They have sufficient size to host a large and heterogeneous labour market, as well as a great portion of the required supply chain. The local market helps to take full advantage of increasing returns to scale, while the diverse environment incentivizes the creation of new ideas through continuous recombination of knowledge.

When large regions have such advantages, the risk that small regions are overshadowed is high. To avoid this happening, smaller conurbations are expected to make use of agglomeration economies in different ways. The first way is through specialization. Specialization in a small number of sectors is seen as an effective way of making use of agglomeration advantages for small regions. In this case the region would focus on sector-specific urban returns to scale: localization economies.

In the first part of this chapter we go around Europe to carefully observe how economic activities are distributed over the territory. We pinpoint which regions are specialized and which are diversified. The observation of specialization/diversification characteristics of European regions can give an indirect suggestion of what kind of agglomeration economies (urbanization or localization) are in place in different parts of Europe.

A second way of making use of agglomeration economies, especially for small regions, is to establish a set of relevant interactions with agglomerated areas in order to 'borrow size' from them. One mechanism that is believed to be a carrier of knowledge externalities is input–output relations (Venables, 2006). In this way regions may gain a significant advantage by establishing a large network of supply relations outside their territory. However, it is not possible to say beforehand whether opening regional economies in this way is convenient. In fact, the economic literature has also associated the use of local inputs with regional development. If an industry mainly uses locally produced inputs, its growth will also boost the growth of its suppliers and subcontractors, which may cluster in the same region, and therefore contribute to create those beneficial cumulative effects of agglomeration (Porter, 1990).

In the second part of this chapter, we look at regional input–output interactions to see when European regions have ended up with a mainly localized (clustered) input–output network and when, instead, they display an international and varied network of supply relations (open). The input–output mechanism is certainly not exhaustive of all types of interactions which are relevant for agglomeration economies. However, it can give an indication of which European regions benefit from agglomeration by opening up the economy (try to capture someone else's mass advantage) and which focus only on local resources (try to have the relevant mass by themselves). In this book, we call the first case openness and the second one clustering.

In the third part of this chapter, the two dimensions of specialization/diversification and openness/clustering are combined into one framework to show more clearly the different nature of agglomeration economies in European regions. The chapter sheds light on how the size of a region and its geographical position in Europe influence the path taken with respect to specialization/diversification and openness/clustering.

The closing section also brings the discussion back to competition and place-based development policies. Following our arguments, all combinations of specialization (diversification) and openness (clustering) have a potential for growth. However, the kinds of circumstances that can trigger this potential are necessarily different. First, there are differences between specialized and diversified regions, as the transmission of localization and urbanization economies often follows different channels. Second, there are differences even between two specialized regions, as they may be focused on the production of different products. Third, there are differences between open and clustered regions, as the former try to share agglomeration advantages, while the latter try to appropriate them. We previously pointed out that regional competitiveness is seen as the capacity of a region to attract and retain mobile resources (such as FDI and human capital). In the light of the above discussion, we conclude that, according to the specialization/diversification and openness/clustering patterns, different regions may compete for different mobile resources, with different strategies. Place-based development policies at regional level should take these elements into account, as they provide an additional useful perspective to identify regional characteristics and potential assets. A comprehensive strategy can also benefit from smart specialization policies. For instance coordination of economic policies would help to avoid the situation where many regions compete to attract the same mobile resources.

4.2 SPECIALIZATION AND DIVERSIFICATION IN EUROPE

In the introduction, we noticed that agglomeration does not necessarily go one-on-one with productivity. Among the possible explanations we claimed that, while agglomerated areas are likely to diversify and make use of urbanization economies, small regions may perform just as well by specializing and making use of localization economies.

In this perspective, one of the main purposes of this section is to go around Europe and observe which regions are diversified and which are specialized. We try to understand if it is correct to make the link between agglomeration and diversification. In addition, we deepen the scope of the analysis to see in which kinds of activities European regions are specialized. Going into this level of detail is also important for this book's discussion on competition. With the overview of this chapter we can give a first snapshot on competition among European regions. In the next chapter (Chapter 5), we describe competition in more detail. Using trade data, we show that not every region is competing on the same markets. This section, by showing what Europe produces and where, can provide an initial indication, as well as additional guidance, towards understanding regional competition.

After exploring regional specialization, the section ends with a discussion on geographical concentration. In fact, concentration and specialization are two faces of the same coin. With specialization we look at distribution of activities from the point of view of the regions, which can be either specialized or diversified. With concentration we observe distribution from the point of view of economic sectors, which are either concentrated or spread.

4.2.1 Concept and Measurement

In this section we want to study the degree of sector concentration and region specialization in Europe. A distinction is made between concentration and specialization. The concept of concentration takes sectors as central units of reference. The focus is on the supply of a certain product or service and the way it is spread across the territory (Duranton and Overman, 2005). If a sector is found only in a few locations, we say that it is concentrated, while we call a sector spread if it can be found in many regions in Europe.

When a regional perspective is taken, we can observe that some regions host most sectors while others focus on particular industries. Regions that display a disproportionate presence of a specific kind of firm are referred to as specialized regions. Conversely, diversified regions are those that engage in the production of a wide range of activities.

We feel the need to highlight that in economic literature, the term 'concentration' refers to another, distinct, but related, concept. In this chapter we study geographical concentration, which focuses on the spatial distribution of activities. Industrial concentration, instead, concerns the distribution of production among firms, asking whether there is a high number of firms producing a comparable quantity of output (competitive market, for example bars and restaurants) or whether the production is concentrated in the hands of a few players (monopolistic market, for example aerospace). Given the confusion that this vocabulary might generate, in this study we are precise in our use of the term 'concentration': unless stated otherwise, we employ the word in its geographical sense.

A useful way to look at specialization and concentration is in relative terms. Despite the fact that sometimes one may be interested in the absolute size of, for instance, textile production in a region, we find it more informative, for the purposes of this chapter, to observe whether a region has an output of textiles which is larger than average. Therefore, region–sector specialization and concentration are measured through the Location Quotients (LQ) based on total output. This indicator is obtained with the share of sector s on the total production of region r, divided by the share of sector s in the whole of Europe.[3]

$$LQ_{r,s} = \frac{x_{r,s} / \sum_{s} x_{r,s}}{\sum_{r} x_{r,s} / \sum_{r,s} x_{r,s}}$$

A high LQ indicates that region r is specialized in sector s. Equivalently, it also indicates that sector s is concentrated in region r.

LQs are the starting point for the measurement of the overall regional specialization and sectoral concentration. To assess regional specialization, we want to compare the economic structure of region r with the economic structure of the whole of Europe. If a region resembles the production structure of Europe as a whole, then it is diversified. If, conversely, a region has a structure which differs significantly from Europe (for example more agriculture, less textiles, more machinery), we call it specialized. To measure specialization, then, we look at the structure of LQs in a region. If a region has most of its LQs close to 1, then it resembles the average region, and it is diversified. A region with many LQs above 1 (and many below) is, subsequently, a specialized region.

To assess regional concentration we look at the distribution of production across regions. If a sector matches the spatial distribution of the economy as a whole, then we call this sector spread. When a sector does not match population and it is, for instance, found only in much agglomerated areas or, perhaps, only in uninhabited regions, we define this sector as concentrated. Also to measure concentration we look at LQs. A sector with many LQs close to 1 is a spread sector, while a sector with many high and many low LQs is concentrated.

To quantify the distance from 1 of LQs effectively (and assess regional specialization and sectoral concentration) we need a measure of entropy-diversity. For this purpose, we use the Theil index.[4] Specialization is defined as follows:

$$\text{Specialization}_r = \left[\frac{1}{S}\frac{1}{\ln(S)}\right]\sum_s\left[\left(\frac{LQ_{r,s}}{\frac{1}{S}\sum_s LQ_{r,s}}\right)\ln\left(\frac{LQ_{r,s}}{\frac{1}{S}\sum_s LQ_{r,s}}\right)\right]$$

where S is the total number of sectors under analysis. The index assumes a value of 0 in case of perfect diversification and 1 for perfect specialization. Similarly, concentration is measured in the following way:

$$\text{Concentration}_s = \left[\frac{1}{R}\frac{1}{\ln(R)}\right]\sum_r\left[\left(\frac{LQ_{r,s}}{\frac{1}{R}\sum_r LQ_{r,s}}\right)\ln\left(\frac{LQ_{r,s}}{\frac{1}{R}\sum_r LQ_{r,s}}\right)\right]$$

where R is the total number of regions. This time a value of 0 corresponds to perfect spread and 1 to perfect concentration.

Our measurements are embedded in a burgeoning literature on specialization and concentration. Combes and Overman (2004) perform an extensive review and discuss the seven properties of an ideal index of spatial concentration/specialization. The Theil index falls short in some of these properties. In particular, it is sensitive to arbitrary changes in geographical and industrial classification.

Throughout the years the specialist literature has suggested several sophisticated indicators to satisfy unmatched requirements of this ideal measure. Duranton and Overman (2005) create a measure based on continuous space that gets rid of the problem of regional classification. The Ellison and Glaeser (1997) index of specialization, instead, controls for industrial concentration. The shortcoming of these indices is that they are very expensive with respect to data requirements. Given the range of European countries that we would like to cover, it is not possible for us to have a consistent dataset allowing such sophisticated measures.

However, the lack of data is not the only motive to choose for the LQs-based Theil index. In this book we focus on regional competition and development policies. The geographical unit of analysis is the NUTS-2 region, not uniquely because of data constraints, but also because NUTS-2 regions often coincide with the administrative territories targeted by the European Union with the regional development funds (cohesion policies). Consistently with the rest of the book, this section shows specialization/diversification of the territorial units we chose to analyse: NUTS-2 regions. The Theil index over the LQ fully satisfies our needs, as it provides a way of comparing the selected regions. Next, we are not entirely sure whether it is desirable to neutralize the effect of industrial concentration (as in Ellison and Glaeser, 1997) since we consider it as a relevant determinant of geographical concentration.[5] From this perspective, the Theil index also permits a meaningful comparison among chosen economic sectors.

Having said that, to better interpret the results, it is important to keep in mind the shortcomings of measuring specialization and concentration with LQs-based Theil indices. In the following pages, we present computations of the indices based on our dataset on European regional output. The dataset, as better explained in the Appendix, is obtained through an elaboration of Cambridge Econometrics and Eurostat statistics.

4.2.2 Specialization in Europe

We defined specialization and diversification in relative terms. A diversified region is a region that, with respect to production structure, looks like the average region. A specialized region deviates from the average structure. To clarify this, Table 4.1 shows the average production structure in Europe, with the economy divided into 11 large categories. We recall that the indicator of specialization/diversification we employ (Theil index) is based on 59 goods and services. Table 4.1 is intended to provide guidance to facilitate the interpretation of the indicator.

The table shows the primacy of the service sector in European economies, followed by the manufacturing sector. Within the manufacturing sector, the medium–low tech (MLT) and medium–high tech (MHT) subsectors are the most important. The primary sector's output is, instead, marginal if we compare its shares with those of the secondary and tertiary sectors. The difference between the value of output of services and

Table 4.1 Composition of output for Europe (2000)

SECTOR	Share (%)
Agriculture	2.3
Extraction of raw materials	1.0
Total primary sector	3.3
Knowledge-intensive manufacturing: medium–low tech	21.5
Knowledge-intensive manufacturing: medium–high tech	12.0
Knowledge-intensive manufacturing: high tech	3.0
Construction	8.6
Total secondary sector	45.0
Wholesale trade and transport services	10.7
Retail	6.0
Financial and business services	12.5
Other market services	8.7
Other non-market services	13.9
Total tertiary sector	51.7

manufacturing is just below seven percentage points. This margin would have been larger if we had used value-added instead of value of output to compile this table. The reason is that, in their production process, manufacturing sectors use relatively more intermediate inputs than the service sector. The mark-up is lower; hence the ratio output on added value is larger than it is for services.

Figure 4.2 shows the levels of specialization based on our data for 2000, featuring the distribution of activities over Europe. It may be recalled that the indicator employed assumes a value of 0 in the case of perfect diversification (in line with the European benchmark) and a value of 1 in the case of perfect specialization. Three large core nations, Germany, France and the UK, are close to the European benchmark: the distribution of activities in their regions resembles each other's and also resembles the aggregate European average (compare Combes and Overman, 2004).[6] The most diversified of all is Germany. This implies that German production shares across sectors are comparable to those in Table 4.1. It must be highlighted, though, that German regions, even if they appear to be similar to the average, are not exactly identical to it. The largest differences are found in the primary sector, especially in the resource-based industries.

Given the relatively low availability of resources, German regions have a lower share of output in the resource-based sub-sector. On the other hand,

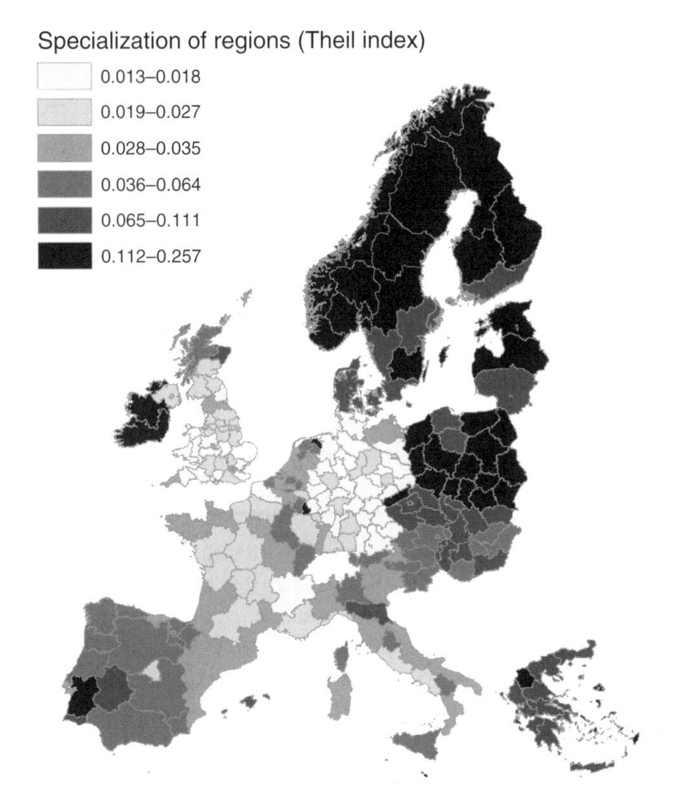

Figure 4.2 Specialization and diversification in Europe

Germany is stronger than average in the manufacturing sector, especially in the medium–high and high-tech industries. This is largely explained by the production of motor vehicles, which is, with some regional variation, up to 2.3 times greater in German regions than the European aggregate average. We also distinguish regions in eastern Germany as less industrial and more dependent on agriculture, construction and non-market services.

France shows an analogous pattern. The nation hosts a variety of activities, which is comparable to Germany, the UK and the European average. They also have a weaker resource-based sector and a stronger position in the services sector. However, the regional differences within the nation are greater than in Germany. Some regions, such as Bourgogne or Champagne-Ardenne, are more agricultural, while others, such as Franche-Comté and Rhône-Alpes, are more industrial.

The UK also has a range of activities close to the aggregate European average. Compared to Germany and France, the United Kingdom excels in the service sector, which constitutes 58 per cent of the value of output. Regional differences are also important in the UK, with the north of the country markedly specialized in the resource-based industry.

Next to these three core nations, Belgium, The Netherlands and Austria (small central economies) along with Italy and Spain (large, partially peripheral economies) are mid-way between specialization and diversification. Belgium scores relatively highly on MLT manufacturing and trade and transport services. The Netherlands is specialized in the resource-based sector (natural gas), trade and transport services and financial services (particularly in private insurance). Austria and Italy have high LQs in MLT manufacturing, Austria specifically in wood and paper products and Italy in textiles, leather and wearing apparel. A distinction is made between the north and south of Italy. While most of the manufacturing is concentrated in the north, the south of the peninsula is more agricultural. Some alpine regions (Valle d'Aosta, Trentino e Alto-Adige) and some coastal ones (Liguria and Toscana) are strong in tourism. Spain is specialized in agriculture, the construction industry and tourism. Important manufacturing niches are found in Cataluña and Pais Vasco. Spain has a peculiar regional pattern of specialization, possibly due to its position between the core and the periphery of Europe: the regions bordering with France are relatively diversified and the regions next to Portugal are more specialized.

At the periphery of Europe, we find the most specialized regions. Greece and Portugal are more specialized in the primary sector and tourism. Ireland is strong in knowledge-intensive activities, such as the chemical industry, manufacturing of computers and supply of computer services. The northern countries can be divided in two blocks: Sweden and Finland have significant specialization of firms in high-tech knowledge-intensive manufacturing and services. Denmark and Norway rely more heavily on the primary sector: agriculture, fishery and oil extraction. In Norway, the resource-based sector accounts for more than 14 per cent of the national output (the European average is below 1 per cent). Finally, the Eastern European countries are characterized by high shares in agriculture and MLT manufacturing and low shares in MHT manufacturing and services. Nonetheless, exceptional niches can be noticed. Hungary, for instance, hosts a number of MHT and HT firms in manufacturing of computers, machinery and electrical equipment.

Figure 4.3 attempts to show what European regions are specialized in. To obtain the map, the economy is divided into 11 categories of goods and services and LQs are re-computed according to this division. Next, a different type of shading is assigned according to the macro-sector each

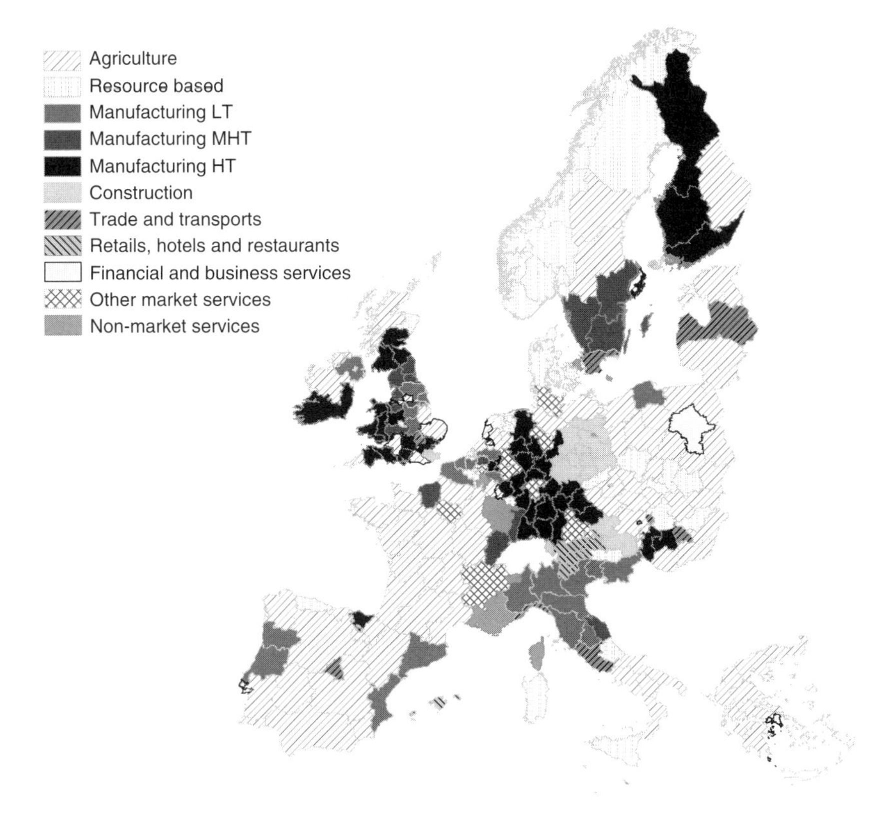

Figure 4.3 Main specialization of European regions

region is the most specialized in (highest LQ). This method provides an interesting overview of what European firms produce and where, although it only shows the first sector with the highest LQ.

It is also interesting to focus on the specialization patterns of the case study regions that will accompany us throughout this book. We present these regions maintaining the division in three groups: large agglomerations, strong medium sized regions and peripheral regions.

We observe that the agglomerations of London and Paris have a marked specialization in services. In particular financial services dominate the landscape of these regions, with inner London hosting more than twice the average share of these activities in Europe. Other services, such as real estate, also emerge.

The region of Munich is, in line with the other German regions, rather diversified. Other than a sizeable service sector, the activities of this region include the production of cars (BMW) and other medium–high or high-tech manufacturing.

The region of Milan is a large agglomeration with a distinct focus on manufacturing, especially in low tech. It excels in furniture, textiles and leather production. Higher-tech niches are also present, with a chemical sector, plastic production and electrical equipment. The share of financial services is low if compared to Paris and London, though it is still larger than the European average. Interestingly, the specialization of Barcelona resembles the one of Milan in many aspects. It differentiates itself with a larger construction sector, its food industry and with a smaller presence of financial services.

With respect to economically wealthy medium sized regions, we encounter a variety of specialization patterns. Brussels is decidedly service oriented, with the LQ of financial services scoring higher than 3. Helsinki is a peripheral region with relatively low density. With few services, little resources and almost no agriculture, the region finds a great part of its strength from the manufacturing of high-tech activities (among which we find Nokia). Another specialized niche can be found in activities related to forestry, the working of wood and pulp and the production of paper products.

Lyon is a rather diversified region with many LQs close to 1. In Figure 4.3 it is seen that the region is mostly specialized in services. However, one needs to be careful in reading this, since the risk is to obscure the manufacturing vocation of the region. In fact the Lyon area has a large presence of firms in textiles, chemicals, production of electrical machinery, medical and precision instruments.

The region of Rotterdam–The Hague is very peculiar in the European panorama. It is highly urbanized and densely inhabited, but it has managed, nonetheless, to become one of Europe's largest agricultural producers. The region is also known to be an important logistic hub for goods shipped from Europe to the rest of the world and vice versa.

Noord-Brabant is primarily a low-tech manufacturing region, with the strongest assets lying in the food industry (for example Mars), tobacco (Philip Morris) and chemicals (divisions of Shell, GE Plastics). The expected strong specialization in traditional electronic equipment produced by Philips is not observed in our data, most likely because the assembly part of the production is outsourced abroad (Atzema, 2007). However, Philips does show up in the HT sector with the supply of medical instruments.

Lastly, it is worth discussing a handful of peripheral and emerging regions, to get a feeling of which kind of specialization is typically observed in these cases.

Dresden is a region in East Germany, which shares borders with Poland and the Czech Republic. It has low shares of agriculture and few resources. Also manufacturing is not extremely developed, although we observe interesting niches of automotive and electric machinery. The main specialization of the region lies, however, in non-market services and construction.

Hungarian regions have relatively high shares of medium and high-tech firms. Specifically, we observe a concentration of firms in the production of radio, TV and communication equipment, electrical machinery and computers. Some regions also engage in a modest level of production of cars. Budapest, the capital, is where most of the country's services are concentrated, while in the rest of the country (as in Pécs, one of our case studies) we note high LQs in agriculture and resource-based activities. Nowhere in the country have we observed important clusters of financial services. These activities seem to have concentrated in Prague and, even more, in Warsaw. The Polish capital is also strong in transportation and distribution, while its extensive surroundings are mostly dedicated to the primary activities of agriculture and mining.

The regions of Thessaloniki in Greece and Andalucía in Spain make our case for that part of peripheral Europe that is currently undergoing major struggle. Thessaloniki is essentially relying on three macro activities: agriculture, textiles and tourism. A significant concentration of construction firms is also observed. Andalucía is to a certain extent similar, but on a different scale, since the region is inhabited by more than 8 million people. The region, in fact, is specialized in agriculture, tourism, construction and traditional low-tech manufacturing: food production. It is interesting to notice that similar specialization patterns are found in southern Italy and in Portugal.

4.2.3 Concentration in Europe

Although the main goal of this section is to understand the levels of specialization and diversity in European regions, it is important to be aware of the general geographical concentration/spread of sectors. The same methodology used for specialization is employed to obtain an indicator of concentration. The more regions' sectoral shares deviate from the average sector, the more they are concentrated. The index of overall sector concentration is constructed by observing, sector by sector, the deviations from the average.

Table 4.2 displays the share of output for different regions. This is also what the average sector looks like. Since 4.14 per cent of total output is in Paris, 2.98 per cent in Milan, 1.84 per cent in Inner London (and so forth),

Table 4.2 Top 20 regions by output

Region	Rank	Code	Share (%)
Île de France	1	FR10	4.14
Lombardia	2	ITC4	2.98
Inner London	3	UKI1	1.84
Rhône-Alpes	4	FR71	1.56
Oberbayern	5	DE21	1.50
Düsseldorf	6	DEA1	1.47
Cataluña	7	ES51	1.39
Veneto	8	ITD3	1.35
Stuttgart	9	DE11	1.31
Darmstadt	10	DE71	1.28
Emilia-Romagna	11	ITD5	1.26
Lazio	12	ITE4	1.25
Outer London	13	UKI2	1.25
Piemonte	14	ITC1	1.22
Comunidad de Madrid	15	ES30	1.17
Köln	16	DEA2	1.13
Provence-Alpes-Côte d'Azur	17	FR82	1.00
Southern and Eastern	18	IE02	0.97
Zuid-Holland	19	NL33	0.94
Arnsberg	20	DEA5	0.93

a spread sector is the sector that replicates this structure. A concentrated sector deviates from the pattern. Table 4.2 is mainly illustrative. For this reason (and because we study 256 regions) only the top 20 are shown.

Again, as we did for specialization, we quantify concentration by the Theil index over the Location Quotients. The measure employed gives for each region a score on specialization that ranges from 0 (complete diversification) to 1 (perfect specialization). Comparably, the concentration levels shown in Figure 4.4 range from 0 (spread) to 1 (concentration).

The services sector is, with the exception of financial services, rather evenly spread across European regions. It is most likely that the prohibitive cost of trading most services means there is a strong incentive to supply one's activities locally. Trading of services can be done primarily in three ways (Sampson and Snape, 1985): electronically; with the supplier travelling to the customer; or in the opposite direction, from the customer to the supplier. With many services still requiring face-to-face interaction, there are reasons to believe that trading services is quite expensive. This may be reflected in the higher degree of spread that services display, if confronted with goods.

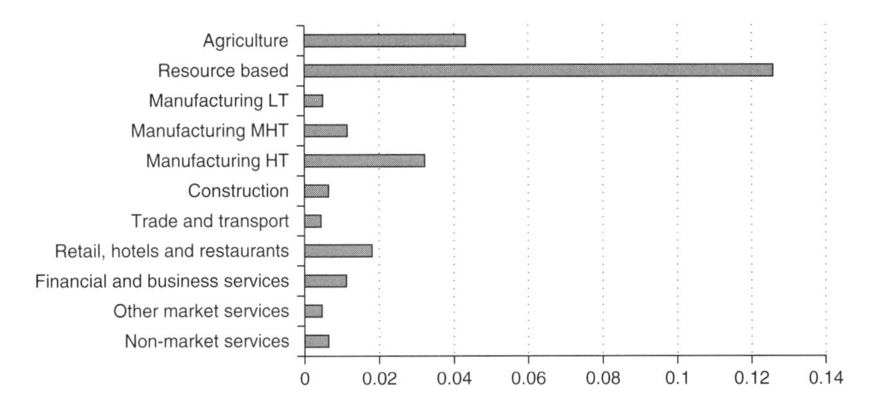

Figure 4.4 Concentration in Europe

The category *Retail, hotels and restaurants* is more concentrated than other services. We expected retailers to be rather spread, to match population. In fact, if we look at wholesale services, we notice that this sector is quite spread. Hotels and restaurants, on the other hand, are expected to be found in abundance in tourist areas, which will not match the distribution of population.

Within the tertiary sector, finance and business services are, after retail, hotel and restaurants, the most concentrated. It is hard to precisely isolate the reasons behind this. However, we can venture to propose a number of (ex-post) explanations. The puzzling part is that for banks, pension funds and insurance companies, proximity to clients and the possibility to access the market is an asset, in this way pushing the sector to spread where clients are situated. Nonetheless, The majority of financial services do not really require face-to-face interactions and can be provided electronically. Next, there is a difference between branch offices and headquarters' activities. While a firm has the incentive to spread its offices, the location of its headquarters is based on specific locational characteristics. In this case, firms in financial and business services may be looking for agglomeration benefits, the most important of which is likely to be the access to highly skilled workers.

High-tech manufacturing is concentrated, while the rest of the manufacturing sector is relatively spread. While the concentration of high-tech manufacturing could have been anticipated, the same cannot be said for low-tech manufacturing, which is subject to opposing economic forces that cause the geographical distribution of this industry. On one hand, medium and low-tech manufacturing is mostly mature industry, with economies of scale and low costs of trading that generally induce industrial concentration (Brakman et al., 2009). On the other hand, the output of the industry is relatively undifferentiated. When firms have to face a high degree of competition, trade costs become important, even if they are relatively low (Krugman, 1991b). Observing a medium and low-tech sector perceivably spread throughout European regions suggests that the latter force is prevailing: trade and transport costs appear to have a significant weight in the location of medium and low-tech firms, pushing the demand for their products to be served locally. In support of this explanation we notice that the degree of concentration of manufacturing increases proportionally with the level of technology involved, with low tech being the most spread, medium–high tech more concentrated, and the high-tech sector, the most concentrated.

The primary sector, especially the resource-based sub-sector, is highly concentrated. For the resource-based sector this is easily explained by the uneven distribution of oil and natural gas across Europe, with the largest repositories in Norway and northern UK. For agriculture it is somewhat more complex to explain the high degree of concentration. Common experience and perception suggests that the sector is scattered over the entire European territory. One explanation might be that, even though agricultural land is spread in the continent, high value-added agriculture (especially fruits and vegetables) is concentrated in a limited number of regions. This may very much be the case. However, we think that the majority of the explanation lies somewhere else: the way concentration has been measured. We define a sector as concentrated if its distribution on the territory deviates from the average. This average (which is given by the distribution of population and its activity) is more concentrated than agriculture. As a consequence, our measure of concentration detects agriculture to be concentrated for the simple reason that, unlike the population, it is quite evenly distributed in the territory.

This observation highlights a potential problem in interpreting the measure of concentration we use. It is embedded in our definition of concentration (as relative to the average distribution of economic activities) that a sector that is geographically too spread will be considered concentrated. From the strict point of view we take, this is correct: agriculture is concentrated in those regions that lack other economic activities, exactly because we defined concentration relative to the average distribution of economic activities. However, the reader must have noticed that interpreting concentration gets trickier in this case. For a sector that is more evenly spread than population, our measure of concentration may deceive those who still bear in mind a definition of concentration based on a different benchmark (for example, regional land area).[7]

To explore whether other sectors may trick our understanding of concentration/spread we run a simple test. We order the 256 regions by sectoral output share. It is observed that the distribution of output share for all 11 sectors considered roughly follows the typical skewed distribution known as the Zipf law (rather unsurprisingly). The intention of this test is to assess whether the distribution of a sector is flatter (more even) than the average distribution. To quantify it, the logarithm of the ranking is regressed on the logarithm of the output share. This is repeated for every sector and finally for the whole economy (the average sector). Confronting the slopes of the distribution, we see that agriculture is the only sector with the marked characteristic of being more evenly distributed (flat) than the average sector, while being concentrated at the same time. Other sectors (construction, trade and transportation) also have flatter distribution than the average sector. However, they are close enough to the average sector to be detected as spread by the LQ-based Theil index. All remaining sectors have steeper slopes than the average.

From the perspective of place-based development and smart specialization policies getting a grip on which sectors are geographically concentrated and which are spread is not just a theoretical exercise. It has been discussed that some sectors have the tendency to spread across the territory to match the population. Some sectors, instead, appear to be inclined to concentrate in a limited number of locations. Finally, other sectors rely on natural resources and they are forced to be located near those resources. The distinction among these three cases is of great importance for regional development policies aimed at attracting mobile resources.

If market forces push a sector to be spread, policies that attempt to concentrate this sector in a region may have higher chances of failure. By contrast, a sector that is prone to concentrate in space could in some cases justify the effort to attract (or retain) firms and specialized workers. This could be, for instance, the case if the sector has yet to reach maturity and it is still not clear which regions will come out as the winners of this competition for mobile resources. As an example, think of the production of solar panels. This is a growing industry that uses highly qualified workers, produces differentiated goods that are not too expensive to transport and it is subject to economy of scale. It is probable that in the following years this industry will consolidate in some regions, but it is still not clear where.

We notice that there is a difference between being specialized in sectors that are found in only a few places, and being specialized in sectors that are spread over Europe. Regions that are specialized in those sectors that are generally spread over Europe are likely to be specialized because of the lack of other activities. On the other hand, a region that is specialized in a concentrated sector holds some kind of monopolistic power, which may be highly advantageous for its citizens. We conclude that, to a certain extent, concentration qualifies specialization and that it is important that these elements are taken into account in the design of smart specialization policies.

4.3 CLUSTERING AND OPENNESS

Agglomeration economies 'amplify with density' and 'attenuate with distance', says a World Bank report of 2009, 'Reshaping economic geography'. The question on our minds is: what distance? We have been observing agglomeration for pre-determined NUTS-2 regions, but what if benefits of agglomeration spill over across these borders? Even if NUTS-2 regions are relatively large units of analysis, there may be some agglomeration externalities that do not exhaust their effect when they reach the regional boundaries. From this perspective, even a region with low density of activities may benefit from agglomeration economies of another region, if they have enough interactions. In the words of Alonso (1973), a region may 'borrow size' from another.

In our discussion on agglomeration and competitive advantages, we claim that there are at least two aspects which need to be analysed to comprehend agglomeration economies better. These aspects are the sectoral and geographical scope of agglomeration economies. With respect to the sectoral scope we looked in the previous section (4.2) at specialization and diversification around Europe in an attempt to understand which kind of agglomeration externalities (localization or urbanization) are giving benefits to which regions. In the current section, we observe which regions are clustered (to appropriate agglomeration advantages) and which are open (to borrow size), in this way trying to assess the geographical scope of agglomeration economies.

4.3.1 Concept and Measurement

A recent stream of literature in evolutionary economics stressed that agglomeration spillovers cannot be assimilated by simply standing next to a cluster of economic activities, but they are acquired through the establishment of relevant interactions. It is argued, for instance, that knowledge is not simply 'in the air' (as in Marshall's metaphor, Principles of Economics, Book IV, Ch. X, 1890), but it is transmitted through formal or informal relations, like collaborations, intermediate supply, labour mobility and so forth (Breschi and Lissoni, 2009; Neffke and Henning, 2012). These contributions suggest that physical proximity facilitates the exchange of externalities, but it is neither a sufficient nor a necessary condition for agglomeration economies to materialize.

From this perspective, looking at the network of interactions in which a regional economy is engaged can be seen as an effective way to assess whether the region's agglomeration economies are locally bound (clustered) or outward oriented (open). If economic agents maintain a large majority of interactions within the region's borders, then we can see the region as clustered. Conversely, if a large range of relations are found with neighbouring regions or, better still, international actors, then it is likely that the scope of agglomeration economies are beyond the administrative borders. We associate this second case to borrowing size and we refer to it as regional openness.

In this research, we study the regional-sectoral network of intermediate supply to obtain an indication of the degree of openness or clustering in a region. There are three main reasons why we believe that exploring regional input–output relations can provide a reasonable proxy to understand whether a region's agglomeration advantages are predominantly contained in its borders or borrowed from somewhere else. First, the access to specialized suppliers is, by itself, one of the mechanisms which are believed to be at the root of agglomeration economies, ever since Marshall (1890). Large markets can host a greater variety of input suppliers that can tailor production to the needs of other firms. These suppliers are also put into a position of stronger competition with each other, pushing down prices and driving up efficiency (Venables, 2006). Second, input–output relations are thought to be an important mechanism of knowledge transfer. In *The Competitive Advantage of the Nations* (1990), Porter reports a body of anecdotal evidence of this phenomenon: regional clusters, which initially were forced to import a relevant portion of intermediate inputs, with time acquired with the knowledge to produce these intermediates themselves. Third, the analysis of input–output structure allows sectors to be isolated and the geographical scope of agglomeration externalities of different economic compartments to be studied in detail.

We want to stress that input–output flows cannot capture all the relevant mechanisms that are supposed to be the cause of agglomeration economies. The most important element that our indicator does not account for is the agglomeration effect given by the labour market (for example, knowledge transfer through labour mobility or through informal ties among workers of different companies). However, for the reasons explained, we believe that suppliers' interactions do provide a reliable indicator of the geographical scope of agglomeration economies.

The analysis makes use of an original dataset constructed for the purpose. Regional use and supply tables, together with bilateral trade data, are employed to build a large regional/sectoral input–output matrix. To adapt the use and supply matrices to the input–output framework, we follow the industry technology assumption (Miller and Blair, 2009).[8]

Two new indicators have been developed using this input–output matrix. The first indicator is based on the backward linkage and illustrates how much intermediate inputs come from the same region. We call this the indicator of clustering[9] and it can be computed for the whole region or per sector in every region. It measures the intermediate production in a region, which is used to produce one unit of final demand. So if the market demands 1 (million euros) of the product sector s in region r, the indicator measures all the intermediate output that region r produces in order to satisfy this demand.

If we define A as the input requirement matrix, with $r \times s$ sectors of destinations and $r2 \times s2$ sectors of origins, formally we have:

$$\text{Clustering}_{r,s} = \left[\sum_{s2 \in r} (I - A_{r,s2,r,s})^{-1} \right] - 1$$

In other words, the A matrix is first cleaned of interregional links. Then the Leontief inverse is taken. Next, we take the column sum of the elements of the inverse; however, not of all the elements, only the ones that refer to intermediate sectors that are located in the same region as the sector demanding the inputs. Lastly the value of final output (which equals 1) is subtracted, to have a measure that focuses uniquely on the inputs.

The second indicator we use in this section captures the variety of sources that a sector uses for its inputs. We call this the openness indicator. The methodology for measuring this concept is derived from economic theory: a theoretical optimal use of inputs from various sources[10] is confronted with the actual expenditure on inputs. If a sector purchases its inputs from a relatively large range of suppliers, the indicator will score highly. Instead, if a sector depends on a small number of intermediate producers, the indicator will get low values. The following equation describes the approach:

$$W^{s2}_{r,s} = \left[\sum_{r2} \left((X_{r2,s2})^{\frac{1}{\sigma}} (E^{r2,s2}_{r,s})^{\frac{\sigma-1}{\sigma}} \right) \right]^{\frac{\sigma}{\sigma-1}}$$

W indicates the ideal theoretical use of input $s2$ (by region r, sector s), in a production function with love-for-variety.[11] Parameter E is the actual observed input $s2$, coming from region $r2$, used by sector s in region r. The larger is the number of regions that are providing this input (and the larger is the output X of those regions), the larger is W. We note that W is the ideal use of one input type only. If we want to make useful statements on how open or clustered a sector or a region is, we must aggregate over the different inputs employed by this sector/region. The final indicator of input openness is:

$$\text{Openness}_{r,s} = \frac{\sum_{s2} K^{s2} W_{r,s}^{s2}}{\sum_{r2,s2} E_{r,s}^{r2,s2}}$$

where K is an estimated parameter that serves us to scale the measurement. The rationale of the division comes from the necessity of accounting for size.

If the inputs of a sector-region come only from one, perhaps small region, the resulting value of the indicator of openness will be small and we can conclude that the input–output network of this region-sector is limited. In this case we do not expect this sector-region to have a geographically wide scope of agglomeration economies. The expectations are different when a sector-region shows a wide input–output network, connected to many sectors in many regions. This is consistent with the logic we presented to conclude that, in this situation, the scope of agglomeration economies goes beyond the regional borders, to assume a more interregional and international connotation.

The indicator of clustering and the indicator of openness will serve us, together, to assess the degree to which a region or a sector is locally focused (to appropriate agglomeration advantages) or internationally oriented (to share these benefits). Although these two indicators are meant to describe two opposing concepts, they are not exactly the mirror image of each other. We do expect, on average, the indicators to be inversely related, for the simple reason that if a region does produce most of the inputs locally, there is not much room for having a large pool of international suppliers; nonetheless, two scores in the same direction (either high–high or low–low) are also possible. To exemplify, a sector which uses only one big foreign supplier will score low on both indicators. Conversely, a high score on both measures can be found in a sector that uses local inputs significantly and also a large variety of foreign inputs. In the analysis we will highlight those cases. Nevertheless, we are more interested in the situations when the two indicators give converging results, as they provide more convincing evidence on whether a region relies on its own mass or tries to borrow it from other regions.

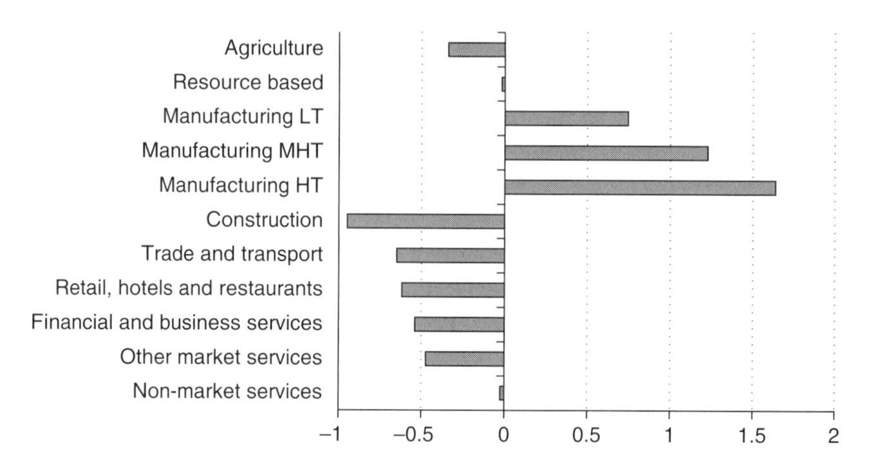

Figure 4.5 Sector clustering (negative scores) and openness (positive scores)

4.3.2 Sector Clustering and Openness

Before focusing on the geographical differences, the overall degree of openness and clustering of sectors is discussed. In fact, some sectors are more internationally oriented than others, while, in contrast, there are sectors in which clustering is more commonly observed. In order to evaluate potential regularities, we developed a synthetic indicator, which takes into account both the concepts of clustering and openness.[12]

Results are rather instructive (see Figure 4.5). First, a general rule that holds all around Europe is that manufacturing sectors display more openness to international markets than services. A quite likely explanation for this phenomenon is that, in the service sectors, the largest part of the inputs used are other services, which are in general less tradable than goods. Manufacturing, instead, makes extensive use of goods as inputs. This allows the sector to be more independent from the limits of local production and permits the supply chain to be more open to international markets.

The primary sector is somewhere in between, more clustered than the manufacturing sector, but more open than the service sector. More in detail, agriculture shows a supply chain that is rather embedded locally, resembling almost the structure of services rather than that of goods. This is somewhat less expected, taking into account that inputs of agriculture are tradable in nature (other agricultural products, chemicals). If we look in depth, we discover that these results are driven by the lack of variety of source (the openness component) rather than by a strongly clustered supply chain. The resource-based sector has an average score, led by moderately scarce levels of both clustering and openness.

Next, it appears that the more a sector is knowledge intensive, the more it is open to international markets. This is especially true for the manufacturing sector, in which the score of the indicator increases proportionally with the advancement of the technology, with high-tech firms having the most open production structure. It is also possible to observe this trend in services. High-tech services (telecommunications, computer-related services and research and development) are among the most open sectors in the service category. Many theories, especially within the field of economic geography, have claimed the importance of networks in knowledge creation and diffusion (Ponds et al., 2010). Our data strongly support this view.

It is also worth noticing a few peculiarities. The construction industries are an exception within the manufacturing sector, as they show a rather clustered structure. Most construction materials can be traded (basic metals, fabricated metals, machinery and so on). In spite of this, the sector still has a tendency to purchase its inputs locally. This may be due to the low level of technology, high transport costs and low economy of scales of some important inputs, like cement. Retail, wholesale trade and transport are the most clustered among services. It must be noted that the goods distributed by these sectors are not accounted as inputs in the ESA95 system. Typical inputs of the trade and transport sectors are other trade and transport services, financial and business services and transportation equipment.

Finance, business and other market services are clustered as well. It appears to be customary for these sectors to make abundant use of other services (or even of services in the same aggregated category) as intermediate input. Again, low tradability of many services provides an incentive to cluster.

Third, the category named in Figure 4.5 as 'Non-market services' is an aggregate of a number of services: education, health, social work and, lastly, recreational, cultural and sporting activities. Given the public nature that these sectors have in Europe, it is surprising to spot them as the most internationally open services. Analysing the data in more detail suggests that this unexpected result is driven by two factors: first, recreational, cultural and sporting activities seem to be a rather open sector, whose services are traded significantly over Europe. Second, the health sector uses two very internationally traded inputs in abundance: medicines and medical instruments.

4.3.3 Clustering and Openness in Europe

In some sectors, such as high-tech knowledge-intensive manufacturing (HT), we observed a strong tendency to openness. For some others, such as the financial sector, we verified the existence of a rather clustered structure. It might be tempting to conclude that in open sectors like manufacturing, being an open region is an advantage. Similarly, one can conclude that in clustered sectors like services, a clustered supply chain is beneficial. These conclusions may be inexact, though. There is no convincing a priori reason for which a predominantly clustered sector could not be outperformed by a concentration of firms with a more open conformation. We therefore do not make any assumption on whether clustering is more convenient than openness or vice versa. In section 4.4, an effort is made to understand why some regions are more clustered or open than others, and we argue for some possible interpretation. The current section remains descriptive in nature. We investigate how regions are performing with respect to openness/clustering in different key sectors. The three macro-sectors we selected to represent different compartments of the economy are presented: agriculture, manufacturing and financial and business services.

Unlike other sectors, agriculture has been found to be neither strongly oriented to international markets nor particularly clustered. The synthetic indicator shows that the weight is slightly unbalanced towards clustering (mostly for lack of input variety), but all in all agriculture is in between the two extremes. Since these are average results, it is important to highlight that agriculture does have a wide regional variation in the scores of openness and clustering. It is, hence, instructive to look at the patterns across Europe. The map presented in Figure 4.6 depicts the measures of clustering and openness for different regions in the agricultural sector. In this map we did not aggregate the two indicators into one synthetic score.

The comparison between the two maps gives a visual insight into the opposite nature of the indicators we are presenting, with clustering being almost the mirror image of openness. Nevertheless, this is not always true. A number of regions have positive scores on both indicators, while some other regions perform quite poorly from either perspective. Positive performance on both indicators are found for instance in the regions of Munich and Lyon, with high scores in clustering and openness. Notable counter examples can be seen in the regions of Milan or Barcelona.

Although we can see that there is an important degree of difference among regions in the same nation, clustering and openness in agriculture is rather dominated by country effects. In particular, France (except the region of Paris), Hungary, Slovakia, Czech Republic, Poland, Denmark, Finland, Norway and the Baltic states are very *clustered* in agriculture.

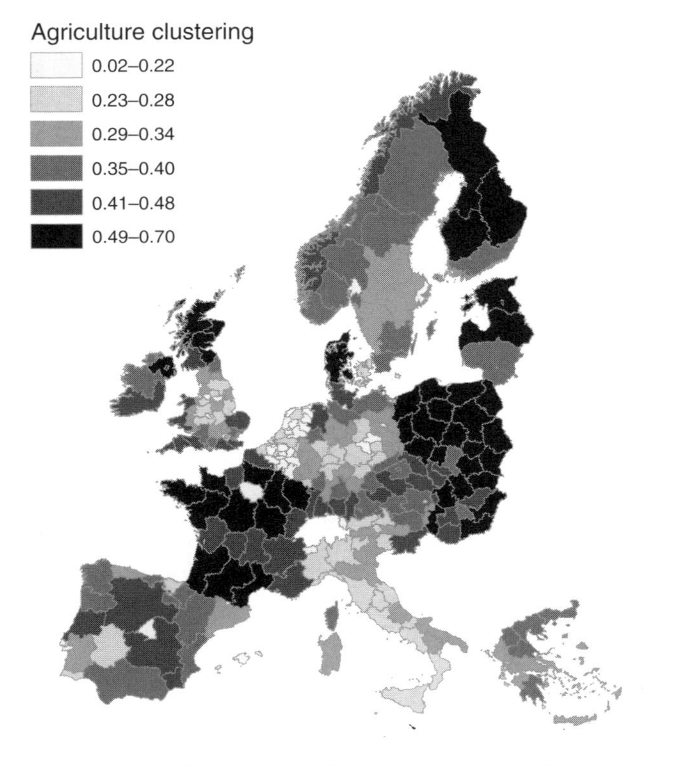

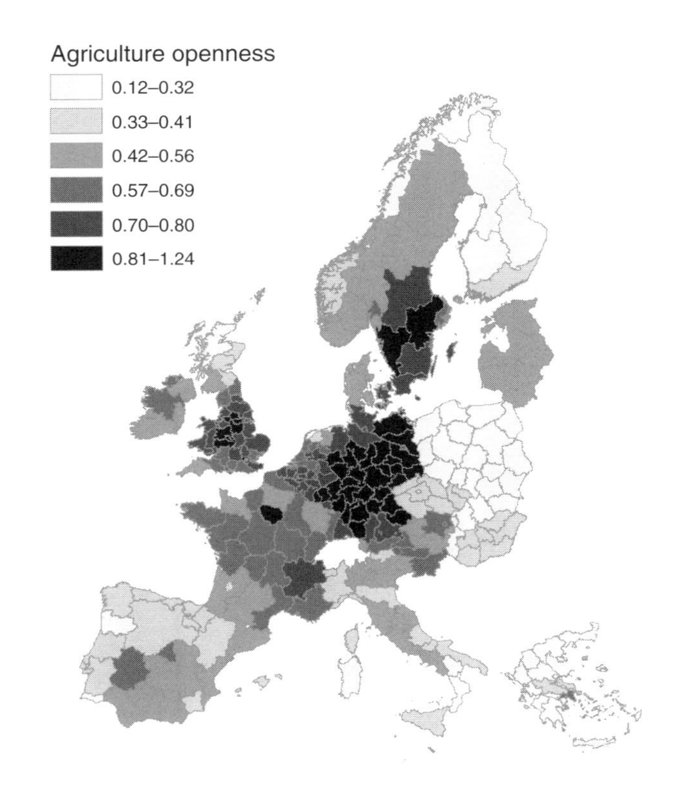

Figure 4.6 Clustering and openness in agriculture

On the other hand we observe The Netherlands, Belgium and large parts of Germany as the most open. The United Kingdom appears to be open in the south (England and Wales), while clustered in the north (Scotland and Ulster).

Italy, Spain, Portugal, Ireland, Greece and Sweden stand in the middle, neither clustered nor open. In some cases, as in Italy or certain regions of Spain and Greece, we can identify low results in both indicators.

It has been pointed out that on average manufacturing is characterized by a larger degree of openness, given the higher tradability of its inputs. Our analysis shows empirically that the knowledge content of a sector increases its openness towards international markets. The score of openness/clustering differs across Europe, according to the knowledge content of the sector. Although the overall pattern is comparable, there are regional dissimilarities, which are worth discussing separately. For this reason, our analysis first discusses aggregate manufacturing, but subsequently we differentiate between medium–low, medium–high and high-tech manufacturing (MLT, MHT and HT).[13]

Openness in manufacturing presents a core–periphery structure, with a centre identifiable on an imaginary North-West to South-East diagonal that crosses Ireland, England, Belgium, The Netherlands, Germany, Slovenia and Hungary. Near to the core, Denmark, Czech Republic, Slovakia, Austria and Italy are less open relative to the top performing regions, but still rather open in absolute terms. The degree of openness in this sector seems to attenuate with distance from the core. At the periphery of Europe, we observe the lowest scores: Poland, Finland, north Sweden, north Norway, Greece and Scotland. An intermediate position is held by south Norway, south Sweden, the Baltic States, central France, Spain and Portugal.

Some relevant changes are found when we study the openness of only MLT firms. In this sector (which represents 59 per cent of manufacturing output), the pattern is fairly similar to overall manufacturing, although we witness a strong contraction of the core. This contraction reduces the area in which firms are very open, to only four countries: Germany, Belgium, The Netherlands and England. Because of the shrinkage of the centre, the core–periphery structure gets accentuated. On the other hand, if only HT firms are considered (8 per cent of manufacturing output) new areas become part of the *open* centre. The general structure is maintained, but the relative openness of Germany, The Netherlands and England is eroded. Austria, Italy and to some extent Spain are in comparison characterized by a considerably internationally open HT sector.

Data on clustering is consistent with the figures on openness. We can see in Figure 4.7 that the core regions of Europe, on the diagonal between Ireland and Hungary, score low on self-sufficiency. There is a

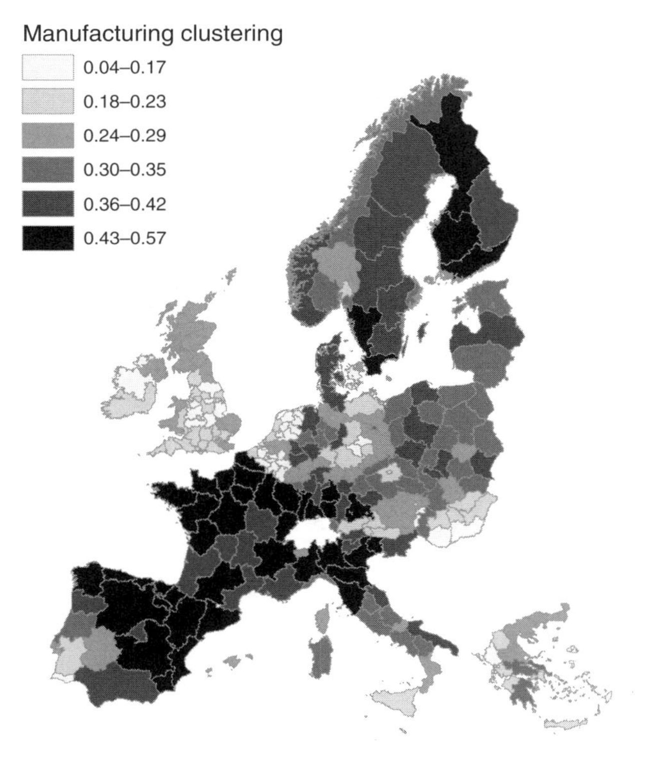

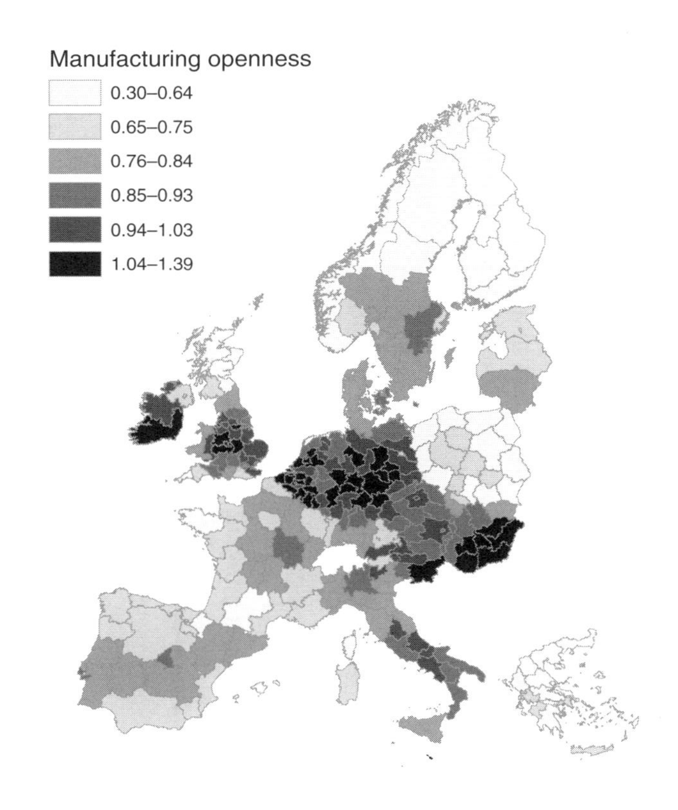

Figure 4.7 Clustering and openness in manufacturing

dominant South-Western European block, constituting Spain, France, south Germany and the north of Italy, that is relatively more clustered in manufacturing. Another important block is identified in Finland and, partially, Sweden. While the variation of openness according to the knowledge classification (MLT, MHT and HT) is significant, in the case of *clustering* the outcome is much less influenced by this factor. Only in Spain and Sweden do we perceive a strong fluctuation. While east Spain is always relatively self-sufficient, the remainder of the country is so only with respect to MLT. Instead, Sweden shows strong local autonomy in HT more than in any other knowledge-intensive manufacturing sector.

As expected, we observe that regions that score highly on the clustering index perform poorly on openness, and vice versa. However, we spotted a few important exceptions: all Greek regions appear to be lacking in both openness and clustering. On the other hand, there are some regions in Europe that score highly on both dimensions. The north of Italy and east of Spain achieve rather positive scores on both indicators, with the manufacturing centres of Milan and Barcelona in the forefront. Other regions with a significant presence of manufacturing also display remarkably high levels of openness and clustering. This includes the regions of southern and western Germany, southern Sweden and Slovenia.

Lastly, we discuss financial and business services. As stated above, this sector is characterized by a marked degree of clustering. The general core–periphery pattern that was observed in agriculture and manufacturing is also observed in this case. Regions in proximity of the blue banana tend to be more open than regions at the edges of the continent.

However, in a break with the two previous cases, we notice that the national patterns are less dominant, especially with respect to clustering. Among the most *clustered* regions we often find the financial centres of each nation. We see, among others, Lisbon, Madrid, Barcelona, Milan, Paris, London, Berlin, Frankfurt, Munich, Brussels, Prague, Bratislava, Budapest, Warsaw, Stockholm and Helsinki. These centres are also, in many cases, rather open to international markets. With a few exceptions (for example Helsinki, Bratislava), all the above-mentioned financial centres appear to have a positive mix of clustering and openness.

Another significant exception is seen in The Netherlands, which is, along with Belgium and Greece, the least *clustered* nation in Europe for financial and business services. It is worth noting that the financial and business centres of the Randstad (North-Holland, South-Holland and Utrecht) score poorly on clustering, while positively on openness.

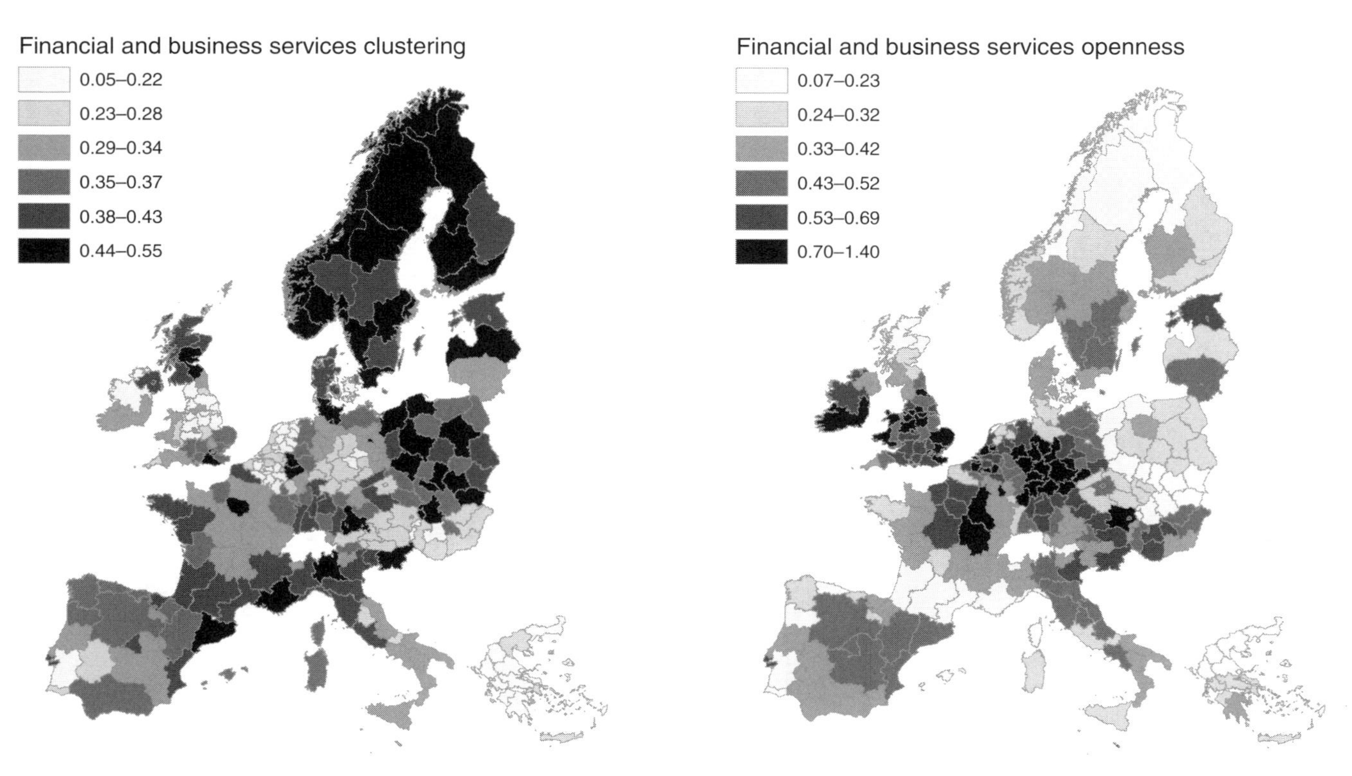

Figure 4.8 Clustering and openness in financial and business services

4.4 DEVELOPMENT STRATEGIES

In this chapter, we argue that agglomerated regions have a significant economic advantage if compared with their scarcely populated counterparts. We discuss that this advantage may as well be absolute (in contrast with classical and neoclassical models), which raises the question concerning the prospects of small, low-density regions. Sections 4.2 and 4.3 suggest two ways in which small regions can avoid being entirely outcompeted by dominant agglomerations. First, through specialization small regions can make use of localization economies, which are sector-specific agglomeration economies. We refer to this first dimension as the sectoral scope of agglomeration economies. Second, through interactions with large agglomerations, small regions can benefit from someone else's urban returns to scale (Alonso's concept of borrowing mass). This second dimension concerns the geographical scope of agglomeration economies.

If in the previous two sections we have looked at the concepts of specialization/diversification and clustering/openness separately (with primarily a descriptive purpose), in the following pages we cross these two dimensions to evaluate their relevance simultaneously. We argue that the concepts of specialization/diversification and clustering/openness can be used as a framework to analyse which path of development regions have taken. These paths will be named *strategies*, although the reader must be warned that we do not want to imply that there is a political process or decision behind it. We analyse 'observed strategies' knowing that in many cases they are likely to be the results of market forces.

The purpose of a simultaneous analysis of specialization/diversification and clustering/openness is threefold: first, to observe the different strategies of European regions and have a better perspective of what was discussed in sections 4.2 and 4.3. Second, we attempt to identify regularities and patterns, to understand whether we can explain the differences in sectoral and geographical scope of agglomeration economies. The underlying hypothesis we want to verify is whether it is true that the mass of a region, and its central or peripheral position, have an influence on its strategy with respect to specialization/diversification and clustering/openness. Third, the development strategies can be useful guidelines in the design of place-based policies.

We identify four strategies that arise from crossing the conceptualizations of specialization/diversification and clustering/openness. In Figure 4.9, these two dimensions are crossed against each other. On the horizontal axis we have the synthetic clustering/openness indicator for an aggregation of all sectors, while on the vertical axis there is the specialization index employed (Theil on Location Quotient). The

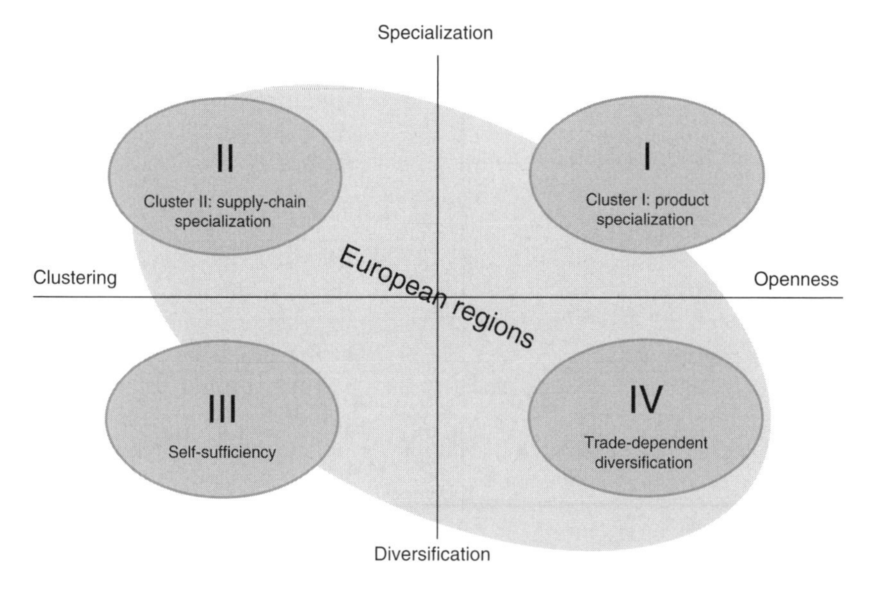

Figure 4.9 Development strategies

intersection of the axis defines four quadrants, to which we attribute the different strategies.

I. *Cluster I: Product specialization.* A region in this situation is specialized in a relatively limited number of sectors. However, suppliers are not clustered in the area, but provide their intermediate goods or services through trade from somewhere else.

II. *Cluster II: Supply chain specialization.* Unlike the previous case, this type of cluster involves the presence of intermediate suppliers in the proximity. They are comparable to rather mature industrial districts as described in Porter (1990), in which various elements of the supply-chain group together in the same region.

III. *Self-sufficiency.* Regions in this quadrant have the characteristic of producing all sorts of goods and services, including the intermediate inputs required for the final product. The name naturally derives from the fact that this type of region benefits from large margins of economic autonomy.

IV. *Trade-dependent diversification.* The last category we identify derives from the crossing of diversification and openness. In this case, regions exhibit wide and various varieties of economic activities, while engaging in a wide array of importing and exporting activities of intermediates.

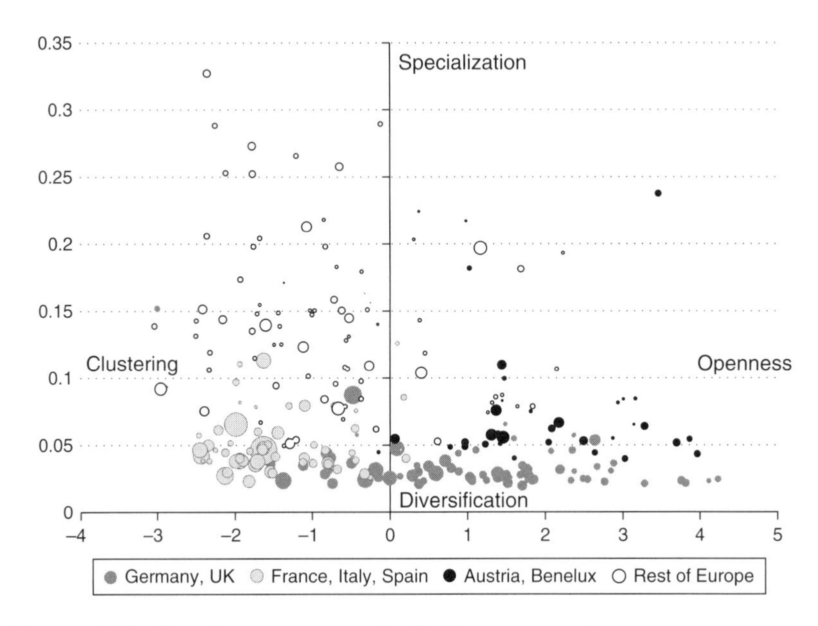

Figure 4.10 Development strategies in European regions

4.4.1 The Strategies in Europe

What strategies with respect to sectoral and geographical scope of agglomeration economies are followed in Europe? Using the framework discussed, in Figure 4.10 the 256 European regions in the analysis are plotted. On the horizontal axis we have the synthetic indicator of clustering/openness by region. On the vertical axis there is the level of specialization/diversification. To include more information in the graph, we vary the size of the bubbles in proportion to regional output. Moreover, regions are gathered in four macro-groups with different shades of grey: (a) Germany and UK; (b) France, Italy and Spain; (c) Austria and Benelux; and (d) the rest of Europe. The groups have been selected on a practical basis, by looking at revealed strategies, and they are meant as a tool to facilitate the reading of results.

At first glance, we note that the majority of European regions (because of the skewedness of the distribution) are relatively diversified. That means that a large number of regions follow either strategy III or strategy IV, to various degrees. A significant group of regions, instead, can be found in the group of type II, being specialized and clustered. We finally observe that the strategy we named product specialization (strategy I, a specialization characterized by abundant use of external intermediate inputs) is not very commonly adopted in Europe: only a few outliers are positioned in this quadrant.

Next, it was shown, in paragraph 4.2, that Europe's big corc has a relatively diversified economy. While this is particularly true for Germany, France and the UK, it also holds to a large extent for two other large nations: Italy and Spain (compare with Figure 4.2). Crossing specialization with openness for the five large Western European countries suggests that the group can be classified in two sub-categories. Figure 4.10 shows that the regions belonging to France, Italy and Spain show high levels of clustering. This group follows almost in its entirety a self-sufficiency strategy (III) and only a few regions are found in other quadrants. Even these regions are relatively close to quadrant III and their position in other strategies largely depends on the arbitrary choice of drawing the boundaries of the different strategies.

In the case of Germany and the UK. We observe a mix of openness/clustering strategies, with a moderate tendency towards openness and, consequently, for strategy number IV: trade-dependent diversification. The city of London represents a clear outlier. The level of specialization of this region is significantly higher than that of its reference group. These findings can be partially explained by the strong position of London in financial and business services. North-eastern Scotland also shows exceptional level of specialization for the heavy presence of resource-based activities.

The third group represents the regions of the small core European countries: Austria, Belgium, The Netherlands and Luxemburg. With few exceptions, the regions in this group are mostly oriented to strategy IV, openness and diversification. We notice that this group could be, to some extent, compared to Germany and the UK, for their central location in Europe, for the average size of their regions, and for their preferred strategy. The two clear outliers are Luxemburg (strong specialization in business services) and Groningen (for the significant presence of fossil fuels).

The last group constitutes all remaining regions in Greece, Portugal, Ireland, Northern and Eastern Europe. A common feature of these countries is to be located rather at the geographical edges of Europe. For this group we can verify that the dominant strategy is the type-II of clustering. Two specific large outliers are visible in the first quadrant, the atypical strategy I. These two regions are the NUTS-2 subdivision of Ireland. This atypical position may be justified by the fact that Ireland is a well-known case study (Barry, 2004; Buckley and Ruane, 2006) of a specialized export platform.

Figure 4.10 helps us also to have a first, rough picture of what might lead to certain development strategies. As we have said, the size of the bubbles is proportional to regional output. Visual inspection suggests that the largest regions in Europe end up with an approach of self-sufficiency (strategy III). In an economic sense, this can be explained by the fact that large regions may have the critical size to produce everything internally. Looking at different nation groups, it seems that the position of regions within Europe also has an effect on regional strategies. Central regions tend towards diversification and openness (strategies III and IV), while peripheral regions appear to be more oriented to supply-chain specialization (type II). We want to investigate these intuitions further.

4.4.2 Mass, Position and Strategies

Our hypothesis is that there is a connection between the type of strategy adopted by different European regions and two important geographical characteristics of these regions: the mass and the position. By looking at Figure 4.9, we get some interesting hints that these elements may, in fact, be connected.

In order to better evaluate the influence of mass and position, we combined the two elements into one, well-known, indicator: market potential (MP).

$$MP_o = \sum_d (X_d dist_{od}^{-1})$$

where X represents the output of region d and $dist$ the distance between region o and region d. The advantage of this indicator is that it can capture agglomeration economies, partially solving for regional classification. In fact, normally we would underestimate the urban externalities of a small region, which is surrounded by a number of large agglomerations. MP, instead, takes this element into account and corrects for it.

The shortcoming of this indicator is that its measurement relies on a number of arbitrary choices that need to be made by the researcher. In particular, two important choices are the slope of distance decay and how to account for the distance of the own region. In the measurement we present the exponent on distance is set to −1 (linear decay), while the distance of the own region (the diagonal) is measured with the formula: $dist_{oo} = (2/3)\sqrt{A_o/\pi}$, where A is land area in square kilometres.[14]

In Figure 4.11, we map our measurement of MP in Europe. We can see that the central, populous and wealthy regions (blue banana) have the highest MP, while peripheral Europe shows the lowest values. Next to it we have a rearrangement of the previous figure (Figure 4.10). The dimensions of specialization/diversification and clustering/openness are kept the same, but the size and the shade of the bubbles have been changed. Now

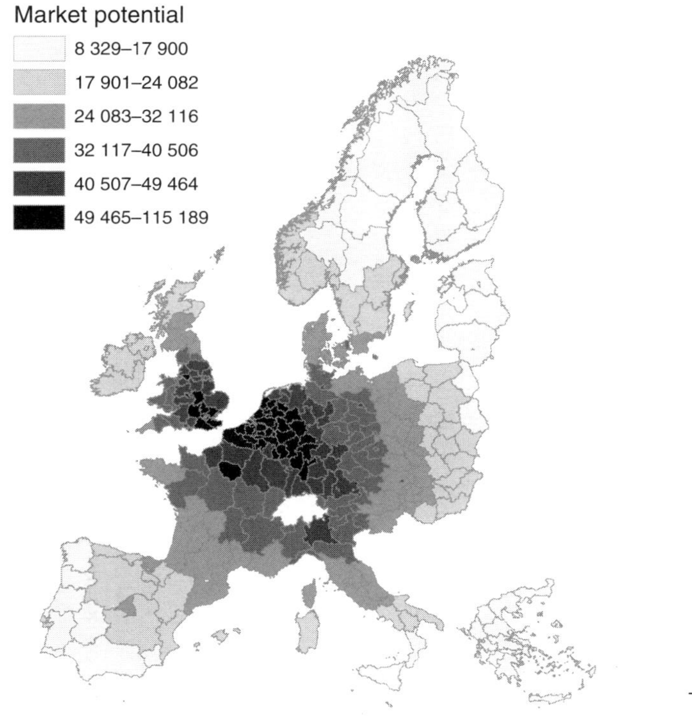

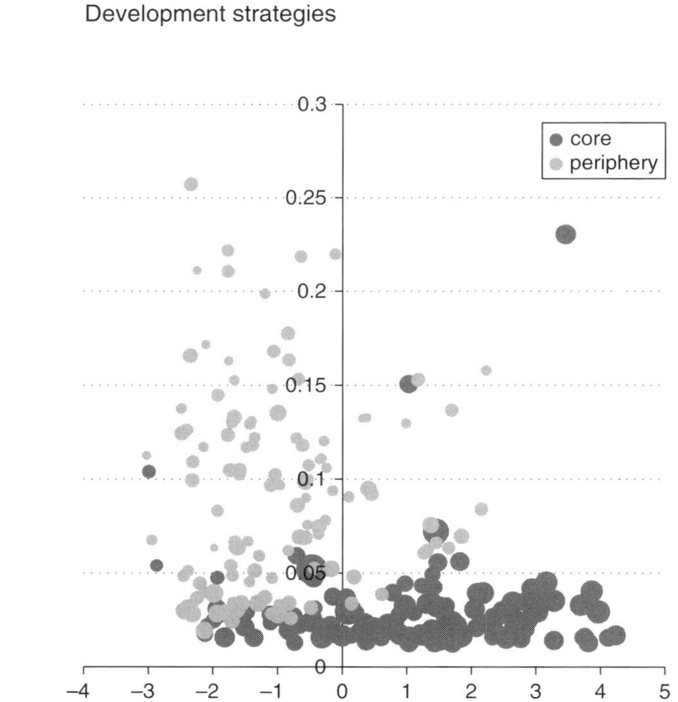

Figure 4.11 Market potential and development strategies

Table 4.3 Different OLS regressions with all variables in logarithms

Dependent variable	Regression 1	Regression 2	Regression 3	Regression 4
	Specialization		Openness	
Size	−0.3819***		−0.0212	
	(−9.36)		(−0.40)	
Market potential		−1.0781***		0.8709***
		(−14.27)		(8.56)
Constant	1.4144**	11.5053***	1.5897*	−11.6969***
	(2.22)	(10.23)	(1.89)	(−7.72)
Adj. R-squared	0.2535	0.4428	−0.0033	0.2207
# observations	256	256	256	256

Notes: t-statistics are presented in brackets. *, ** and *** denote levels of significance of 10%, 5% and 1% respectively.

the bubbles are proportional to MP, while the two shades of grey are used to distinguish the core of Europe from the periphery.

The division between core and periphery is done on a conventional basis. Germany, UK, France, the Benelux and Austria are labelled as core, the rest as periphery. It could be argued that the north of Italy should be considered core, or that the north of the UK should be included in the periphery, but these are issues that do not modify the main conclusions. These conclusions are that core regions are in the bottom-right part of the framework (diversified and open) while peripheral regions are in the top-left (specialized and clustered). There are some exceptions, that is regions that are in strategy III (diversified and clustered) and some exceptions in the top-right quadrant, but considering Figure 4.3, the overall message is clear. Next to the classification in core or peripheral regions represented by the shade of the bubbles we can look at the size of the bubbles (proportional to MP) to find a comparable message. It appears that there is a gradual proportionality between MP and the position of regions on the graph. The higher the MP, the more regions are diversified and open. Vice versa, the lower the MP, the more regions are specialized and clustered. We want to put this interesting regularity to the scrutiny of statistics. In Table 4.3 we report the outcome of a number of regressions.

The idea behind these simple regressions is to test the following questions: does an increase in size or market potential increase the level of diversification? And does an increase in the same two explanatory variables lead to more openness? By taking the logarithms of all variables, we model the relationship among regressors and regressand in a log-linear fashion. The parameters of the models are estimated through Ordinary Least Squares (OLS).

With respect to diversification/specialization, we find what we expect: both size and MP have a statistically significant negative effect on our indicator (the Theil index). That implies that the larger the mass (or the centrality), the more diversified is the region. As we said, both size and MP are statistically significant, but we note that the model with MP (regression 2) has a larger explanatory power (Adj-R^2 = 44%) and larger t-statistics than the model with just size (regression 1).

With respect to clustering/openness, the model with size as independent variable carries no explanatory power (Adj-R^2 is negative). Instead, the results with MP are in line with expectation from Figure 4.11 (right-hand side): the larger the MP, the more open is the economy.

We conclude that MP is a better predictor of both diversification (specialization) and clustering (openness) than size. The reason is that when using MP the geographical position of a region is taken into account. We notice that it is possible to give an interpretation on the estimated magnitude of the betas. For the log-linear regressions, the estimated parameters are to be read as the exponents of a power function. Therefore, the model of regression 2 claims that if we halve the MP, the Theil coefficient, the measure of specialization, more than doubles ($0.5^{-1.078} - 1 = +111\%$). Similarly, regression 4 suggests that if we double MP, the synthetic indicator of clustering/openness increases by 82 per cent ($2^{0.871} - 1$).

Despite the fact that with these regressions we are looking at rather simple (if not basic) correlations, the results strongly suggest that the dynamics of specialization and clustering, which we called – perhaps improperly – 'strategies', might be in large part driven by geographical forces. We can distinguish between two kinds of forces, using common terminology often used in the literature: first and second nature geography. In fact, it appears that specialization and clustering depend on the position of regions in Europe (exogenous, first nature) and the distribution of activities in those regions (endogenous, second nature).

4.4.3 Sector-specific Strategies

The simplified four-quadrant framework we presented was applied at the regional level. Nonetheless, it is also interesting to perform a similar type of analysis on specialization and openness at the regional-sectoral level. In fact, the relations between specialization, openness and size differ perceivably by sector, suggesting that it is interesting to take this dimension into account when analysing regional development strategies. Each of the 256 regions in Europe will have a specific strategy, according to the segment of the economy we focus on. Consistently with the rest of the book, the key and representative sectors of agriculture, manufacturing and financial and business services are discussed.

The conceptual framework needs to be slightly modified to perform an analysis by sector. The concept of diversification loses its meaning at the sectoral scale. On the other hand, indicators such as the location quotient are able to capture the sector specialization. Consequently the framework's vertical axis won't range, as in the regional case, between specialization and diversification, but it will vary between specialization and non-specialization. The clustering/openness indicator, instead, can be calculated at sector level, as we did in section 4.3. In this setting, the sectoral framework confronts the level of specialization of a sector-region with its level of clustering/openness. Furthermore, in the same fashion as the regional framework, we will depict a graph with bubbles, whose size is proportional to the total output in that particular sector. In this way connections between specialization, openness and size can be investigated.

In Figure 4.12 the framework for agriculture is represented. As an illustration, four regions are highlighted in the graph. We selected four specialized in agriculture from the set of regions in the study.

In the agricultural sector it appears that there is a direct relationship between clustering and specialization; the more specialized a region is, the more the sectors in the region are characterized by clustering. It is also seen that a region is more open if it is less specialized. This relationship is fairly clear and it can be verified in the graph that almost all regions lie in the

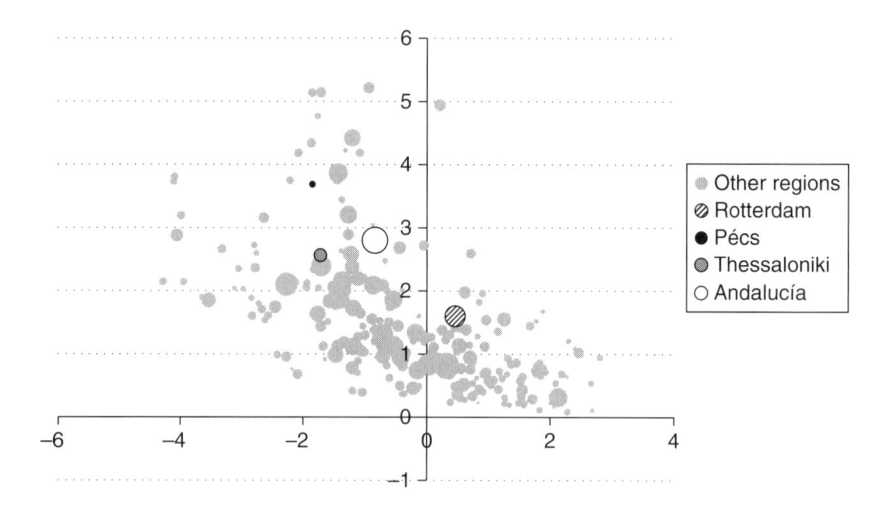

Figure 4.12 Agriculture strategies

second and fourth quadrant of the framework. This suggests that in most cases regions specialized in agriculture also specialize in the supply of the necessary inputs, while regions that are not specialized in agriculture tend to import the intermediate components of the supply chain. An explanation for the pattern we observe could be that when a region specializes in agriculture, suppliers of intermediates are attracted to cluster in this region. However, this is not the only possible explanation. We have noted in section 4.2 that the regions that are more at the periphery of Europe are mostly specialized in agriculture (see Figure 4.3). An alternative explanation, then, for the positive correlation between specialization and clustering in agriculture reflects the fact that peripheral regions in general are more inclined to clustering. With this interpretation, it is not the case that specializing in agriculture attracts suppliers. It is rather the case that peripheral regions are prone to clustering, given their less convenient geographical position. They also tend to be specialized in agriculture, because of the lack of other activities. From this perspective we cannot see the link between specialization and clustering as a causal relationship, but more as a coincidental one. Finally, we notice that the size of regional output in agriculture does not have a marked influence on the strategy.

The cases examined do not show any surprising findings. The small region of Pécs, in emerging Hungary, has very high scores of LQ in agriculture and remarkable levels of clustering. A similar situation (though to a lesser extent) is observed for two large, but peripheral regions of Europe: Andalucía and Thessaloniki. The region of Rotterdam makes the case for a central region specialized in agriculture and we notice that, unlike its peripheral counterparts, the sector is rather open.

The analysis of the manufacturing sector shows a different pattern. The first thing we notice is that this segment of the economy is on average more open than other sectors. Next, the relationship between openness and specialization is weak, with the two variables being almost orthogonal to each other: more open regions are neither more nor less specialized than clustered regions. Why is that? We have seen that, contrary to agriculture, the core of manufacturing production in Europe is in its geographical centre. Since we made a connection between centrality and openness, we would have expected to observe regions specialized in manufacturing to be rather open (especially considering that the manufacturing sector is on average more open than other sectors).

However, things don't appear to be that simple. First, we should take into account that a number of non-core regions are also specialized in manufacturing. Among these we recall the regions of Spain, Italy, Hungary, Sweden and Finland. Second, even with this in mind, we need to acknowledge that the clustering/openness pattern for manufacturing follows only partially

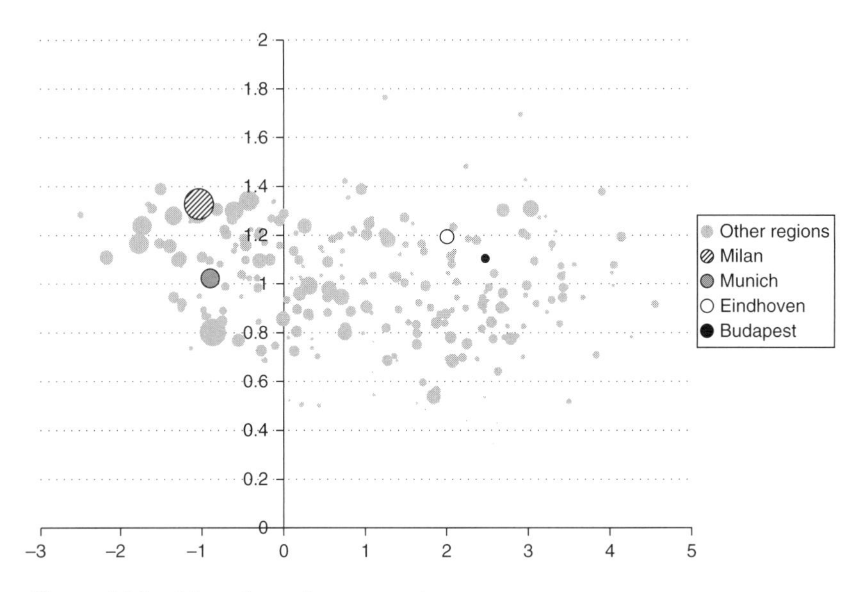

Figure 4.13 Manufacturing strategies

the periphery/core scheme we identified. For instance, in Figure 4.13 we can see Milan and Munich, two blue banana regions, being clustered, while a third blue banana region, Eindhoven, is rather open. Next to it, we also see Budapest being more open than expected.

If neither centrality nor specialization appears to be correlated to the level of openness and clustering in manufacturing, it looks as if the effect of size is stronger. Perhaps also this relationship is not particularly strong, but we do spot that the largest manufacturing centres are clustered.

The third sector we focus on, financial and business services, also displays unique dynamics. These activities are characterized by a high degree of concentration, with few large specialized regions and many others in which this part of the economy is not represented.

By observing Figure 4.14, we do not detect a strong connection between specialization and openness, similarly to the case of manufacturing. The size effect, instead, plays a rather important role: the dimension of financial and business service correlates positively with both specialization and clustering. Among the possible ways of interpreting these findings, we believe there might be a causal link between sector size and clustering running both ways, that is the growth of financial sector induces clustering, and vice versa.

Imagine that a region enlarges its financial and business sector. This particular segment of the economy, even more than others, has the

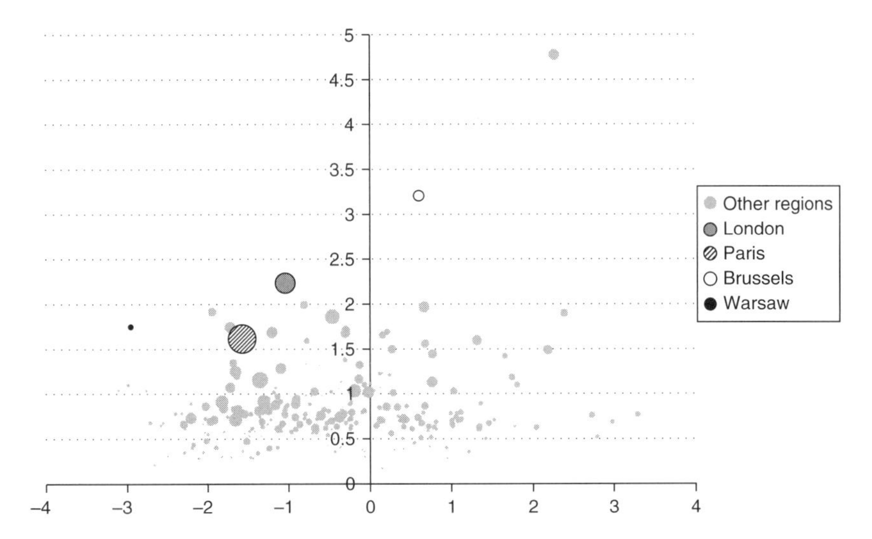

Figure 4.14 Financial and business services strategies

peculiarity of using intermediate inputs which come from the same sector, hence using other financial and business services. But services are very expensive to import because they require, in most cases, the movement of the customer or the supplier. Consequently, an increase in the financial and business sector will most likely attract the required suppliers in the region. Since these suppliers are also part of the financial and business sector, they will determine the causality in the other direction, enlarging the overall size of this part of the economy. This effect directly influences the absolute size of financial and business services in a region, but also indirectly influences the relative size of it, which we detect through the specialization index. We note that the two most important financial centres, London and Paris, have characteristics consistent with this interpretation. The emerging financial centre of Eastern Europe, Warsaw, also appears to be going down the same path, although its nominal absolute size is still not comparable to the levels of Western Europe financial hubs. Two clear outliers stand out in Figure 4.14: Brussels and, at the top of the graph (with a specialization of 4.8), Luxemburg.

4.5 CONCLUSIONS

The degree of agglomeration has important consequences for the discussion on regional development and regional competitiveness. In fact, theoretical considerations, together with empirical evidence, suggest that more populous areas may have a large competition advantage due to increasing returns to agglomeration. NEG-based models suggest that, in some situations, this advantage may be absolute (and not comparative, as in neoclassical trade models).

Nonetheless, small regions are not sentenced to decline. Through specialization, small regions can make use of sector-specific agglomeration economies (Marshall–Arrow–Romer externalities). Moreover, a small region can open its economy to a large range of interactions and attempt to 'borrow size' from other agglomerations. Or, alternatively, a region can cluster, by also specializing in important sections of the supply chain. The open approach and the cluster approach fundamentally differ from each other. If in the former agglomeration advantages are shared among a group of different regions, in the latter a region tries to capture and appropriate the agglomeration benefits by itself.

In this chapter, we argue that according to the level of agglomeration, and according to location within Europe, regions have followed different paths of development.

1. Large regions in the core of Europe are diversified and open. The significant mass allows them to engage in a range of activities, while their central position fosters trade of inputs with neighbours.
2. Small regions in the core are rather diversified and open. These regions have a limited internal mass, but since they are positioned in the core of Europe close to larger agglomerations, they appear to 'borrow size' from them. In fact, the strategy of a small central region recalls closely that of a large central one: diversification and openness. The only difference is that small regions appear to be slightly more specialized than large regions in the core. However, they are still far more diversified than peripheral regions.
3. Large regions in more peripheral position show fair diversification and clustering. Internal mass is an important driver of diversification. Consequently, and in spite of the less convenient position, many large peripheral regions are diversified, especially in Western Europe (for example Madrid, Naples). The location outside the core, though, seems to be a crucial determinant of the clustered structure of production.
4. Small, peripheral regions are specialized and clustered. They cannot rely on their own mass or on someone else's. Perhaps because of this, they appear to make use of the full extent of localization economies, with specialization on limited range of products, as well on their relevant inputs.

The debate on regional development and regional competition has inspired a number of place-based policies aimed at attracting and retaining mobile resources, such as physical and human capital. Among many, we recall the fiscal incentive for Foreign Direct Investment or the creation of an optimal environment for business to flourish. Next, local governments have been attempting to increase the level of amenities their regions offer, since mobile, highly educated workers are sensitive to this. In addition, some policies have been aimed at the creation or fostering of clusters (real estate projects, incentives for firms to group together, collaborations with local universities), while some others have been incentivizing networking (collaborations with international actors in business and academia).

We argue that these policies have much to gain from taking into account the framework presented in these pages. The awareness of the level of specialization/diversification and clustering/openness, together with the comparison with other similar regions, can be of great help to the design of place-based (tailor-made) regional policies. For instance for a small, peripheral region, it may prove convenient to focus its resources and policies on a limited number of sectors (specialization and cluster strategies). But if these sectors have a natural tendency to spread (construction, low-tech firms, most services) it is harder for the efforts to be repaid. On the other hand, if a region has the right pre-conditions, investment in sectors that have the tendency to concentrate (high-tech, tourism, financial and business) may be repaid with the appropriation of localization economies. However, it is very hard to move a sector agglomeration when it has already concentrated in certain specific regions.

The discussion on openness/clustering, in addition, should remind policy-makers that some regions, especially in the core of Europe, benefit from a dense network of interactions with their neighbours. A smart policy should take into account regional interactions and regional complementarities. It should also attempt to achieve a good level of coordination with policies of other regions: a situation in which too many regions compete for the clustering of the same sector may result in a disastrous waste of public resources.

In this chapter we identify different development paths of European regions and we claim that this knowledge can help identify strategies to tailor regional policies. In the next chapters – by including a more thorough analysis of trade networks – we can go a step further and identify which regions are competing with each other. This will be helpful (from the point of view of policies on regional competitiveness) to identify what competing regions are good at, and then to design place-based development strategies with greater awareness.

NOTES

1. Rosenthal and Strange (2004), Melo et al. (2009).
2. Heckscher–Ohlin (see Ohlin, 1933), Samuelson (1948).
3. Alternatively, it can be seen as the share of region r on the output of sector s, divided by the share of region r in the whole of Europe. Mathematically, this is identical.
4. Alternative indicators of diversity used in literature with LQs are the Krugman index or the Gini index. The properties of these indices are rather similar (Combes et al., 2009, pp. 255–74).
5. Sticking to the conceptualization of Combes and Overman (2004), this is equivalent to saying that we have a different null hypothesis.
6. As also noted by these authors, in part the results are driven by the fact that these nations have the heaviest weight in determining what the average region looks like.
7. Also specialization/diversification is defined relative to the distribution of economic activities and it has the potential to play this trick. However, it is our belief that the risk is much lower. It is easier, for instance, to accept that a region that produces even shares of products (9 per cent agriculture, 9 per cent resources, 9 per cent manufacturing MLT and so on) is specialized.
8. The reason for the industry assumption is twofold. The first reason is practical. We work with rectangular supply and use tables which prohibits most of the other methodologies. The second reason is related to our study which is mainly focused on trade networks. Trade takes place in commodities, and a commodity by commodity table resulting from the industry assumption seems therefore to be more appropriate than an industry by industry table.
9. The word 'cluster' has also been used in the literature (specialist and non-specialist) to indicate a large presence of firms of the same kind in a region. For this concept, we use the word 'concentration'. When we use 'cluster' in this research, we will refer specifically to the concentration of intermediate suppliers. In this case the concept indicates a sector's self-sufficiency in the production chain.
10. Such a model with love-for-variety of inputs can be found in Krugman and Venables (1995), in which a Dixit–Stiglitz constant elasticity of substitution function (1977) is employed as production function.
11. From the literature, we assume elasticity of substitution to be equal to 1.5 (McKitrick, 1998)
12. First, the indicators of clustering and openness have been normalized. Then, the opposite numbers of clustering are taken, such that now low scores indicate high clustering. Lastly, clustering and openness are summed, yielding to a synthetic measure that combines the information of both indicators. Synthetic clustering/openness by sector is simply obtained by taking the average of regions' combined scores.
13. Maps depicting the indicators for MLT, MHT and HT manufacturing are not presented here, but are available upon request.
14. In a perfect circle, the formula represents the average distance of a random point to the centre.

5. Revealed competition in European regions

5.1 INTRODUCTION

As discussed earlier, competitive advantage is throughout Europe predominantly envisioned as a place-based (regional) investment strategy by European, national and regional policy-makers, providing optimal locational circumstances to attract mobile capital, knowledge and footloose firms (Basile et al., 2008). By looking at the actual competition between regions in terms of trade, we add the network dimension to this discussion. This can provide us with suggestions about the network determinacy of regional competitiveness – the main goal of this research project. We applied the regional competitiveness analysis to regional-sectoral high-potential combinations, so-called clusters. Cluster policies are present in practically all countries and regions in the European Union, initiated by either local, national or even European governments (Borras and Tsagdis, 2008). In local clusters, firms specialized in certain products and operating on the same market are located in proximity to each other. Local clusters are thought to enhance growth and innovation potential by local linkages and embedding – self-augmenting processes of network and firm-related development. These local specialized centres of specialization and excellence are perceived to compete with many similarly specialized clusters elsewhere. Cities and regions are compared with each other in rankings on competitiveness (see Chapter 1). In this chapter we analyse to what extent this multi-regional competition actually is the case in specific clusters.

Competition is traditionally related to the contest between firms for customer goodwill, either from consumers or other industries, and a firm is considered to have a good competitive position if it succeeds in improving or maintaining its market share. In this chapter, we interpret the newly developed trade network approach to determine in which regions in Europe firms best succeed in gathering a share of the European market. As we do not look at productivity of firms but at their trade networks overlapping with those of their competitors, we talk about revealed competition. By investigating market overlap, we learn which markets are most important for firms, and from which regions there is strongest competition. We do not look at individual firms but at economic sectors, and investigate to what extent a sector in a region has competition from the same sector in other regions. Throughout the text, we talk about competition between regions; this, in fact, is a short way of saying that firms within a region compete with firms located in another region.

By stimulating particular sectors and particular regions, the European Commission has an objective to further strengthen strong localized sectoral specializations. It is hypothesized that by stimulating these sectors and improving particular bottlenecks, new firms are attracted and growth is expected to increase (compare Delgado et al., 2010). This, in its turn, is expected to trickle down to the rest of the economy and in other (neighbouring) regions as well. Even though each region in principle contains all economic sectors, a certain degree of specialization can be observed in each region. Well-known examples of important clusters are the financial district in London, the manufacturing cluster in the Ruhr area in Germany and in Milan (region Lombardia), the high-tech clusters in Eindhoven (Noord-Brabant) and Helsinki, the horticultural hotspots in the Rotterdam–The Hague region (Zuid Holland) in The Netherlands, and business services in Amsterdam (Noord-Holland) and Frankfurt (Raspe and Van den Berge, 2010).

In this chapter, in section 5.2 the term 'revealed competition' is defined. Section 5.3 provides a general discussion of the regions which have the strongest competitive trade position in Europe in three broadly defined basic sectors: agriculture, manufacturing and services.[1] We will discuss how these clusters are seen as important competitors by a selected number of regions in Europe. The regions considered in more detail are:

- agglomerations: regions of London, Paris, Milan, Barcelona and Munich;
- strong medium sized regions: regions of Brussels, Helsinki, Lyon, Rotterdam–The Hague and Eindhoven;
- peripheral and emerging regions: regions of Budapest, Pécs, Dresden, Warsaw, Thessaloniki and Andalucía.

For this range of European regions, we assess and discuss how important they are in terms of trade network relatedness, and from which regions in Europe they have the strongest competition.

5.2 REVEALED COMPETITION DEFINED

The principle of revealed competition between regions concerns their market overlap. The competition that a region A has from a region B depends on two factors. First, it depends on the market share of firms from region B in each region. Secondly, it depends on the importance of each of these markets for firms in region A, where a market is important for A if it sells a substantial share of its production on that market. So, A receives strong competition from B, if region B has a large market share in the regions which are important for region A. If B had a large market share in the regions which are unimportant for A or if B had a low market share in the regions which are important for A, competition between A and B would be less strong. After all, in that situation, there is only a limited market overlap and firms from A and B would have fewer opportunities to take market shares from each other. In Figure 5.1 region A has strong competition from region B because region B holds a strong position in market C, which is an important export market for region A. Region A does not have strong competition

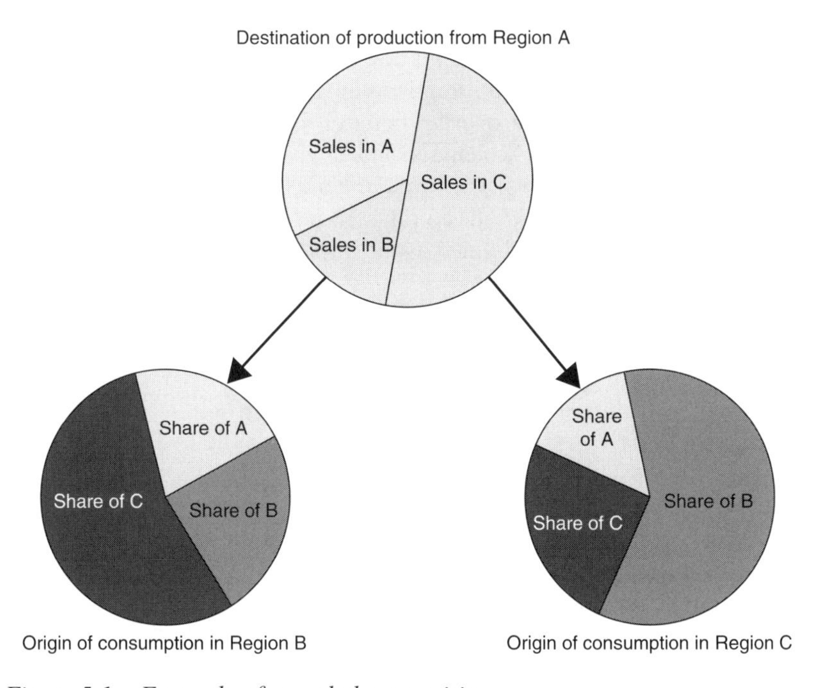

Figure 5.1 Example of revealed competition

from region C. Even though region C holds a strong position in market B, region A only exports a small amount to region B.

To define revealed competition properly, introduce the following sets and variables:

$i,j,k,l \in I$ sets of regions
a_{ij} = quantity traded by the firms in region i to the market in region j

It follows that $\sum_{j \in I} a_{ij}$ is production of the firms in region i, $\sum_{i \in I} a_{ij}$ are sales in the market on region j, $\sum_{j \neq i} a_{ij}$ are exports from the firms in region i, and $\sum_{i \neq j} a_{ij}$ are the imports into region j. Moreover, the following features can be defined:

$$I_{kj} = \frac{a_{kj}}{\sum_{i \in I} a_{ki}}$$ = share of total production of the firms in region k that is sold in region j

$$M_{lj} = \frac{a_{lj}}{\sum_{i \in I} a_{ij}}$$ = share of the total sales in region j that comes from firms in region l

We can also define I_{kj} as the importance of region j for the firms in region k and M_{lj} as the dependence of the market in region j on the firms in region l. The level of revealed competition firms in region k experience from firms in region l depends on the overlap between the markets in which firms from both regions sell, in which account is given for (1) the importance of the respective markets for the firms in k and (2) the dependence of the respective markets on the goods coming from region l. Competition experienced by k from l can be defined as the importance of the market shares of l for the sales of k.

$$C_{kl} = \sum_{j \in I} M_{lj} \cdot I_{kj} = \sum_{j \in I} \left[\frac{a_{lj}}{\sum_{i \in I} a_{ij}} \cdot \frac{a_{kj}}{\sum_{i \in I} a_{ki}} \right]$$

It can be proven that $\sum_{l \in I} C_{kl} = 1$. As a result, C_{kl} can be interpreted as the percentage competition region k experiences from the sales from region I.

If firms in region k have strong competition from firms in region l, they will benefit from improvements in the regional characteristics in their region that affect their productivity. If l scores better on particular characteristics that are deemed important, it would be good if the authorities in k also invested more in these characteristics.

5.3 THE MAJOR COMPETITIVE REGIONS IN EUROPE

Before discussing the international trade position of a selected number of European regions and sectors, we assess which European regions are seen as important competitors. Table 5.1 gives the top 30 competitive regions in Europe for a number of sectors. The complete ranking of competitive regions for the sectors discussed in this book is presented in Figure 5.2. For this, an aggregate competition score is calculated for each region, indicating the total level of competition a region poses for all other European regions. The table shows some interesting features. First, it can be concluded that the regions of Paris (Île de France), Milan (Lombardy) and Dublin (south/east Ireland) are important as trade nodes in almost all sectors.[2] Moreover, it evidently follows from our conceptualization that larger regions have larger trade networks and therefore are more important. Despite the fact that, for instance, the Dutch province of Utrecht contains a strong marketing and financial services sector, it is not among the top 30 European competitive regions because the province is rather small and can therefore only host a limited number of internationally operating firms. A result of this mass effect is that London, which is divided into inner and outer London, holds a lower position than Paris and Milan in several sectors. Another result is that the importance of the Ruhr area in Germany appears small because the area is divided into several regions. In our research we stick to the NUTS-2 regional division because of comparability with earlier research (for example Moreno et al., 2005), and because of its rather clear policy connotation as in practically every country this represents a legal institutional level of governance.

Secondly, regions which are considered to be important competitors by many regions form a band from north-western Europe to north-eastern and south-central Europe. For Ireland, all sectors belong to the European top regions whereas Germany and Italy are especially strong in industry. The Dutch regions are seen as important competitors especially in the agricultural sector, but also for financial and business services, while Danish regions are characterized by their competitiveness in a large number of sectors. France and the UK are dominated by a few very strong regions and a large number of regions mainly producing for national consumption and to a lesser extent for exports. Even though the agricultural sector is strong in a number of large rural regions, the major agricultural regions are characterized by highly diversified and developed regions with a large, export-oriented industrial sector (for example regions of Milan, Paris, Rotterdam–The Hague, Amsterdam and Barcelona). The major manufacturing areas are concentrated in a conglomerate of connected and

Table 5.1 Top 30 regions which are seen as important competitors by many other regions

	All sectors	Agriculture	Low-tech manufacturing	Medium-tech manufacturing
1	Paris – FR	Rotterdam – NL	Milan – IT	Milan – IT
2	Milan – IT	Danish mainland – DK	Paris – FR	Paris – FR
3	Dublin – IE	Andalucía – ES	Stuttgart – DE	Stuttgart – DE
4	Düsseldorf – DE	Eindhoven – NL	Emilia Romagna – IT	Düsseldorf – DE
5	Stuttgart – DE	Milan – IT	Düsseldorf – DE	Munich – DE
6	Munich – DE	Amsterdam – NL	Veneto – IT	Dublin – IE
7	Frankfurt – DE	Gelderland – NL	Munich – DE	Lyon – FR
8	Lyon – FR	Paris – FR	Dublin – IE	Arnsberg – DE
9	Veneto – IT	Aquitaine – FR	Danish mainland – DK	Frankfurt – DE
10	Köln – DE	Barcelona – ES	Eindhoven – NL	Veneto – IT
11	Barcelona – ES	Champagne – FR	Barcelona – ES	Köln – DE
12	Inner London – UK	Veneto – IT	Lyon – FR	Barcelona – ES
13	Arnsberg – DE	Pays de la Loire – FR	Piemonte – IT	Karlsruhe – DE
14	Emilia Romagna – IT	Castilla y Leon – ES	Helsinki – FI	Piemonte – IT
15	Danish mainland – DK	Lyon – FR	Frankfurt – DE	Antwerp – BE
16	Rotterdam – NL	Bretagne – FR	Köln – DE	Emilia Romagna – IT
17	Piemonte – IT	Limburg – NL	Arnsberg – DE	Freiburg – DE
18	Eindhoven – NL	Emilia Romagna – IT	Antwerp – BE	Nord Pas Calais – FR
19	Antwerp – BE	Overijssel – NL	Rotterdam – NL	Madrid – ES
20	Karlsruhe – DE	Castilla Mancha – ES	Karlsruhe – DE	Eindhoven – NL
21	Helsinki – FI	Friesland – NL	Toscana – IT	Detmold – DE
22	Madrid – ES	Dublin – IE	Nord Pas Calais – FR	Tübingen – DE
23	Outer London – UK	Piemonte – IT	Lazio – IT	Mittelfranken – DE

High-tech manufacturing	Services sector – total	Marketing and financial services	Other marketing services
Dublin – IE	Paris – FR	Luxembourg –LU	S.E. Ireland – IE
Paris – FR	Luxembourg – LU	Paris – FR	Milan – IT
Helsinki – FI	Inner London – UK	Inner London – UK	Inner London – UK
Milan – IT	Dublin – IE	Dublin – IE	Luxembourg – LU
Lyon – FR	Outer London – UK	Outer London – UK	Frankfurt – DE
Stuttgart – DE	Copenhagen – DK	Stockholm – SE	Brussels – BE
Göteborg – SE	Stockholm – SE	Brussels – BE	Paris – FR
Düsseldorf – DE	Rotterdam – NL	Oxfordshire – UK	Amsterdam – NL
Munich – DE	Amsterdam – NL	Frankfurt – DE	Rotterdam – NL
Border Midlands – IE	Frankfurt – DE	Rotterdam – NL	Lazio – IT
Lansi Suomi – FI	Danish mainland – DK	Amsterdam – NL	Düsseldorf – DE
Inner London – UK	Oxfordshire – UK	Surrey/Sussex – UK	Wien – AT
Frankfurt – DE	Düsseldorf – DE	Düsseldorf – DE	Helsinki – FI
Veneto – IT	Brussels – BE	Helsinki – FI	Stockholm – SE
Upsalla – SE	Surrey/Sussex – UK	West Midlands – UK	Outer London – UK
Stockholm – SE	Helsinki – FI	Madrid – ES	Copenhagen – DE
Köln – DE	Milan – IT	Milan – IT	Veneto – IT
Oxfordshire – UK	Munich – DE	Manchester – UK	Antwerp – BE
Arnsberg – DE	Madrid – ES	Munich – DE	Piemonte – IT
Outer London – UK	Oslo – NO	Utrecht – NL	Utrecht – NL
Eindhoven – NL	Eindhoven – NL	Wien – AT	Eindhoven – NL
Piemonte – IT	West Midlands – UK	Copenhagen – DK	Vest for Stor. – DK
Karlsruhe – DE	Manchester – UK	Eindhoven – NL	Munich – DE

Table 5.1 (continued)

	All sectors	Agriculture	Low-tech manufacturing	Medium-tech manufacturing
24	Amsterdam – NL	Nord Pas Calais – FR	Copenhagen – DK	Rheinhes. Pfalz – DE
25	Copenhagen – DK	Provence Alpes – FR	Amsterdam – NL	Weser Ems – DE
26	Stockholm – SE	Valencia – ES	Göteborg – SE	Danish mainland – DK
27	Lazio – IT	Centre – FR	Madrid – ES	Basque country – ES
28	Göteborg – SE	Weser Ems – DE	Oberösterreich – AT	Braunschweig – DE
29	Nord Pas Calais – FR	Bourgogne – FR	East Flanders – BE	Schwaben – DE
30	Toscana – IT	Galicia – ES	Pays de la Loire – FR	Göteborg – SE

highly urbanized regions which runs from northern Italy, through western Germany to The Netherlands and to Denmark and Sweden and in the large agglomerations around Paris, Barcelona and Dublin. The financial and business services are mainly concentrated in the large agglomerations. As argued above, the larger financial and business services companies need the presence of other, competing and complementary financial and business services as well as a substantial industrial sector requiring their services.

5.4 REVEALED COMPETITION FOR THE EUROPEAN REGIONS

In this section the major competitors are presented for a selection of the European NUTS-2 regions and a selection of the sectors. As follows from the method explained above, each region has competition from different regions. Moreover, each sector within a region competes with different regions because the network structure of each region's exports differs. To find out which regions operate on the same markets as the companies in your region, Table 5.1 does not provide any relevant information. For every region separately, it has to be indicated with which regions your market is overlapping. In this section we present the regions that are the major competitors for some of the European agglomerations (regions of London, Paris, Milan, Barcelona and Munich), the strong medium-sized regions (regions of Brussels, Helsinki, Lyon, Rotterdam and Eindhoven) and the peripheral and emerging regions (regions of Budapest, Pécs, Dresden, Warsaw, Thessaloniki and Andalucía).

High-tech manufacturing	Services sector – total	Marketing and financial services	Other marketing services
Rotterdam – NL	Wien – AT	Barcelona – ES	Campania – IT
S./W. Scotland – UK	Athens – GR	Stuttgart – DE	Toscane – IT
Malmö – SE	Barcelona – ES	Gloucestershire – UK	Puglia – IT
Gloucestershire – UK	Utrecht – NL	Danish mainland – DK	Sicilia – IT
West Midlands – UK	Köln – DE	Antwerp – BE	Niederösterreich – AT
Nord Pas Calais – FR	Stuttgart – DE	Bedfordshire – UK	Emilia Romagna – IT
East Scotland – UK	Lyon – FR	Gelderland – NL	Gelderland – NL

5.4.1 Regional Characterization

Before discussing from which regions the selected regions receive most competition, first some general statistics of the regions are discussed which characterize the economic structure of the regions. A first observation is that all the selected regions only export 10 to 20 per cent of their production, where the smaller countries generally are the larger exporters – see Table 5.2. The majority of the production remains in the own country and even remains in the own and surrounding regions. This is especially so for the less knowledge-intensive sectors. Moreover, generally more than 50 per cent of the exports go to only five countries. The major trade partners are Germany, the United States, the United Kingdom, France and Italy, usually followed by the surrounding countries.

If a few selected regions are investigated in more detail, see Table 5.3, it can be observed that the sector structure differs substantially between the different regions, and the export orientation differs between the sectors. The *agricultural sector* is mainly Europe oriented and regions export mainly to the neighbouring countries. Generally, in the more peripheral and emerging regions the agricultural sector represents a larger share of the economy than in the agglomerations. This does not mean, however, that they also produce a large share of total agricultural production. High value crop production and greenhouses which require more and high value inputs as well as high quality transport infrastructure and logistic services are often located in the richer and more industrialized regions. Export orientation of the agricultural sector differs substantially between the regions. The majority of the regions process or consume the largest part of

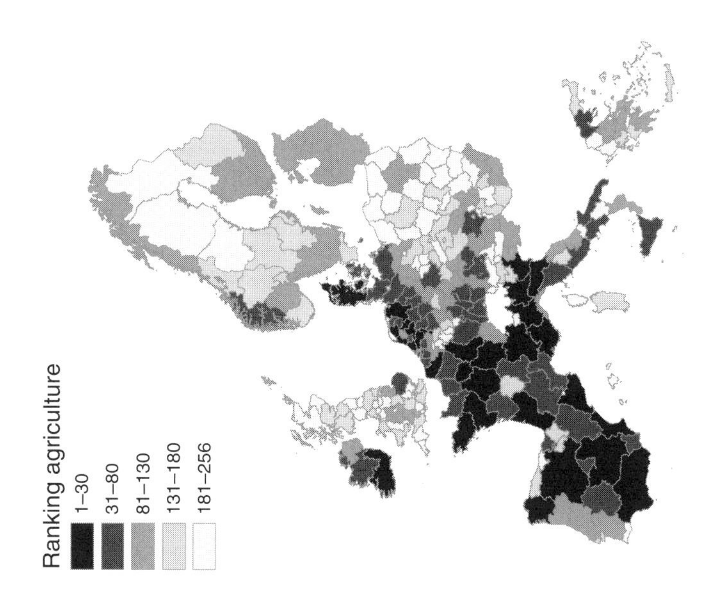
Ranking agriculture
1–30
31–80
81–130
131–180
181–256

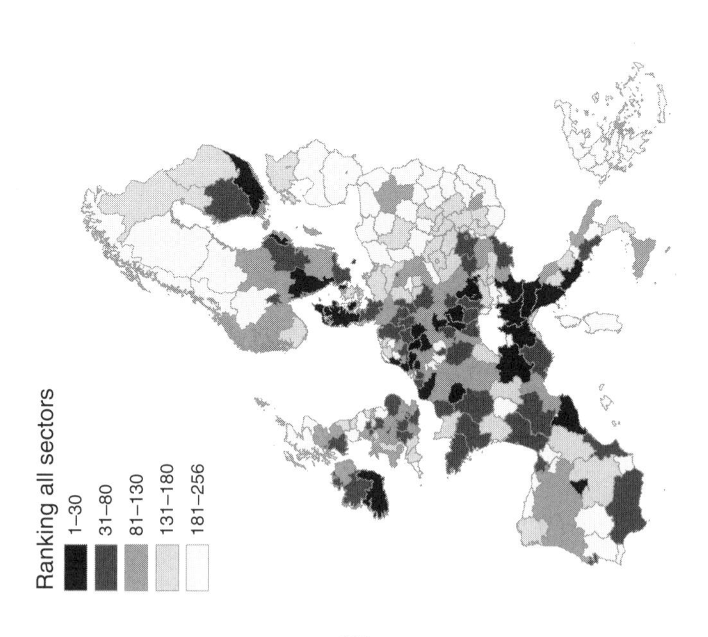
Ranking all sectors
1–30
31–80
81–130
131–180
181–256

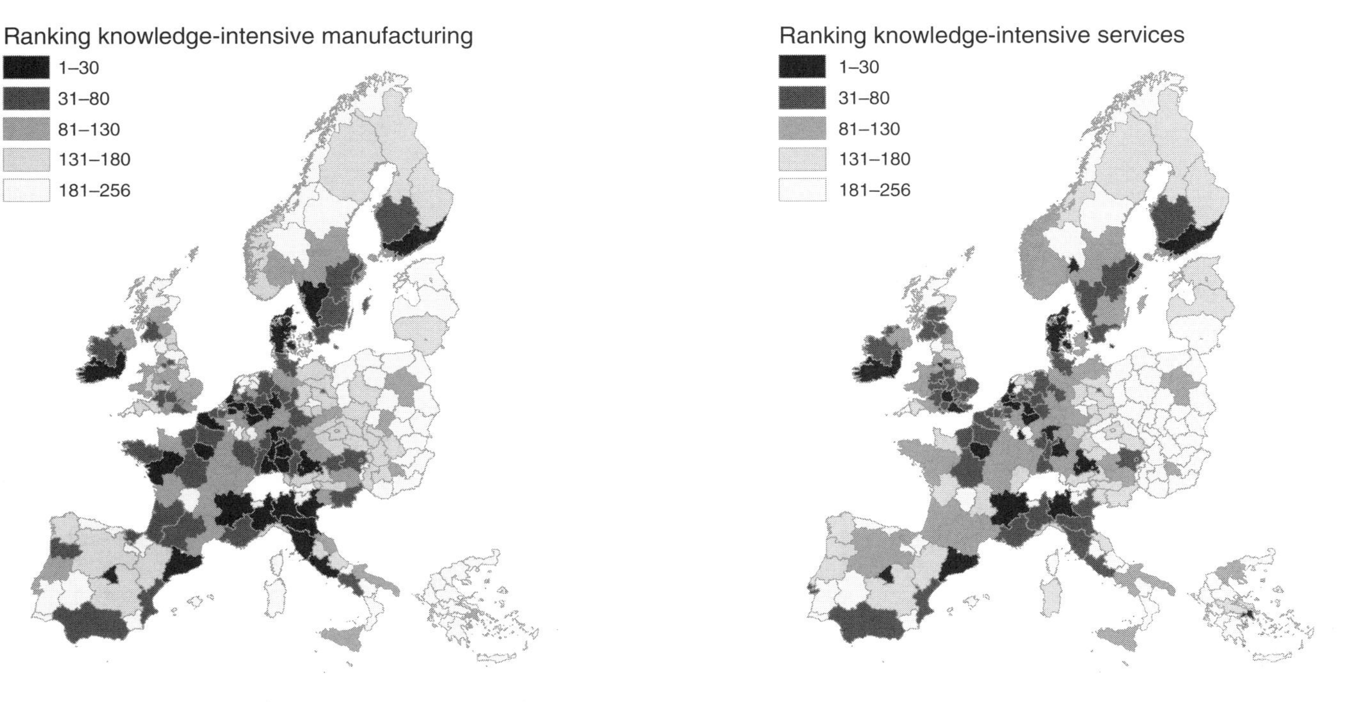

Figure 5.2 Ranking of competitive position of each region in Europe

Table 5.2 Export characteristics of selected regions for the total economy

Agglomerations					
	Inner London	Milan	Barcelona	Munich	Paris
Prod. remaining in own region	62%	71%	75%	72%	73%
Prod. remaining in own country	90%	87%	85%	86%	89%
Major export partners	USA – 17% Germany – 9% Asia – 8% France – 7% Netherlands – 5%	USA – 13% Germany – 12% France – 10% UK – 7% Spain – 6%	France – 15% Germany – 14% UK – 11% Italy – 8% USA – 7%	USA – 13% France – 8% Italy – 8% UK – 8% Austria – 5%	Germany – 12% USA – 12% UK – 11% Italy – 9% Spain – 7%
Strong medium-sized regions					
	Brussels	Eindhoven	Lyon	Helsinki	Rotterdam–The Hague
Prod. remaining in own region	46%	47%	76%	75%	52%
Prod. remaining in own country	80%	75%	86%	82%	79%
Major export partners	Germany – 15% UK – 12% USA – 11% France – 11% Netherlands – 7%	Germany – 18% UK – 12% Belgium – 8% France – 8% USA – 8%	Germany – 12% USA – 11% UK – 10% Spain – 9% Italy – 9%	Germany – 10% Sweden – 8% Rest World – 8% UK – 8% USA – 7%	Germany – 18% UK – 11% Belgium – 8% USA – 8% France – 7%

Peripheral and emerging regions

	Budapest	Dresden	Pécs	Warsaw	Thessaloniki	Andalucia
Prod. remaining in own region	57%	71%	48%	72%	76%	83%
Prod. remaining in own country	76%	88%	74%	89%	88%	89%
Major export partners	Germany – 28% USA – 9% Austria – 8% France – 7% Italy – 6%	USA – 12% France – 9% UK – 8% Italy – 8% Asia – 5%	Germany – 30% Austria – 9% USA – 8% France – 7% Italy – 6%	Germany – 30% USA – 8% Italy – 6% Russia – 5% France – 5%	USA – 22% Rest World – 16% Germany – 11% Italy – 8% Rest Europe – 7%	Germany – 15% France – 12% UK – 12% USA – 8% Italy – 7%

Table 5.3 Export characteristics of selected regions for several economic sectors

Agglomeration: Barcelona		Industry			
% of production	Agriculture	Low-tech	Medium-tech	High-tech	Services
Importance of sector for region	2.0%	29.2%	14.4%	1.7%	22.3%
Prod. remaining in own region	84%	62%	49%	45%	90%
Prod. remaining in own country	85%	84%	62%	61%	93%
Major export partners	Germany – 22% France – 18% Italy – 11% UK – 11% Portugal – 8%	France – 15% Portugal – 11% Germany – 10% USA – 9% Italy – 8%	France – 21% Germany – 13% Italy – 10% UK – 9% Portugal – 7%	Germany – 13% France – 11% Portugal – 11% UK – 10% Italy – 8%	UK – 19% USA – 13% Germany – 11% France – 10% Switzerland – 9%

Strong medium-sized region: Rotterdam–The Hague		Industry			
% of production	Agriculture	Low-tech	Medium-tech	High-tech	Services
Importance of sector for region	3.7%	16.6%	9.3%	2.4%	33.4%
Prod. remaining in own region	27%	35%	29%	14%	58%
Prod. remaining in own country	60%	64%	46%	22%	88%
Major export partners	Germany – 34% UK – 12% France – 8% Italy – 8% Belgium – 5%	Germany – 28% Belgium – 12% UK – 10% France – 10% Italy – 6%	Germany – 14% UK – 13% France – 8% USA – 8% Italy – 7%	UK – 19% Rest World – 13% USA – 9% Italy – 9% Asia – 7%	USA – 10% UK – 10% Asia – 9% Germany – 7% Africa – 6%
Peripheral and emerging region: Region Pécs		Industry			
% of production	Agriculture	Low-tech	Medium-tech	High-tech	Services
Importance of sector for region	8.5%	21.7%	12.8%	7.1%	19.3%
Prod. remaining in own region	44%	40%	20%	4%	67%
Prod. remaining in own country	85%	68%	33%	20%	90%
Major export partners	Rest Europe – 14% Austria – 13% Germany – 13% Italy – 11% Slovenia – 7%	Germany – 26% Rest Europe – 12% Austria – 11% Italy – 9% France – 5%	Germany – 45% USA – 8% Austria – 7% Italy – 5% France – 5%	Germany – 19% France – 15% USA – 12% UK – 8% Austria – 5%	USA – 18% Germany – 18% Austria – 8% Spain – 6% UK – 5%

the agricultural production in the own region. Only a few regions, such as the Dutch regions, are more outside oriented.

The *industrial sector* is one of the major sectors in almost all regions. Some regions that are highly specialized in the services sector, like London, Brussels and Luxembourg, have smaller industrial sectors. For the others, this sector generally accounts for 30 to 50 per cent of regional value-added. The majority of the industrial production, generally 50 to 70 per cent of total industrial production, can be classified as low-tech production. Even in regions with relatively higher shares of high-tech industries, like Helsinki but also Budapest and Pécs in Hungary, low-tech industries are much larger sectors than the high-tech industries. For the industrial sector, it follows for almost all regions that exports increase with knowledge intensity of the sector. As already discussed above, the larger countries export less as they have a larger market already in their own country, whereas the smaller countries are more dependent on foreign demand. Knowledge intensity also affects the countries which are nominated as major export partners. The less knowledge-intensive low-tech industries export to more nearby regions whereas the high-tech industries export to more distant regions and to the more important industrial countries.

One might expect that the *services sector* is a more important sector for the agglomerations than for the peripheral and emerging regions. Except for London, Paris and Brussels, however, which do have large services sectors, in most regions the services sector accounts for 20 to 30 per cent of total value-added. This is even the case in the more rural regions of Pécs and Andalucía. Export orientation of the services sector is generally low. In most cases, services are provided to local or national companies. Many of the international activities of the large financial and marketing services companies are performed by national tributaries of the international holdings and are therefore not counted as exports. Nationally, the services companies in particular provide their services within the own region and the neighbouring regions. Those services that are exported are not constrained by distance and even the peripheral and emerging regions export to non-European regions.

5.4.2 Major Competitors

As argued above, the major competitors differ per region and within each region even per sector because market overlap differs per region and per sector. Table 5.4 and Figure 5.3 show which regions are seen as the major competitors for the group of regions that are analysed in more detail in this book if the entire economy is considered. It is noted that for determining the competition scores, only market overlap with foreign regions is considered. So, to derive their competition scores, we compare the markets in which, for example, Paris and Brussels are selling their products. We do not compare market overlap between, for example, Paris and Lyon. As all regions sell the majority of their produce within their own country, it can generally be stated that a region has the strongest competition from the regions within its own country.

As already shown in Table 5.1, Table 5.4 shows that the major European agglomerations of Paris, Milan and Dublin are seen as important competitors by almost all regions, independently of whether regions are large agglomerations themselves or smaller peripheral or emerging regions. The top 10 competitors of the major European agglomerations of London, Milan and Paris all are major European economic regions. For Barcelona and Munich, this is somewhat different. Next to competition from the European top regions, they also receive competition from regions from the neighbouring countries that can be classified as secondary top regions. Examples are Lisbon and Norte in Portugal, Lyon and Provence Alpes in France, Veneto and Emilia Romagna in Italy, the Danish mainland region, and Oberösterreich in Austria. This shows that Barcelona and Munich play a more regional function than regions such as London, Milan and Paris.

The strong medium-sized regions and the peripheral and emerging regions especially receive more competition from the strong regions in their neighbouring countries. Compared to the large agglomerations, they seem to have a less widespread international market network but especially focus on the nearby customers. Economic focus affects the list of major competitors. For example, the German regions in the Ruhr area, which have a strong manufacturing profile, are among the list of major competitors for several regions. In particular the regions with a strong low- and medium-tech manufacturing profile, such as Noord-Brabant, Zuid Holland, Dresden, Warsaw and Thessaloniki see these German regions as important competitors. The export markets of Brussels, which has a more services oriented economy, differ from those of the manufacturing oriented regions. Next to that, also the more high-tech oriented regions of Lyon and Helsinki have different competitors. This phenomenon is partly explained by their location within Europe. The peripheral regions of Budapest, Pécs, Warsaw and Thessaloniki in particular compete with their neighbours. Due to their geographical and economic position in Europe, the majority of their economies are regionally focused.

Table 5.3 already showed that the list of major competitors is influenced by the economic structure of the region. The competition ranking is especially dominated by the competitors of the manufacturing sector. Generally, the manufacturing sector is the largest exporter and therefore

Table 5.4 Top 10 of major competitors for the total economy

Agglomerations					
	Inner London	Milan	Barcelona	Munich	Paris
1	Paris – FR	Paris – FR	Paris – FR	Milan – IT	Milan – IT
2	Dublin – IE	Lyon – FR	Milan – IT	Paris – FR	Inner London – UK
3	Milan – IT	Dublin – IE	Lyon – FR	Dublin – IE	Barcelona – ES
4	Rotterdam – NL	Barcelona – ES	Lisbon – PT	Wien – AT	Dublin – IE
5	Düsseldorf – DE	Stuttgart – DE	Provence Alpes – FR	Veneto – IT	Madrid – ES
6	Antwerp – BE	Munich – DE	Norte – PT	Oberösterreich – AT	Antwerp – BE
7	Mainland – DK	Düsseldorf – DE	Düsseldorf – DE	Lyon – FR	Düsseldorf – DE
8	Brussels – BE	Provence Alpes – FR	Stuttgart – DE	Emilia Romagna – IT	Stuttgart – DE
9	Barcelona – ES	Inner London – UK	Dublin – IE	Mainland – DK	Outer London – UK
10	Luxembourg – LU	Madrid – ES	Inner London – UK	Barcelona – ES	Piemonte – IT
Strong medium-sized regions					
	Brussels	Eindhoven	Lyon	Helsinki	Rotterdam–The Hague
1	Paris – FR	Paris – FR	Milan – IT	Eesti – EE	Paris – FR
2	Luxembourg – LU	Milan – IT	Barcelona – ES	Mainland – DK	Inner London – UK
3	Inner London – UK	Düsseldorf – DE	Piemonte – IT	Stockholm – SE	Milan – IT
4	Rotterdam – NL	Antwerp – BE	Dublin – IE	Göteborg – SE	Antwerp – BE
5	Milan – IT	Dublin – IE	Madrid – ES	Paris – FR	Düsseldorf – DE
6	Eindhoven – NL	Köln – DE	Veneto – IT	Milan – IT	Dublin – IE
7	Lyon – FR	Arnsberg – DE	Antwerp – BE	Copenhagen – DK	Frankfurt – DE
8	Amsterdam – NL	Lyon – FR	Emilia Romagna – IT	Sydsverige – SE	Stuttgart – DE
9	Dublin – IE	Stuttgart – DE	Düsseldorf – DE	Dublin – IE	Köln – DE
10	Düsseldorf – DE	Inner London – UK	Stuttgart – DE	Upsalla – SE	Arnsberg – DE

Peripheral and emerging regions

	Budapest	Dresden	Pécs	Warsaw	Thessaloniki	Andalucía
1	Milan – IT	Paris – FR	Munich – DE	Milan – IT	Milan – IT	Paris – FR
2	Munich – DE	Dublin – IE	Stuttgart – DE	Paris – FR	Paris – FR	Milan – IT
3	Stuttgart – DE	Milan – IT	Milan – IT	Düsseldorf – DE	Veneto – IT	Lyon – FR
4	Paris – FR	Mainland – DK	Paris – FR	Stuttgart – DE	Em. Romagna – IT	Lisbon – PT
5	Niederöster. – AT	Copenhag. – DK	Düsseldorf – DE	Munich – DE	Stuttgart – DE	Prov. Alpes – FR
6	Wien – AT	Barcelona – ES	Frankfurt – DE	Frankfurt – DE	Piemonte – IT	Dublin – IE
7	Düsseldorf – DE	Lyon – FR	Niederöster. – AT	Helsinki – FI	Düsseldorf – DE	Düsseldorf – DE
8	Frankfurt – DE	Rotterdam – NL	Wien – AT	Köln – DE	Dublin – IE	Veneto – IT
9	Oberöster. – AT	Veneto – IT	Oberöster. – AT	Arnsberg – DE	Munich – DE	Munich – DE
10	Dublin – IE	Oberöster. – AT	Köln – DE	Mainland – DK	Inn. London – UK	Stuttgart – DE

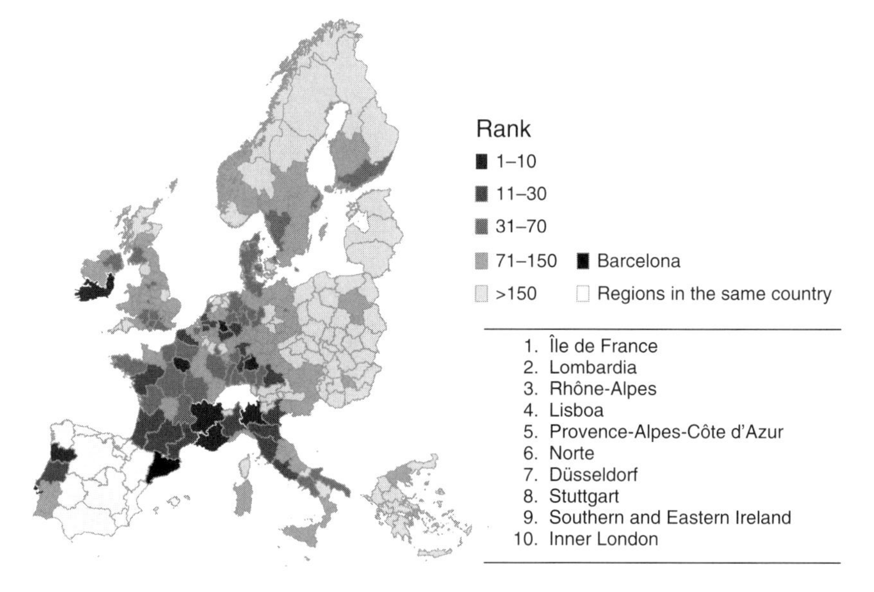

Figure 5.3 Major international competitors for the total economy: Barcelona (2000)

dominates the overall competitor ranking for the total regional economy. If the major competitors are listed per economic sector, we see some interesting differences in the rankings. First, for the agricultural sector, the major competitors come especially from a few strong European agricultural regions such as Zuid-Holland in the Rotterdam–The Hague region, Milan in Italy and Andalucía in Spain and a number of regions in the neighbouring countries. As already argued above, the major competitors are generally among the stronger regions in their own country. The geographical pattern in international competitors for different region–sectors combination is shown in Figures 5.3–5.7. High value-added agriculture is concentrated in regions with better infrastructure and those close to suppliers and markets. Regions classified as rural areas often have lower value-added agricultural activities, being more dependent on the availability of cheap land and less so on good connections.

Secondly, where Milan has the strongest network of markets in the low-tech manufacturing sector, Dublin has the strongest network in the high-tech sector. The low-tech sector has a rather strong regional focus where most competition comes from regions in the neighbouring countries. Also the low-tech manufacturing firms in the large agglomerations obtain the strongest competition from nearby countries. This relates

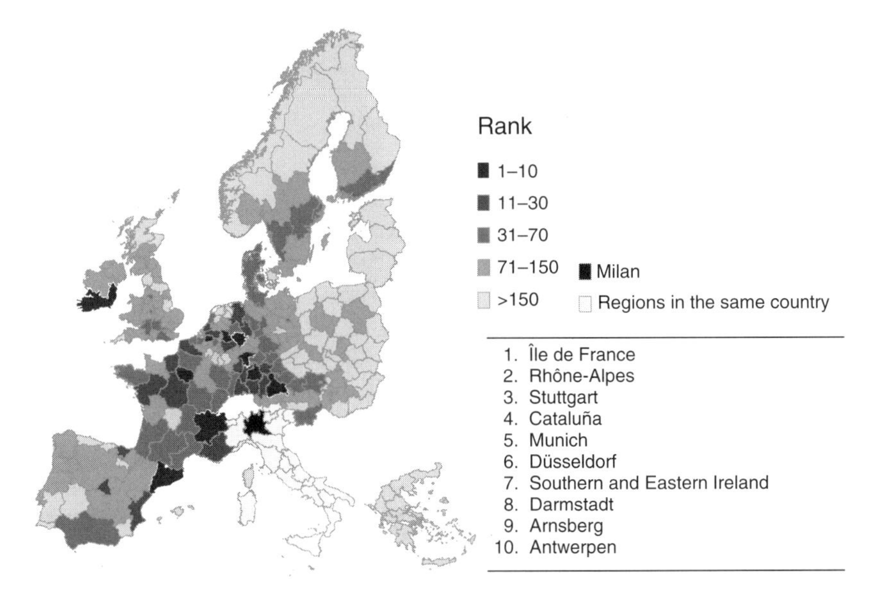

Figure 5.4 Major international competitors for medium-tech manufacturing: Milan (2000)

to the low concentration of firms in the low-tech manufacturing as we have seen in Chapter 4. The low concentration of low-tech manufacturing results in small market areas with overlap with nearby competitors. For the medium-tech manufacturing, trade networks seem to be already more elaborated. In particular the position of the German Ruhr area is important for almost all regions considered, regardless of whether they are agglomerations or peripheral regions. The high-tech manufacturing sector has the most widespread network.

For most regions, the list of top 10 high-tech competitors is almost the same, except for the order in which they appear. This list of major high-tech competitors immediately shows which regions have the strongest positions in this sector. It is noted that the high-tech sector is only a small sector in almost all regions. Low-tech manufacturing is the largest sector, employing a large number of employees. Policy attention, however, is more focused on high- and medium-tech manufacturing because these firms are expected to have higher export and growth potential. As will be discussed in the next section, characteristics of regions being strong in the high-tech sector may differ from those of the regions focusing more on low- or medium-tech.

For the financial and business services sector, Table 5.3 shows that

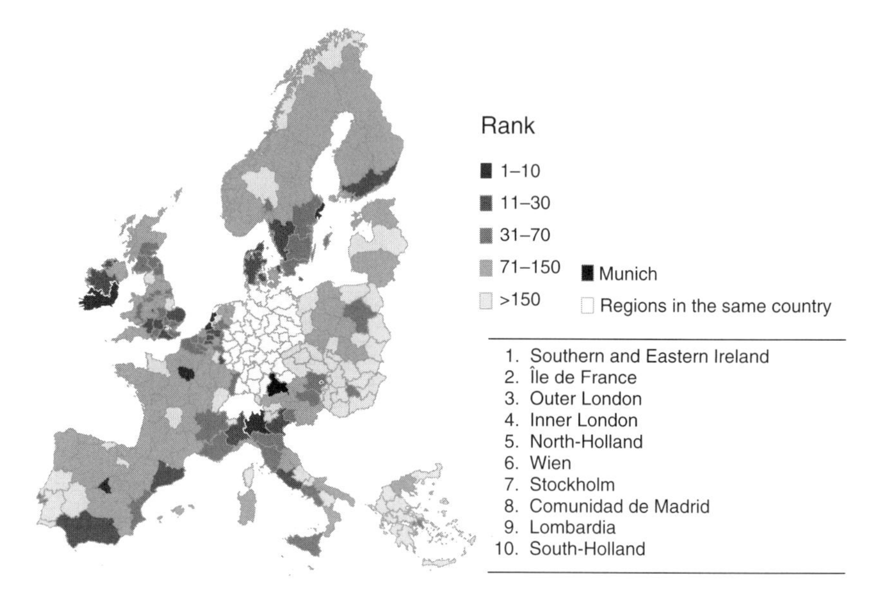

Figure 5.5 Major international competitors for high-tech manufacturing: Munich (2000)

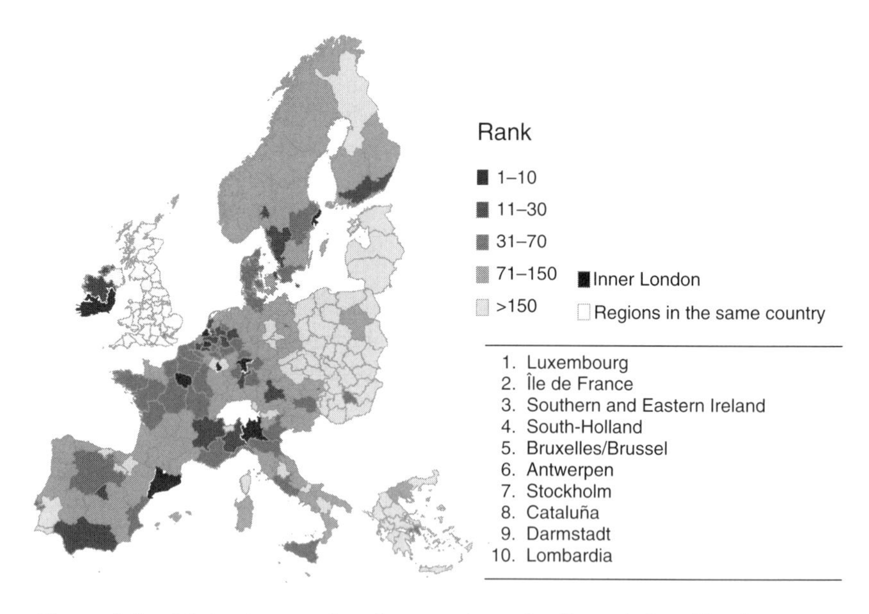

Figure 5.6 Major international competitors for financial and business services: inner London (2000)

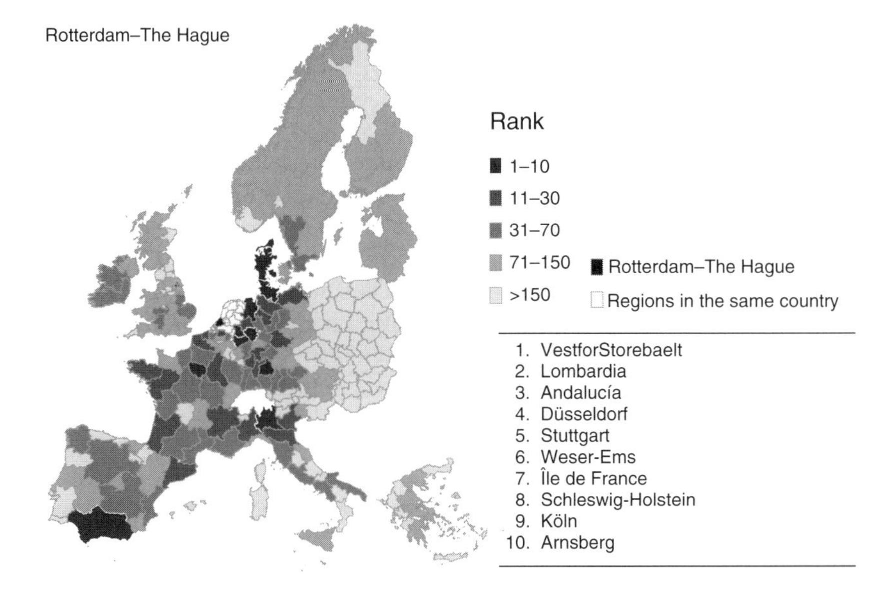

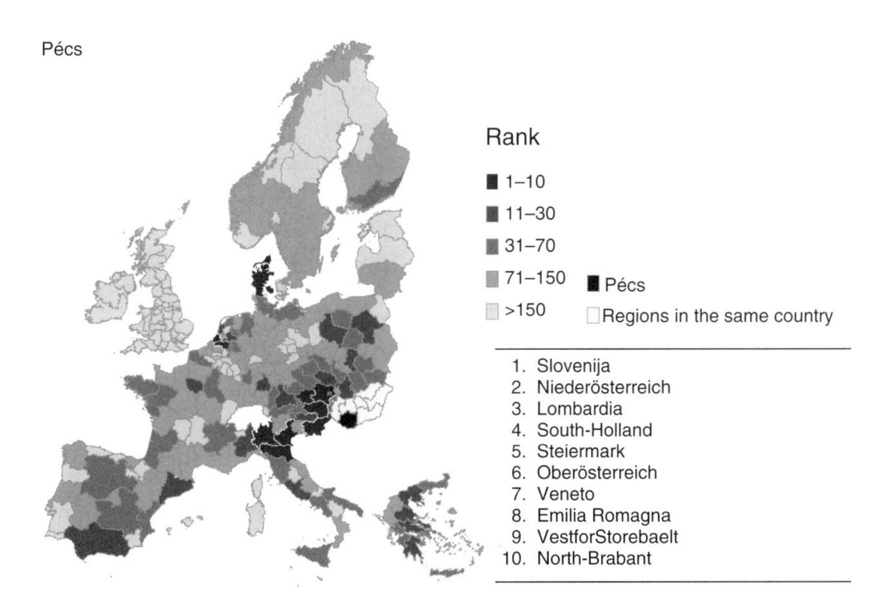

Figure 5.7 Major international competitors for agriculture: Rotterdam–The Hague and Pécs

exports only constitute a small part of total production. The majority remains in the own or neighbouring regions. Table 5.5 shows that for the part that is exported, regions have competition from all over Europe. For the part exported, distance does not play a role. The strong European economic centres are the major competitor for almost all regions. In particular Luxembourg and London have strong positions. Moreover, we observe some surprising market overlaps. Surprising examples are the competition Brussels has from Gelderland in The Netherlands, a region which is not renowned for its financial and business services sector, or the competition Thessaloniki has from Helsinki, two regions that are distant from each other and that have different economic structures. The relation between Budapest and Vienna is expected due to their close proximity and the growing role Budapest plays as an intermediary between Western and Central Europe.

5.5 CONCLUSIONS

From the analyses in this chapter, it becomes clear that competition is location-specific because competition is determined by the trade connections between regions. The overlap in trade connections shows with whom a region competes, on what, and where. The context specificity of the market where firms are active is therefore important in determining their regional competitiveness. We applied the introduced revealed competition measure to region-sector high-potential combinations introduced in the first chapter. Local factors are supposed to be important in the competition of firms from different regions which may lead to a self-augmenting process of network and firm-related development (Brenner, 2004) and attract foreign direct investments (Basile et al., 2008). Cities and regions are therefore compared with each other in rankings on competitiveness (see Chapter 1). In this chapter we analysed to what extent this multi-regional competition actually is the case and whether these comparisons between regions are indeed based on common markets of local firms.

The case studies presented in this chapter show that there are many differences with whom, where and on what firms from different regions compete. Similarly specialized clusters may face competition from different competitive regions in their respective network. The regions of Eindhoven, Helsinki and Milan all have strong medium- and high-tech production sectors but do not face mutual competition in the same degree. Dutch regions face a lot of competition from firms in Milan, but those in Milan do not face the same competition from Dutch regions. They also

Table 5.5 Top 10 of major competitors for selected sectors and selected regions

	Agricultural sector			Low-tech manufacturing		
	Rotterdam–The Hague	Pécs	Andalucía	Warsaw	Dresden	Pécs
1	Mainland – DK	Slovenia – SI	Languedoc – FR	Milan – IT	Milan – IT	Milan – IT
2	Reg. Milan – IT	Niederöster. – AT	Rotterdam – NL	Stuttgart – DE	Mainland – DK	Oberöster. – AT
3	Andalucía – ES	Milan – IT	Prov. Alpes – FR	Düsseldorf – DE	Paris – FR	Niederöster. – AT
4	Düsseldorf – DE	Rotterdam – NL	Lyon – FR	Munich – DE	Eindhoven – NL	Stuttgart – DE
5	Stuttgart – DE	Steiermark – AT	Paris – FR	Arnsberg – DE	Copenhagen – DK	Wien – AT
6	Weser Ems – DE	Oberöster.– AT	Milan – IT	Helsinki – FI	Emil. Romagna – IT	Emil.Romag. – IT
7	Reg. Paris – FR	Veneto – IT	Alentejo – PT	Frankfurt – DE	Rotterdam – NL	Munich – DE
8	Schles. Hols. – DE	Emil. Romag. – IT	Aquitaine – FR	Köln – DE	Veneto – IT	Steiermark – AT
9	Köln – DE	Mainland – DK	Mainland – DK	Emil. Romagna – IT	Oberöster. – AT	Veneto – IT
10	Arnsberg – DE	Eindhoven – NL	Champagne – FR	Paris – FR	Antwerp – BE	Düsseldorf – DE
	Medium-tech manufacturing			**High-tech manufacturing**		
	Milan	Eindhoven	Budapest	Munich	Lyon	Helsinki
1	Paris – FR	Paris – FR	Stuttgart – DE	Dublin – IE	Dublin – IE	Dublin – IE
2	Lyon – FR	Milan – IT	Munich – DE	Paris – FR	Milan – IT	Paris – FR
3	Stuttgart – DE	Düsseldorf – DE	Milan – IT	Milan – IT	Helsinki – FI	Eesti – EE
4	Barcelona – ES	Stuttgart – DE	Düsseldorf – DE	Lyon – FR	Göteborg – SE	Milan – IT
5	Munich – DE	Antwerp – BE	Frankfurt – DE	Helsinki – FI	Stuttgart – DE	Lyon – FR
6	Düsseldorf – DE	Arnsberg – DE	Paris – FR	Veneto – IT	Piemonte – IT	Göteborg – SE
7	Dublin – IE	Köln – DE	Arnsberg – DE	Göteborg – SE	Düsseldorf – DE	Stuttgart – DE

Table 5.5 (continued)

	Medium-tech manufacturing			**High-tech manufacturing**		
	Milan	Eindhoven	Budapest	Munich	Lyon	Helsinki
8	Frankfurt – DE	Lyon – FR	Karlsruhe – DE	Inn. London – UK	Munich – DE	Upsalla – SE
9	Arnsberg – DE	Munich – DE	Köln – DE	Border Midlan. – IE	Veneto – IT	Stockholm – SE
10	Antwerp – BE	Barcelona – ES	Niederöster. – AT	Piemonte – IT	Inn. London – UK	Düsseldorf – DE
	Financial and business services					
	Inner London	Paris	Brussels	Rotterdam–The Hague	Budapest	Thessaloniki
1	Luxembourg – LU	Inn. London – UK	Luxembourg – LU	Inn. London – UK	Wien – AT	Inn. London – UK
2	Paris – FR	Luxembourg – LU	Inn. London – UK	Dublin – IE	Paris – FR	Paris – FR
3	Dublin – IE	Dublin – IE	Paris – FR	Paris – FR	Inn. London – UK	Surrey – UK
4	Rotterdam – NL	Out. London – UK	Rotterdam – NL	Luxembourg – LU	Luxembourg – LU	Luxembourg – LU
5	Brussels – BE	Madrid – ES	Dublin – IE	Surrey – UK	Dublin – IE	Helsinki – FI
6	Antwerp – BE	Milan – IT	Utrecht – NL	Brussels – BE	Amsterdam – NL	Out. London – UK
7	Stockholm – SE	Brussels – BE	Amsterdam – NL	Frankfurt – DE	Frankfurt – DE	Stuttgart – DE
8	Barcelona – ES	Amsterdam – NL	Out. London – UK	Out. London – UK	Düsseldorf – DE	Dublin – IE
9	Frankfurt – DE	Barcelona – ES	Gelderland – NL	Stockholm – SE	Out. London – UK	Düsseldorf – DE
10	Milan – IT	Stockholm – SE	Eindhoven – NL	Madrid – ES	Munich – DE	Amsterdam – NL

compete with firms from other regions. Specialized firms in the Budapest region show a lot of similarities in magnitude and reach of their export orientation in comparison with, for example, the Danish regions, but they focus on different regions and markets altogether. Geographical proximity for manufacturing goods and hierarchical functional proximity for (high-end) services coincide in practically all regional trade patterns analysed. Although services are mainly produced for local markets, a small proportion is traded internationally, between firms and institutions in global financial and business service centres such as London, Frankfurt and Paris (Thissen et al., 2011).

The trade network-based applications and descriptions in this chapter show the wealth of heterogeneity present in relative competitiveness linkages between regions in Europe. This calls for a careful addressing and evaluating of the cluster-based strategies of regional, national and European governments in a smart specialization type of framework. In Chapter 7 we will extensively discuss a smart specialization-based benchmark approach to carry out regional competitiveness analyses of the specific region–sector combinations introduced in the introduction.

NOTES

1. We first focus on the three broad basic sectors of agriculture, (knowledge-intensive) manufacturing and (knowledge-intensive) business services. See Van Oort (2004) on why these broadly defined sectors are hypothesized to have different spatial footprints from the outset. Within these three broad sectors, we pay attention to specific policy-relevant clusters. The construction of our dataset (see Chapter 2) allows us to analyse business and financial services-based clusters – an unprecedented effort in this line of research.
2. It is noted that the trade data on which this table is based are for the year 2000. As follows from the dynamic analysis in Chapter 6, despite the recent crisis and with the exception of Ireland, trade networks have not changed dramatically during the last decade. Quantities traded have changed, but changes to the trade pattern are minor.

6. Dynamics in revealed regional competition between firms in Europe

In this chapter we take a dynamic perspective and analyse revealed competition, market dominance and spatial trade concentration on specific markets in the first decade of the twenty-first century. We apply our methodology to regional competitive trade dynamics in European regions during the period 2000–10, focusing on urban heterogeneity in regional development. We analyse all European regions but especially focus on the sector–region combinations introduced in the first chapter. We will show that over this period European regional development was characterized not only by a catching up of Central and Eastern European regions, but also by a further integration of these regions in the European economy. However, we will also show that this integration did not have unequivocal positive effects for all sector–region combinations in Central and Eastern European regions.

We discuss in depth the revealed competition measure introduced in the previous chapter. We elaborate on the proposed revealed competition measure thereby deriving two indicators that can be derived from the theoretical revealed competition framework. The first additional measure is market dominance. Market dominance is a spatial market share measure. It is comparable to the market share, but weights spatial markets equally and therefore brings a spatial factor in the market share definition. This market dominance represents to what degree firms from a region are seen by others as a strong competitor on all markets. The second additional measure derived in this chapter is the spatial concentration index. The spatial concentration index gives information on the type of markets on which firms of a region are predominantly strong: many small regions or a few very large regions.

In this chapter we compare the revealed competition measure, market dominance and the spatial concentration indicator over time for the selected sector–region combinations.

Our completely new theoretical framework based on revealed completion and the resulting market dominance and spatial concentration indicators resolve four generally known shortcomings of earlier indicators: our indicators appropriately address the difference in regions' economic size and are thereby well equipped to analyse dynamic developments; they handle asymmetry in trade relations, capture competition between specialized and diversified economies, and are able to address sector heterogeneity in network relations.

6.1 REVEALED REGIONAL COMPETITION AND EARLIER MEASURES

Economists have traditionally argued that competition brings out the best in firms and regions and ensures an efficient distribution of production (Glaeser, 2001). Studies on competitiveness are strongly related to recent studies that analyse the competitive threat that strong regional economies face from other less developed regions. The threat of the emerging economies in Asia, and especially China, are recently the most abundant (Blázquez-Lidoy et al., 2006; Jenkins, 2008). Within Europe there are also studies on the threat that emerging Central and Eastern European regions pose to the economically leading Western European regions (Duboz and Le Gallo, 2011).

Conventionally, the international trade literature has focused on the revealed comparative advantage (RCA) as presented by the Balassa (1965) index to measure inter-country competition. In the Balassa index, the shares of different product categories in total exports of a country are compared to a group of reference countries' shares. The Balassa index determines what types of products are overrepresented in a country's exports and indicates which export products a country is relatively 'good' in. Competition between two regions is commonly measured by comparing the export structure of two regions in a specific market using Finger and Kreinin's (1979) export similarity index (ESI). Analogous to the Balassa index, it measures the degree to which two regions have the same comparative advantage in a *specific* regional market. The ESI is, therefore, symmetric and size independent.

The studies on the competitive threat of regions are based on variants of the export similarity index (ESI). The ESI-based indices used in these studies all compare the relative structure in exports to establish an indicator of the degree of competition between regions. They compare the share of, for example, services, industry and agriculture in the export of two competing regions to a specific third region (the market) to determine the degree of competition between these two regions. According to these ESI-based indices there is a high level of competition between two regions if they have a comparable export structure to the same market.

There are several shortcomings of the usage of ESI-based indicators to analyse the competitive threat of regions. These shortcomings are extensively discussed and summarized in Jenkins (2008). We mention four of these shortcomings below.

1. The ESI-based indicators imply symmetry in competition because only export *structures* are compared and the size of regions has no influence on the degree of competition. As a result a small country such as Honduras faces just as much competition from the US as vice versa. It seems, however, highly unlikely that in a market like Venezuela firms from Honduras face the same competition from US firms as the firms from the US face competition from firms from Honduras. The importance of size in the competition between regions is extensively discussed by Camagni (2002) and we will return to this issue later in this chapter.
2. The second problem discussed by Jenkins (2008) is related to measuring competition and a competitive threat over time. The competition between regions does not change as long as the export structures stay the same. The example of the resulting lack of change in the competitive threat of China, despite its strong growth in exports and economic size, seems therefore intuitively a strange result.
3. Firms from specialized regions only compete with other firms from other specialized regions and not with diversified regions. This problem is directly related to the definition of the ESI-based measures that compare the export structure of regions. Suppose a small region is specialized in the production of textiles, and exports these textiles to the same region as another diversified large region. Textile firms from both regions would be competing heavily while the ESI-based indicator would tell us that competition between the regions is low.
4. A final problem relates to the missing trade network in the competition analysis mentioned in Chapter 3. Two regions may be exporting to completely different markets and have a comparable export structure at the same time. This comparable composition of exports may suggest a high degree of competition between these two regions. In reality, however, firms from both regions do not compete at all because they are active in different (geographical) markets. An appropriate analysis of competition between firms from different regions involves therefore the analysis of the entire trade network.

All these shortcomings mentioned in the literature seem to be caused by the underlying assumption of a region as one producing entity in the ESI-based indicators. The ESI-based indicators take the region as the actor creating a mix of products. The degree of competition is seen as the overlap of this product mix with the product mix of other regions. This may be a representation of comparative advantage at the country level. However, comparative advantage is shown by Camagni (2002) to be problematic at the regional level. As argued by Camagni (2002), competition between regions concerns absolute, not relative, advantage because it is quantity adjustment rather than price that occurs at the regional level within currency areas. As a consequence the export *structure* of regions (cf. Storper, 1997) has little to do with the competition between regions, which is solely determined at the firm level.

In Chapter 5 we therefore introduced *revealed competition* as a measure for interregional competition. This measure addresses all the above-mentioned shortcomings of ESI-based measures. The revealed competition measure takes the firm as the actor receiving competition from firms established in other regions. Using the revealed competition between regions is a more unambiguous way to determine which region competes with whom, in which product markets, and where. The measure is based on the overlap in market areas weighted with both the importance of markets and the strength of competitors. It is therefore by definition asymmetric. The measure stays as close as possible to the market where firm-level competition actually occurs as it can be calculated on any level of product aggregation. Changes in size and export markets affect the competition between regions accordingly and this measure is therefore appropriate to analyse the development in revealed competition over time. These developments in regional revealed competition are central in this chapter.

6.2 REVEALED COMPETITION IN EUROPE

The static picture of revealed competition presented in Chapter 4 tells us much about the regional competitors that firms (in a certain industry) face. However, in this chapter we discuss the revealed competition measure in a more formal way and we are particularly interested in the developments in revealed competition over time to analyse whether we can distinguish typical regions that improve their competitive positions in the European economy. Developments may differ across sectors so we will look at the sector–region combination that we discuss throughout this book.

Recapitulating the definition in Chapter 5, revealed competition between regions is defined as follows.[1] Suppose there are two regions A and B. The competition region A has from region B depends on

(1) the market share of firms from region B in all markets and (2) the importance of each of these markets for region A. The importance of a market for region A is given by the share of this market in the total exports of region A. Region A therefore has strong competition from region B if region B has a large market share in those regions that are important to region A.

The competition between regions A and B is strong if region B has a large market share in the regions that are important to region A and if region B has a large market share in the regions that are important to region A. After all, in such situations, there is a large geographical market overlap, and firms from regions A and B have a high likelihood of being active in the same market. An increase in the market share of region A can only be obtained at the cost of the market share of region B, and firms from both regions are therefore competing for the same customers. This information about the markets where firms are active gives us insight in the market overlap with other firms and the competition between firms from different regions. Throughout our analyses, we discuss competition between regions, which is, in fact, a shortcut for saying that firms within a region compete for product markets with firms located in another region (compare the discussed issue of competition between regions or firms). Although we do not examine individual firms but rather economic sectors, the firm is the assumed actor driving these sector results.

The concept of revealed competition *RC* between region *i* and region *k* is more formally defined in equation (6.1).

$$RC_{ik} = \sum_{j} E_{ij} M_{kj}$$
$$E_{ij} = \frac{T_{ij}}{P_i}, M_{kj} = \frac{T_{kj}}{D_j} \tag{6.1}$$

where T_{ij} is the trade from region *i* in region *j*, P_i is the production in region *i*, D_k is the demand in region *k*, E_{ij} is the export share of region *i* to region *j* and M_{kj} is the market share of region *k* in region *j*. As was explained above, revealed competition is the sum of the market shares of a region's competitors weighted with the importance of the different markets for this region. This indicator can be calculated for different aggregates of products, sectors or even total production. The measure is very close to the notion of competition common in business economics, especially in the case of a very detailed and specific product level.

Revealed competition measures the degree of competition of firms from different regions as a percentage of the total competition that a firm in a region faces in all markets. The row sum of the revealed competition is therefore equal to 1 ($\sum_k RC_{ik} = 1$). If RC equals 1, it implies that there is only one competitor that takes the rest of the market in all destination markets of a region's exports.

It was discussed in section 6.1 that earlier ESI-based measures all suffer from four shortcomings. The first shortcoming was that large and small regions faced exactly the same amount of competition vis-à-vis each other (the symmetry problem). The second shortcoming was that regional economic growth does not affect the competition between regions as long as the composition of its exports does not change. The third shortcoming concerned the lack of competition between specialized and diversified regions because both have a very different composition of their exports. The final shortcoming was that an ESI-based indicator may suggest significant competition between two regions, while they export to completely different (geographic) markets and firms from both regions therefore never meet or actually compete with each other. We discuss these shortcomings in relation to our revealed competition measure below.

The revealed competition indicator between regions is clearly asymmetric and size dependent and therefore not susceptible to the symmetry problem. A region faces more competition from larger regions than from smaller ones. The degree of competition between two regions is now inversely related to the relative production share in both regions. We can mathematically describe this situation as follows:

$$RC_{ij} = \frac{P_j}{P_i} RC_{ji} \tag{6.2}$$

The competition that region i faces from region j is higher if the relative production level in region i is higher, while it diminishes when the relative production in region j is lower. Consequently, the larger the size differences between two regions, the larger the difference in competition between them.

The revealed competition measure is also affected by the growth difference between regions. Thus the second shortcoming also does not apply to the revealed competition measure. It follows directly from equation (6.2) that the growth of a region increases its competitive position vis-à-vis regions with less economic growth. The larger the economic size of a region (measured in its market size), the larger the revealed competition it poses to other regions. The recent relatively strong growth of China would therefore result in it being an increased revealed competitor with respect to other countries or regions. Thus, the *RC* measure is appropriate to analyse the change in competition when the relative size of a region changes over time.

The last two mentioned shortcomings associated with the ESI-based methods also do not apply to the revealed competition measure. The revealed competition is directly measured at the specific market and product aggregation. It therefore is not affected by the specialization of diversification of production of a region. It only measures the overlap in the specific product markets and takes the firm and not the region as the representative actor competing with other firms. Accordingly, the region's production or export structure has no influence on the revealed competition measure. Revealed competition is measured at the level of actual trade flows taking the complete trade network into account. Hence, firms from certain regions do not compete with firms from other regions when they are not active in the same geographical markets (although they may produce the same types of goods).[2]

6.2.1 Dynamics in Revealed Competition among European Regions

We first discuss the dynamics in competition among European regions with respect to total production and subsequently the competition in more specific product markets. We discuss the sector–region combinations according to our selection of sectors and regions presented in the introduction to this book (see Table 1.1).

In Table 6.1 we present the dynamics in revealed competition of the total production in our selection of regions using the regional trade data over the period 2000–10 (see the Appendix for a detailed description of the data).[3] In the first row of Table 6.1 we present the competition of Milan with other regions in the year 2000. Thus, the competition of firms from Milan with other firms from Milan equals 0.2137, while its firms face only a 0.0038 revealed competition from firms established in the Barcelona region. In other words, firms from Milan face less than a half per cent of competition from those established in Barcelona. We can translate the revealed competition scores easily into percentages because they sum up to 1. The competition that firms from Milan face from firms established in Paris is therefore more than double the competition from those established in Barcelona and amounts to slightly less than 1 per cent. The percentage growth in the revealed competition over the period 2000–10 is presented in brackets below the revealed competition score. Hence, the competition that firms from Milan face from firms established in Paris has grown by 2 per cent.

The main differences in dynamics of revealed competition in total production of different regions are due to the region's size, sector structure and location in the trade network. The large agglomerations of Milan, Barcelona and Paris are all characterized by increased competition from other regions and less from firms established in the own region over the period 2000–10. This is represented by the negative

Table 6.1 Dynamics in revealed competition between regions from 2000 to 2010 (total regional production)

Total regional Production	Milan	Barcelona	Paris	Warsaw	Dresden	Thessaloniki
Milan	0.2137	0.0038	0.0086	0.0007	0.0009	0.0009
	(−4%)	(11%)	(2%)	(56%)	(−12%)	(1%)
Barcelona	0.0077	0.2070	0.0120	0.0004	0.0010	0.0006
	(−16%)	(−1%)	(−24%)	(129%)	(−147%)	(−12%)
Paris	0.0060	0.0042	0.2549	0.0005	0.0007	0.0005
	(−7%)	(−8%)	(−3%)	(48%)	(53%)	(−15%)
Warsaw	0.0050	0.0015	0.0052	0.2080	0.0018	0.0003
	(−1%)	(91%)	(3%)	(−5%)	(−84%)	(129%)
Dresden	0.0079	0.0042	0.0093	0.0022	0.1756	0.0006
	(2%)	(13%)	(21%)	(47%)	(9%)	(3%)
Thessaloniki	0.0110	0.0034	0.0088	0.0005	0.0009	0.1969
	(−18%)	(−6%)	(−25%)	(193%)	(−161%)	(6%)

growth on the diagonal in Table 6.1. This signifies increased trade integration and more interregional competition of these regions over this period. We also observe that with the exception of Milan, the other two large agglomerations saw a decline in competition among each other. This is shown by the negative growth rates in revealed competition. This was caused by increased competition from smaller regions, mainly from emerging economies and the periphery. An example of this increased competition by emerging economies is given by the large growth rates in the column of Warsaw. Dresden and Thessaloniki give more mixed results with positive and negative growth rates. The strong growth in competition that Warsaw faces from other regions and gives to other regions at the cost of less competition with firms from its own region represents the increasing economic importance and trade integration of this region. The economies of Dresden and Thessaloniki, however, show an opposite pattern, which suggests a loss in their economic performance and competitive position over these years.

The dynamics in revealed competition for the financial and business sector are presented in Table 6.2. We have seen in Chapter 4 that this sector is generally concentrated in the larger cities and there is only limited trade in services with other regions. The large values on the diagonal and thus the high revealed competition of financial and business services firms with other firms from the same region are the consequence of the concentration of this sector. During the first decade of this century the competition between financial and business firms of the own region declined and as a consequence the competition with firms from other regions increased sharply. This is especially the case because in comparison with other sectors the levels of interregional competition were low in the year 2000. The relatively small change in competition within the region of inner London is probably the consequence of the choice to split London up into two areas. The internal competition of firms within London would be higher if both regions had been taken together.

With Andalucía and Rotterdam–The Hague we have two of the main agricultural regions of Europe. In both regions we see that about 30 per cent of the competitors comes from the own region, which is smaller than for the typical Central Eastern European region of Pécs, where more than 40 per cent of the competition comes from agricultural establishments in the same region. We observe that the growth rates in revealed competition are all positive in the Rotterdam–The Hague column of Table 6.2. Thus, agricultural establishments from Rotterdam–The Hague have become stronger competitors to firms from all three regions. Agricultural firms from Andalucía, on the other hand, only gained in their competitive position vis-à-vis agriculture from Pécs. The region of Pécs decreased its

Table 6.2 Dynamics in revealed competition between regions from 2000 to 2010 (sector details)

Financial and Business services	Brussels	Paris	Warsaw	Inner London	Agriculture	Andalucía	Pécs	Rotterdam–The Hague
Brussels	0.3178 (−18%)	0.0023 (370%)	0.0000 (1670%)	0.0024 (138%)	Andalucía	0.3235 (−5%)	0.0003 (107%)	0.0069 (13%)
Paris	0.0003 (393%)	0.4069 (−5%)	0.0005 (−17%)	0.0004 (523%)	Pécs	0.0045 (47%)	0.4111 (−13%)	0.0039 (242%)
Warsaw	0.0001 (1145%)	0.0129 (−45%)	0.3077 (−11%)	0.0008 (144%)	Rotterdam–The Hague	0.0105 (−5%)	0.0004 (300%)	0.2699 (2%)
Inner London	0.0007 (172%)	0.0009 (579%)	0.0001 (297%)	0.2734 (−3%)				
High-tech manufacturing	**Munich**	**Helsinki**	**Lyon**		**Medium-tech manufacturing**	**Budapest**	**Milan**	**North-Brabant**
Munich	0.1915 (−2%)	0.0062 (−24%)	0.0102 (−18%)		Budapest	0.1105 (28%)	0.0087 (23%)	0.0036 (−23%)
Helsinki	0.0041 (−6%)	0.3124 (2%)	0.0046 (−36%)		Milan	0.0004 (161%)	0.2567 (−6%)	0.0017 (0%)
Lyon	0.0068 (2%)	0.0047 (−36%)	0.2269 (−6%)		North-Brabant	0.0008 (45%)	0.0080 (−11%)	0.1907 (−4%)

inward orientation: revealed competition among agricultural establishments in the Pécs region decreased by 13 per cent. The revealed competition with respect to both Andalucía (107 per cent) and Rotterdam–The Hague (300 per cent), however, became stronger.

The medium and high-tech sectors are commonly considered the field of highly productive small to medium-sized cities whose dominant competitive advantage is that they exhibit high degrees of connectivity (Ni and Kresl, 2010; McCann and Acs, 2011) rather than urban or home market scales. There appears to be urban growth, but it is not occurring at a very fast rate and is located in medium-sized rather than the largest conurbations.[4] We see in Table 6.2 that our high-tech regions, Munich, Helsinki and Lyon, all lose competitive position vis-à-vis each other, with the exception of the competition that firms from Lyon face from firms from Munich. This is an indication that other regions are becoming stronger competitors, because the sum over all 273 regions over the rows of Table 6.2 should add up to 1. This may be comparable to the medium-tech sector where both Milan and Eindhoven face decreasing competition among each other while the revealed competition with the emerging economy of Budapest increases sharply.

6.3 MARKET DOMINANCE IN EUROPE

In the discussion of the revealed competition we often looked at the columns of Tables 6.1 and 6.2 to analyse a region's position vis-à-vis other regions. In order to get the overall strength of a region as a competitor with other regions we introduce a new indicator that represents the column sum of the regional revealed competition measure: market dominance (MD_k) of a region k. This market dominance indicator is measured by the weighted importance of a region as a competitor in all markets, corrected for the geographical scope of the market. It reflects the competitive position or dominance of a certain region in all geographically distinguished markets. More formally, it can be described as:

$$MD_k = \frac{\sum_i RC_{ik}}{\#i} \tag{6.3}$$

where $\#i$ equals the number of regions. The sum of the market dominance scores total 1 over all regions.[5] To interpret this indicator for market dominance, we weight it with the importance of every competitor. The importance of every competitor is its share in the world market. This weighted market dominance indicator adds up to the share of a region in the world market,[6] which complies with the fact that the degree of market dominance should reflect the degree of competition a region imposes on all other regions. The market dominance indicator weighted with every competitor's share in the world market is the share of a region in the world market in the absence of any spatial differentiation in markets. We will use this notion when we derive the spatial concentration indicator in the next section.

Table 6.3 gives the market dominance (MD) of our selection of sector–region combinations in Europe in 2000. The average value of the MD equals approximately 0.003,[7] and most sector–region combinations in Table 6.3 have a larger market dominance, representing their dominance of the market. In brackets we present again the percentage change in the market dominance over the period 2000–10. In Table 6.3 we see that the Paris region has the largest market dominance of slightly more than 2 per cent. Barcelona has exactly half the market dominance of the Paris region and the Milan region is in the middle. The Milan region has lost competitive position to other regions while the other two regions have strengthened their position. The peripheral regions and the emerging economies have, of course, a much smaller market dominance. Among these smaller regions Dresden lost in market dominance, while both other regions strengthened their position. This loss of both Milan and Dresden was already visible in the decline in the revealed competition of these regions in the columns of Tables 6.1 and 6.2.

The strong increase in the agricultural market dominance of the Rotterdam–The Hague region with 16 per cent and the small decline of agriculture in Andalucía was also already present in Tables 6.1 and 6.2. The large loss of almost 10 per cent in the Pécs region is largely due to the large decline of 13 per cent in the revealed competition on the home market. Although the opening of the agricultural market of the Pécs region caused a strengthening in its international position it also caused a much stronger decline in its home market.

In the financial market we see that among the large agglomerations only inner London increased its market dominance while Paris stays at a constant level. The regions of Brussels and Warsaw are characterized by a strong decline in their market dominance. We have seen in Table 6.2 that most of this decline is due to reduced revealed competition on the region's home market. While the large agglomerations of Paris and London keep this loss limited, the loss in revealed competition on the home market is large for Brussels and Warsaw. Part of the associated increase in interregional services competition is coming from outside Europe (not shown). This increase from regions outside of Europe is the reason for the limited gains of London and Paris given the decline of other European financial and business services producers.

Table 6.3 Market dominance in European sector–region combinations

	Total production	Agriculture	Financial and Business services	Manufacturing		
				Low-tech	Medium-tech	High-tech
Large agglomerations						
London			0.019 (11%)			
Milan	0.016 (−3%)				0.022 (−4%)	
Barcelona	0.011 (6%)					
Munich						0.013 (−8%)
Paris	0.022 (4%)		0.034 (0%)			
Strong medium-sized economies						
Brussels			0.010 (−8%)			
Eindhoven					0.007 (−7%)	
Lyon						0.014 (−14%)
Helsinki						0.014 (−23%)
Rotterdam		0.014 (16%)				
Peripheral regions and emerging markets						
Budapest					0.003 (33%)	
Warsaw	0.008 (5%)		0.012 (−4%)			
Dresden	0.003 (−5%)			0.002 (−1%)		
Pécs		0.004 (−9%)		0.001 (6%)		
Thessaloniki	0.005 (7%)					
Andalucía		0.017 (−3%)				

In Table 6.3 the selected large manufacturing region combinations with a market dominance larger than 0.003 have all lost in market dominance during the period 2000–10. This is due to the increase in market dominance of smaller regions such as Budapest. Budapest is exactly equal to the average value for market dominance in 2000 and sees its market dominance increase by 33 per cent over the subsequent 10 years. The very small low-tech manufacturing regions see little change and stay far below the average market dominance value.

In Figure 6.1 we give an overview of regional development in market

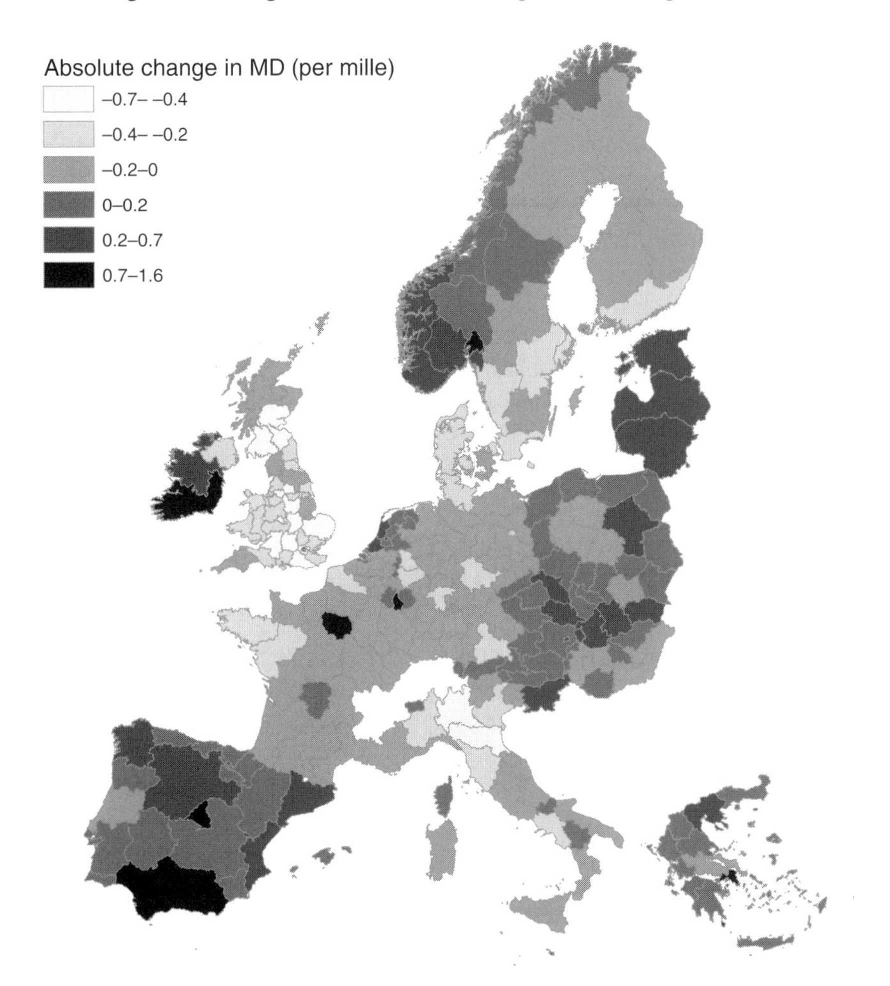

Figure 6.1 The change in market dominance for European regions (2000–10)

dominance by presenting the absolute change for all European regions over the period 2000–10. The figure clearly shows a combination of two occurrences over this period. There was a strong increase in market dominance of the large agglomerations such as Madrid, Dublin, Paris, Barcelona, London, Vienna and the Amsterdam–Rotterdam area. At the same time there was also a strong catching-up of peripheral regions and emerging economies, with more than 30 regions in the top 50 regions with the largest change in market dominance.

6.4 SPATIAL CONCENTRATION IN EUROPE

We have already seen that market dominance is a spatial indicator for market share. Dividing market dominance by European production share therefore gives a spatial concentration in competition indicator SC_k. This indicator provides information on the size of the markets in which a region's industry is strong. The spatial concentration tells us whether a region's industry is strong in a few large markets or strong in a large number of small markets. A value for the spatial concentration indicator close to 1 indicates that the industry in this region has a comparable market share in all European markets. A region is well integrated into the European economy if it manages to get a comparable market share in all European markets and the spatial concentration indicator is close to 1. The SC_k indicator is formally defined as:

$$SC_k = \frac{MD_k}{(P_k / \sum_i P_i)} \tag{6.4}$$

If the spatial concentration indicator is less than 1, the region k has a strong market position in a few large regions where it has a larger than average market share, and a weak market position in many smaller markets where it has a less than average market share. This phenomenon is typical for large agglomerations such as Paris, where local production dominates the market. The size of the Paris region causes Paris's market share in Europe to be large as well, which leads to its market share in many regions being less than that of its European average. If the spatial concentration indicator is larger than 1, the region k has a strong market position in many (economically small) regions where it has a larger than average market share, and a weak market position in the larger regions where it has a less than average market share. This phenomenon is typical for small local-oriented regions. These regions have a relatively large share of the home (own

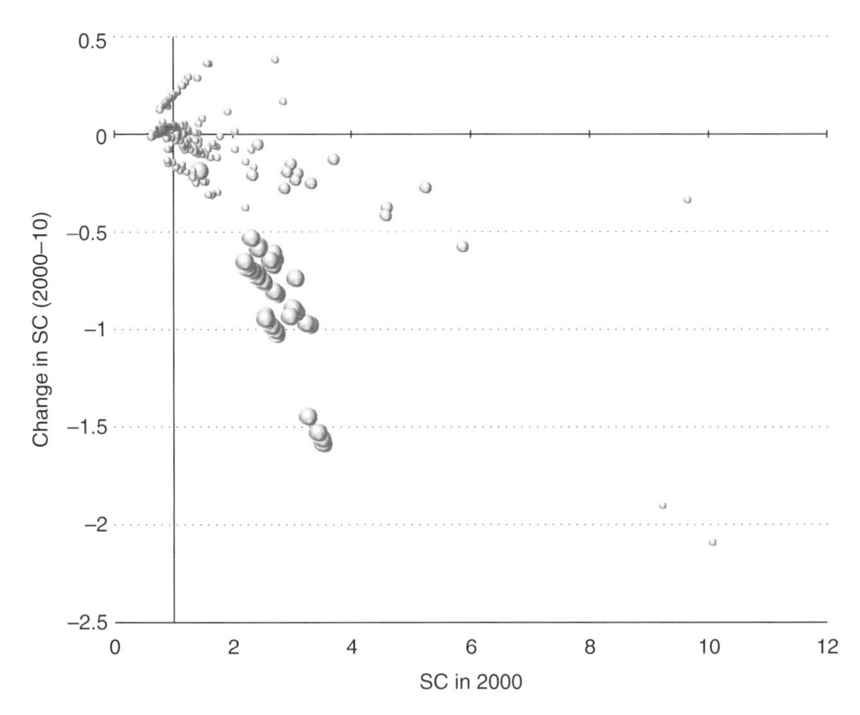

Figure 6.2 The spatial concentration and its change for European regions (2000–10)

region) market and have a reasonable share within their country. These regions have almost no share of the market in the rest of the European economy and are therefore not well integrated in the European economy. Regional economies that are well integrated in the European economy will have market shares in all regions that are close to the European average. They will, therefore, have spatial concentration scores close to 1.

In Figure 6.2 we present the spatial concentration in relation to its change over the period 2000–10. The majority of regions have a value close to 1, which implies that in many regions they have a market share that is close to their total European market share. These regions are, therefore, very well integrated within the European economy. The largest group of regions has values in between 0.75 and 1.25. These regions may gain or lose in the spatial concentration indicator. A second large group of regions consists of the peripheral and Central and Eastern European regions. If we discard the three outliers on the right-hand side, these regions are represented by the large bubbles in the lower right-hand quadrant of the figure. These regions were all characterized by very high values for the spatial concentration indicator in 2000, which declined strongly in the period 2000–10. This signals a tendency towards better integration in the European economy. The medium-sized bubbles in Figure 6.2 give a slightly different picture for Greece. These regions are also not very well integrated, as the spatial concentration measure was very high in 2000. What is worrying, however is that over the period from 2000 to 2010 there is a smaller adjustment than the Central and Eastern European regions towards an average value for the spatial concentration indicator of 1.[8] This implies that the integration of the regional Greek economy in Europe is going more slowly than the integration of the Central and Eastern European countries. Finally we see in Figure 6.2 a few outliers with very high values for the spatial concentration indicator. These are the peripheral Finnish region of Åland and the Spanish regions of Melilla and Ceuta.

We present more detailed results on the dynamics of the spatial concentration index in our sector–region combinations in Table 6.4. The large agglomerations of London, Milan, Barcelona, Munich and Paris all have the expected value for the spatial concentration index lower than 1. This represents their higher than average share of the market in their home regions versus a lower market share in the other regions. This value for the spatial concentration index of lower than 1 is not only for the total regional production but also for the sectoral results, although it should be noticed that Munich's high-tech spatial concentration indicator is approaching 1. Except for the financial and business services in London, the change in the spatial concentration index is negative and the spatial concentration index therefore becomes even smaller over time. The strong and medium-sized economies give a mixed picture, being larger or smaller than 1 in 2000, while the change in the spatial concentration index can be positive or negative and not necessarily in the direction of a value of 1 for the spatial concentration index.

The presented peripheral regions and emerging markets have all, with the exception of the very large Andalusian region, a spatial concentration indicator larger than 1, which declines over the period 2000–10. This change amounts, irrespective of the sector, to approximately 30 per cent of the value for the year 2000 for the regions Budapest, Warsaw and Pécs.

6.5 CONCLUSIONS AND DISCUSSION

In this chapter, we introduced the revealed competition measure more formally. This newly introduced network measure can be used to analyse competitiveness between regions and in different product markets. It will be used in the next chapter to develop smart specialization place-based

Table 6.4 Spatial concentration in European sector–region combinations

	Total production	Agriculture	Financial and Business services	Manufacturing		
				Low-tech	Medium-tech	High-tech
Large agglomerations						
London			0.61 (21%)			
Milan	0.67 (−2%)				0.69 (−7%)	
Barcelona	0.89 (−15%)					
Munich						0.95 (−10%)
Paris	0.63 (0%)		0.47 (−1%)			
Strong medium-sized economies						
Brussels			1.12 (−13%)			
Eindhoven					0.98 (−8%)	
Lyon						0.66 (4%)
Helsinki						0.64 (−7%)
Rotterdam		0.77 (4%)				
Peripheral regions and emerging markets						
Budapest					2.06 (−30%)	
Warsaw	2.18 (30%)		4.24 (−36%)			
Dresden	1.00 (4%)			1.17 (−4%)		
Pécs		1.94 (−30%)		2.01 (−16%)		
Thessaloniki	2.31 (−9%)					
Andalucía		0.65 (4%)				

development benchmarking that can be used in regional development strategies. The newly introduced theoretical framework is based on the geographical market overlap of different product markets and the market share of competitors in these markets. The new theoretical framework solves many of the earlier mentioned drawbacks of alternative measures. Contrary to these earlier ESI–based indicators (Finger and Kreinin, 1979), the proposed revealed competition measure is not symmetric, it can measure competition between specialized and diversified regions, and it can address changes in competition due to economic growth. We also introduced a market dominance indicator providing information on the dominance of sector–region combinations on all distinct regional markets and a spatial concentration indicator that tells us about the type of markets a region has access to.

In this chapter we focused on the dynamics in these indicators after the static revealed competition had already been discussed in the previous chapter. We illustrated the measures by presenting the revealed competition for our sector–region combinations. In general, we found that different sectors in different regions are differently related to each other in dynamic competitive relations: different regions specialized in different sectors and products face competition from other regions, which shows that there is actually no 'one-size-fits-all' strategy in regional economic development. This finding stresses the importance of a place-based smart specialization approach to regional competitiveness where location and networks play an important role. The theoretical framework based on actual network relations between regions trading in goods and services analysing actual revealed competition that was applied in this book and chapter is crucial to the understanding of international competitiveness of European regions and is therefore essential for a smart specialization place-based development strategy.

In general the large agglomerations in Europe have strengthened their position, possibly due to agglomeration economies. There was a strong increase in market dominance of the large agglomerations such as Madrid, Dublin, Paris, Barcelona and London. At the same time there was also a strong catching-up of peripheral regions and emerging economies, with more than 30 regions in the top 50 regions with the largest change in market dominance.

Alongside the region-specific growth patterns, we therefore also found evidence not only for a catching-up of Central and Eastern European regions, but also for increasing integration of Eastern and Central European regions in the European economy over the period 2000–10. The market dominance of the Central and Eastern European regions rose sharply over this period. In sectors such as medium-tech manufacturing we also see an increased importance of Central and Eastern European regions with a sharp increase of the revealed competition in the emerging economy of Budapest.

These Central and Eastern European regions were all characterized by very high values for the spatial concentration indicator in 2000 which declined strongly in the period 2000–10. This signals that these economies became better integrated into the European economy. The strong growth in competition that Warsaw faces from other regions and gives to other regions at the cost of less competition with firms from its own region represents the increasing economic importance and trade integration of this region. However, the results of integration are not always unequivocally positive for these regions: the opening of the agricultural market for the Pécs region caused a strengthening of its international position but has also caused a much stronger decline in its home market.

In the next chapter we will use the developed revealed competition indicators to present smart benchmarks that can be used in developing a smart specialization place-based regional development strategy (Barca et al., 2012). Our newly developed theoretical framework and the associated set of measures based on revealed competition of economic sectors across European regions allow for a more in-depth analysis of the types of regions that are involved in competitive relations in the period 2000–10 and therefore gives a good foundation for regional policies.

NOTES

1. For a similar measure focusing on competition for greenfield FDI, see Burger et al. (2012).
2. This problem occurs with the ESI-based methods because there is no theoretically proper method to aggregate over different markets.
3. Please note that there can be differences in the revealed competition in this chapter if compared to the other chapters. The reason is that we use here a different trade dataset (see the Appendix for details) and we look here at 'total' competition and not only international competition. Total competition implies that competition of firms from the own and from other regions in the same country are also taken into account.
4. Notable exceptions are the capital regions in Eastern European countries.
5. Thus, $\sum_k MD_k = 1$.
6. Thus, $\frac{P_k}{\sum_k P_k} = \sum_i \frac{P_i}{\sum_j P_j} RC_{ik}$, and $\sum_i \frac{P_i}{\sum_j P_j} = 1$.
7. The average value is equal to 1 divided by the number of regions.
8. The large size of the spatial concentration indicator may also be partly due to their reduced trade potential because of the specific island location of Greek regions.

7. A smart specialization strategy: locational and network determinants of international competitiveness

In Chapter 2 we extensively discussed the importance of a smart specialization strategy to implement place-based development to strengthening competitiveness in line with Europe's 2020 strategy and both the Lisbon and Gothenburg Agendas on Innovative Economic Development. In this chapter we show how the key locational and network determinants of competitiveness can play a role in a smart specialization strategy. This goes beyond the well-known benchmarks on locational competition mentioned in Chapter 3, as these do not take interregional network characteristics into account. Neglecting these will overestimate or underestimate certain locational factors and thereby lead to a poor evaluation of the regions' performance. We determine network relations using the trade relations between NUTS-2 regions in the European Union based on a newly structured multi-regional input–output table on that geographical scale, including relations for 60 sectors and products that were introduced in Chapter 4. In the previous chapter we showed which regions actually are competing in different sectors and products. In this chapter we show which locational characteristics – such as accessibility, R&D-intensity of production, labour market conditions and sustainability goals – are related to this competition, and which locational economic structures – such as clusters or specializations – are important for the performance of regions. These insights are useful for guiding and evaluating smart specialization competitiveness policies by correctly identifying important characteristics of every region and correctly evaluating the performance of regions, but also for presenting a common concept in (economic, social and territorial) cohesion policies.

7.1 SMART SPECIALIZATION AND A REGIONAL COMPETITIVENESS BENCHMARK

In Chapter 3 we have seen that the concept of benchmarks and regional competitiveness has become a hegemonic discourse within public policy circles. In this book, competitiveness is considered to be the environment in which productive firms can prosper and the means by which regional economies attract and retain innovative firms, skilled labour and knowledge workers. We have also seen that the literature is not unambiguously positive about the concept. Also the smart specialization initiative was shown in Chapter 2 to focus on embeddedness and network relations, emphasizing specific locational factors in a place-based development approach. Smart specialization therefore follows the critical point of view on the general competitiveness benchmark concept. The main problems with these performance rankings are that they tend to combine unlike locations, industries and indicators into aggregates that obscure important differences. In this chapter we introduce an applied analytical framework that moves beyond the critical stand that has been taken in the literature recently (Kitson et al., 2004).

7.2 AN APPLIED SMART SPECIALIZATION FRAMEWORK: REVEALED COMPETITION BENCHMARKING

Regional competitiveness should not solely be identified by structural characteristics (summarized in benchmarks or listings) of cities and regions, but alternatively by a theoretically informed analytical framework that uses actual networks of competing and economically valued relations between regions. Conceptually, we therefore introduced *revealed competition* in the previous chapter as an important indicator for measuring interregional competitiveness. Measuring revealed competition between regions is an attempt to determine more unambiguously which region competes with whom, on what and where. Our analysis of revealed competition uses interaction data between regions in Europe – interaction by way of the mutual trade in goods and services – to pinpoint market overlap in internationally mobile and traded products, goods and services, and hence measure competition on these markets.

Competitive advantage is predominantly envisioned as a place-based (regional) investment strategy by European, national and regional policymakers, providing optimal locational circumstances to attract mobile capital, knowledge and footloose firms (Basile et al., 2008). By looking at the actual competition between regions in terms of trade, we add the network dimension to this discussion. We do this by comparing locational characteristics of revealed competitors on specific markets after determining the most important locational characteristics on these markets. This provides us with a methodology to include trade networks and geographical markets in the concept of regional competitiveness.

The smart specialization-based benchmark methodology proposed in this chapter can be described as follows. First, we identify those regional characteristics that positively characterize all competitors of a region. These competitors were determined by the principle of revealed competition between regions explained in the previous chapter. In this way we rank regional characteristics in importance for every sector in every region separately. The reason for sector- and region-specific rankings of important locational characteristics is that all region–sector combinations are active on different geographical markets where they meet different competitors and where different characteristics may be important. Second, we analyse the performance of a region on these important indicators in comparison to the average score of its competitors. In this way we avoid comparing a region with 'wrong regions' that are not active on the same market. When two regions are active on completely separate (geographical) markets, different locational characteristics may be of importance and a comparison of the two regions may therefore be of no or limited use. In applying this approach we therefore address two of the main critiques on existing benchmark studies: how to evaluate the different indicators that may have varying effects on competitiveness, and what regions should be compared.

7.2.1 Locational Characteristics in the Benchmark of European NUTS-2 Regions

The smart specialization benchmark of European regions is based on the locational characteristics presented in Table 7.1. We compared competing industries in regions according to locational characteristics that are potential sources of competitiveness as discussed in Chapter 3. They can be subdivided into several groups as they are related to innovation, the functioning of the labour market, infrastructure and the size of regions. The often used indicators on innovation, region size, functioning of the labour market and infrastructure are based on the most recent indicators that are available in the Espon and Eurostat databases.

Besides these standard indicators we introduced new indicators in Chapter 4 that are all related to the economic structure of regions and more specifically different type of clusters and regional specialization.

Table 7.1 Regional characteristics used in the benchmark study

Innovation	*Region size*
R&D business (Eurostat)	Population (Eurostat)
Number of patents per inhabitant (Eurostat)	Active population (Eurostat)
R&D public (Eurostat)	Population density (Eurostat)
Ranking university (the 2008 QS university ranking 600)	*Infrastructure*
Percentage company access broadband internet (Eurostat)	Accessibility by air index (Espon)
	Accessibility by road & rail index (Espon)
Supply chain specialization in:	*Specialization (location quotients) in:*
Agriculture	Agriculture
Knowledge-intensive manufacturing	Knowledge-intensive manufacturing
Knowledge-intensive manufacturing – high-tech	Knowledge-intensive manufacturing – high-tech
Knowledge-intensive manufacturing – medium high-tech	Knowledge-intensive manufacturing – medium high-tech
Knowledge-intensive manufacturing – medium low-tech	Knowledge-intensive manufacturing – medium low-tech
Knowledge-intensive financial services	Knowledge-intensive financial services
Knowledge-intensive services	Knowledge-intensive services
Financial & business services	Financial & business services
Input openness in:	*Labour market*
Agriculture	Percentage employment 55+ (Eurostat)
Knowledge-intensive manufacturing	Participation – percentage employment women (Eurostat)
Knowledge-intensive manufacturing – high-tech	Percentage unemployment* (Eurostat)
Knowledge-intensive manufacturing – medium high-tech	Percentage long-term unemployment* (Eurostat)
Knowledge-intensive manufacturing – medium low-tech	*Regional specialization*
Knowledge-intensive financial services	Product specialization
Knowledge-intensive services	Supply chain specialization
Financial & business services	

Note: * The inverse of the indicator was taken.

They consist of the specialization of regions in the production of one specific type of product or the specialization in a complete supply chain to produce one specific type of product. The product specialization of a region has been based on the Theil index over the location quotients of regional production regarding 59 products and using the European average as a reference. This indicator tells to what extent a region is specialized in producing a certain product if compared to the average distribution of production in Europe. We also introduced sector indicators for specialization in certain types of production based on location quotients (concentration of a typical type of product) or the degree of supply chain production of a typical type of product. Supply chain specialization was determined using the backward linkages of the Leontief inverse of the multiregional input–output table. Finally, we introduced a sector indicator describing the network orientation or openness of a sector in a region regarding its inputs. The input openness indicator is based on the Krugman–Venables NEG model. It compares the actual input to the optimal input given a love of variety in intermediate inputs to the optimal spatial distribution of inputs. It assumes that in every region different varieties of products are produced and access to more varieties via a larger network (more open) will induce higher productivity.

In the benchmarking the sector supply chain and input openness indicators have only been used in the same sector. This implies that we assume that the degree of input openness of, for example, the agricultural sector, is an important factor for the agricultural sector and not for other sectors in the economy. All indicators used have been normalized with respect to the median value and the most recently available value has been taken. In order to keep the benchmark lucid, we present and discuss only the benchmark of the aggregate group of indicators in this chapter. The aggregate was determined as the average of the underlying locational characteristics. We will show the results for a more detailed analysis taking all detailed indicators into account as an illustration of the difference for a few cases.

We have constructed several composite indicators in the analysis. These composite indicators are presented in Table 7.2. The reason for working with composite indicators is mainly to keep the analysis lucid and to prevent superfluous information in the tables. For example, in the benchmark we often find population density and population size in two subsequent numbers in the ranking of regional characteristics. This is caused by the high correlation between these two indicators. A second reason for working with composite indicators is that only a combination of indicators tells us something about the performance of, for instance, the whole local labour market. We have therefore grouped these indicators in

Table 7.2 Composite indicators

Labour market is composed of:	*Agglomeration size is composed of:*
Percentage employment 55+ Participation (percentage employment women) Percentage unemployment Percentage long-term unemployment	Population Active population Population density
Public R&D is composed of:	*Private R&D is composed of:*
R&D public Ranking university	R&D business Number of patents per inhabitant

thematic subjects. The consequences of working with composite indicators will be illustrated in section 7.4.

All regional characteristics used in this chapter have been normalized with respect to the median value. In this way they are made comparable and they can therefore be used in the benchmarking study. The composite indicators are the average values of the normalized characteristics.

7.3 SMART SPECIALIZATION STRATEGIES FOR SELECTED SECTOR–LOCATION COMBINATIONS

Throughout this book we have discussed several exemplary European sector–region combinations. These sector–region combinations were presented in the introduction and are more extensively discussed in the Appendix. In this chapter we will discuss sector–region benchmarks and possible strategies for these sector–region combinations that can be derived from the benchmarks. The strategies are presented from the perspective of different types of locations. We show in this way that specific regional characteristics and location matters for a smart specialization strategy. Successful strategies can therefore not be 'simply' copied from other regions because the location and the network are important factors in determining the importance of different regional characteristics in the economic success of this region.

Alternatively, we might have chosen to present sector strategies from a region perspective. Different regional characteristics are important for different sectors in the same (type) of region because sectors are active on different markets and have different competitors. This shows that the region has to make a choice to facilitate successful and promising sectors or the average of all sectors in the region. We will shortly address this point in section 7.4, but mainly discuss sector strategies from the region perspective in this chapter.

We applied the regional competitiveness analysis to region–sector high-potential combinations, so-called clusters, but also to less successful region–sector combinations in the periphery and in emerging economies. Cluster policies are present in practically all countries and regions in the European Union, initiated by local, national or European governments (Borras and Tsagdis, 2008). In local clusters, firms specialized in certain products and operating on the same market are located in proximity to each other. Local clusters are thought to enhance growth and innovation potential by local linkages and embedding – self-augmenting processes of network- and firm-related development. These local specialized centres of specialization and excellence are perceived to compete with many similarly specialized clusters elsewhere. Cities and regions compare themselves among each other in rankings on competitiveness (see Chapter 3). In this chapter we analyse to what extent this multi-regional competition actually is the case in specific clusters. We illustrate in which regions in Europe firms succeed in gathering a substantial share of the European market in certain products or sectors. As we do not look at productivity of firms but at their trade networks overlapping with that of competitors, we talk about revealed competition. By investigating market overlap, we obtain insight into the markets being most important for the firms and the regions from which they obtain strongest competition. We thus do not look at individual firms, but at economic sectors, and investigate to what extent a sector in a region obtains competition from the same sector in other regions. Throughout the text, we talk about competition between regions; this, in fact, is a short way of saying that firms within a region compete with firms located in another region.

In this book we focus on the international competitiveness of regions. We therefore analyse the international competitors only. The methodology can, however, be easily extended to cover all domestic and international competitors. That is left for future research. In the benchmark figures below, only the top eight most important regional indicators on the typical market for this region–sector combination are given. There are eight more indicators which are considered not important and therefore not presented in the figure. Thus the first regional characteristic is the most important characteristic on the market for this sector–region combination. Please note that the order of importance of the regional characteristics may change in the figures because every region–sector combination has its own market. The length of the bars in the benchmark figures gives the score for every indicator relative to the weighted average score of the competitors. This weight is determined by the degree of competition of a sector–region combination which was determined in the previous chapter. The weighted average of the competitors is set to an index of 100 and is presented by the dotted line in the benchmark figure. A long bar signals that the region outperforms its competitors, while a short bar tells us that the region underperforms when compared to its competitors.

7.3.1 The Regional Economy

We discuss the total regional economy for the large agglomerations of Milan, Barcelona and Paris, and the peripheral and emerging economies of Warsaw, Dresden and Thessaloniki. Large agglomerations have by definition a diverse economy, and a specific sector focus seems therefore less appropriate for these regions. Nevertheless, we will also discuss separate sectors for these regions in some of the following subsections.

In Figures 7.1 and 7.2 we present the benchmark of locational characteristics for the total production in the regions of Milan, Barcelona, Paris, Warsaw, Dresden and Thessaloniki, respectively. The three large metropolitan areas of Western Europe presented in Figure 7.1 have knowledge and size as the most important regional characteristics. In other words, the most important competitors are large and dense agglomerations. The innovation indicators are important for most regions because the large, dominant regions in Europe such as Paris, Milan and London – who compete with most other regions – have many patents and large R&D expenditures. The size of a region may be an indication of strong agglomeration economies, although it may also be the result of the success of a region. Successful regions will attract economic activity and become large. The connectivity via road and air are the next important characteristics for Milan and Barcelona, while the competitors of Paris are more oriented towards attracting foreign capital and are strong in the number of foreign-owned companies. A strong concentration of financial and business services is important for all three large agglomerations. This strong financial and business services sector is needed for other activities and facilitates the presence of large foreign-owned companies.

The performances of these three large agglomerations are different from each other. This represents the strengths and weaknesses of these regions. The agglomeration around Paris is for most characteristics stronger than its competitors except for the amount of private knowledge being generated and the relative amount of foreign companies it attracts. Only the private knowledge performance may be worrying, but all other regional characteristics are better than the competitors and partly explain the strong economic position of the Paris agglomeration. The Barcelona region is

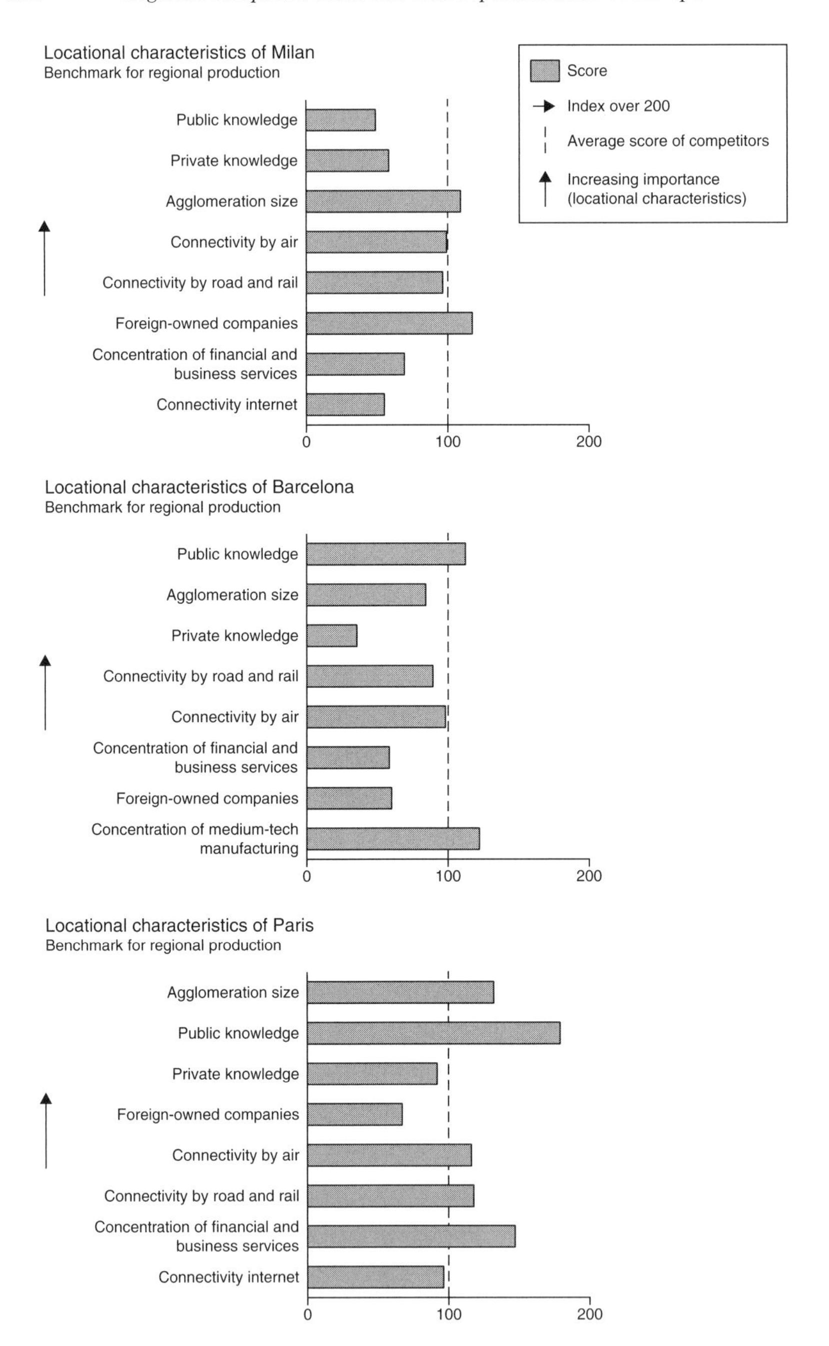

Figure 7.1 A benchmark for the regions of Milan, Barcelona and Paris

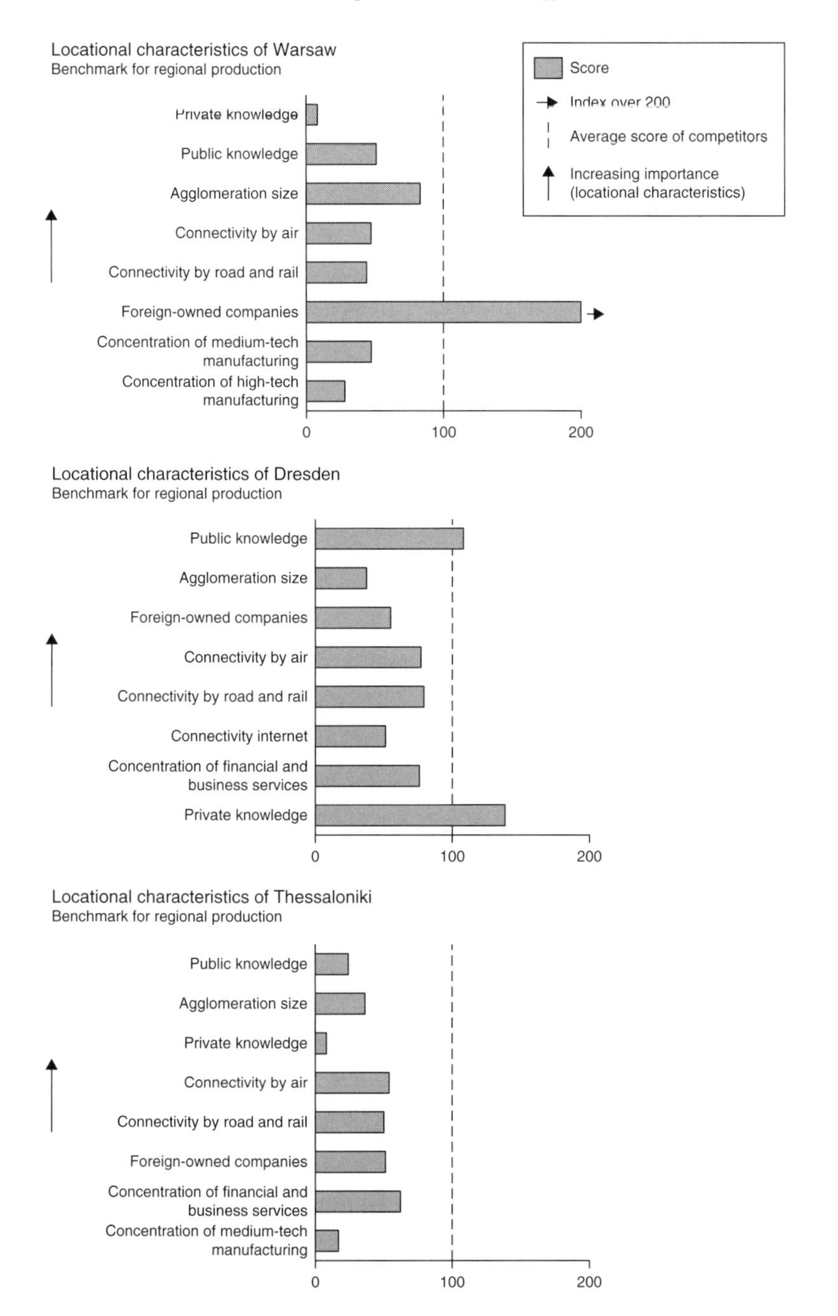

Figure 7.2 A benchmark for the regions of Warsaw, Dresden and Thessaloniki

strong in public knowledge and has a strong concentration of medium-tech manufacturing, but is underperforming on all other indicators when compared to its competitors. The region of Milan can be described as a large and dense region with many foreign-owned companies and a good connectivity. In comparison to its competitors it severely underperforms, however, in the generation of important public and private knowledge and the concentration of financial and business services.

The benchmark for the peripheral region of Thessaloniki and the emerging markets of Warsaw and Dresden presented in Figure 7.2 sketches a more problematic picture. Warsaw is mainly strong in attracting foreign-owned companies, but it lacks strong knowledge creation if compared to its competitors. The other locational characteristics also underperform if compared to its competitors, and the success of the region may be only due to its large market in a more peripheral part of Europe, not very close to Europe's economic axis which goes from London to the Ruhr area, Paris, Milan and Barcelona.

The region of Dresden, on the other hand, outperforms its competitors with strong public and private knowledge although it underperforms on all other important locational factors. It is striking that private knowledge only ranks as the eighth important locational factor. This implies that its competitors are not very strong in private knowledge generation. Clearly, Dresden has chosen knowledge creation as its main asset with which to develop its region. The region of Thessaloniki scores worse than its competitors on all possible locational factors. This region therefore seems extremely problematic from a regional economic perspective.

7.3.2 The Agricultural Sector in European Regions

A large amount of European subsidies are related to the agricultural sector. We therefore specifically focus on three regions with a strong agricultural sector. These regions are Andalucía, Rotterdam–The Hague and Pécs. As we will see in the next chapter, the European agricultural market is dominated by the two regions of Andalucía and Rotterdam–The Hague. We have also seen in the previous chapter that these two regions can be considered strong competitors, although they have different types of agriculture. The Rotterdam–The Hague region has a strong horticulture and land-intensive agricultural sector. Agriculture in Andalucía is more land-extensive. Next to these two regions we also focus on Pécs, a typical agricultural region in one of the emerging economies.

The benchmark of the agricultural sector in these three regions is presented in Figure 7.3. We see in many benchmarks (not shown) that the medium-tech manufacturing sector is located in regions with a strong

Locational characteristics of Rotterdam–The Hague
Benchmark for agriculture

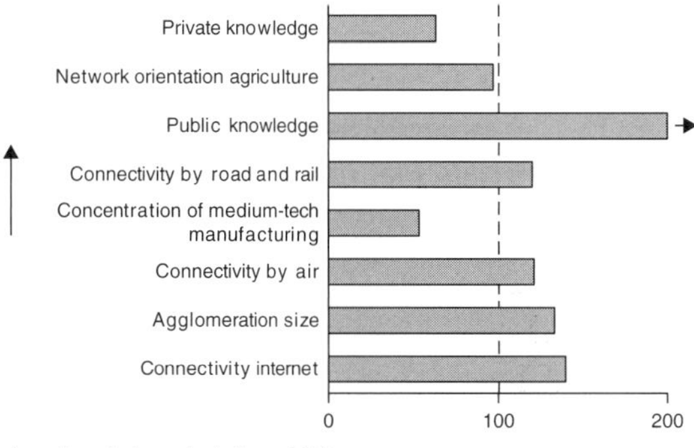

Locational characteristics of Pécs
Benchmark for agriculture

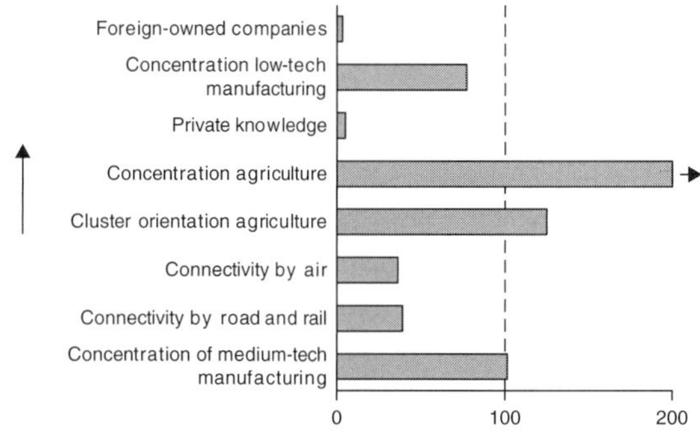

Locational characteristics of Andalucía
Benchmark for agriculture

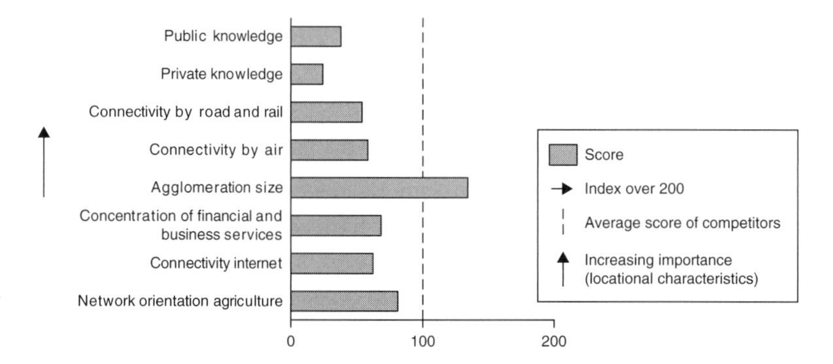

Figure 7.3 A benchmark for the agricultural sector in the regions of Rotterdam–The Hague, Pécs and Andalucía

agricultural sector. We therefore see the concentration of medium-tech manufacturing as an important regional characteristic in both the regions of Rotterdam–The Hague and Pécs. In Pécs we also see a large concentration of low-tech manufacturing. We do not think that there are important relations between these two sectors, but that co-location occurs because both regions are attracted by the same location characteristics. This complicates the analysis because factors that are supposed to be important for the agricultural sector may be important for the medium-tech manufacturing sector. The only reason that they show in the benchmark is because both sectors co-locate in certain areas and have comparable trade patterns.

When we focus on the sector characteristics we see the difference in the agricultural sector in the three regions. Network orientation is especially important for the agricultural sector in Rotterdam–The Hague and to a lesser extent in Andalucía. However, both regions perform worse than their competitors on this sector-specific locational characteristic. This may be due to the fact that both regions can be considered 'the top' competitors in agriculture, reducing the need for obtaining inputs from other regions. The region of Pécs, however, has a very different (smaller scale) agricultural sector where trade is more locally oriented and with more local competitors. As a consequence the concentration and clustering of the sector is more important, and Pécs performs very well on these indicators. With respect to the non-sector-specific locational characteristics, the Rotterdam–The Hague region generally outperforms its competitors while the region of Andalucía underperforms. This is in line with the declining importance of the agricultural sector in Andalucía if compared to the Rotterdam–The Hague region (see next chapter).

7.3.3 The Financial and Business Services Sector in European Regions

The financial and business services sector in Europe is concentrated in the larger agglomerations. We discuss the performance of this sector from the perspective of the large agglomerations of inner London and Paris, the strong medium-sized region of Brussels and the emerging market in Warsaw. The benchmark results of the financial and business services for these regions are presented in Figure 7.4.

Regarding this sector, agglomeration size, foreign-owned companies and public knowledge are always in the top three of the most important locational characteristics. This represents the concentration of this sector in large and dense agglomerations. It also illustrates the importance of a high demand for financial and business services in the presence of foreign companies and in these large and dense agglomerations. The importance of public knowledge in the region is caused by a need for highly educated personnel.

It is important for the financial and business services to be concentrated in one region. Apparently there are strong spillovers within the sector. A probable cause for these spillovers may be labour pooling, but other (knowledge) spillovers discussed in Chapter 3 may also play an important role. At the same time the sector performs well with a good network of relations with suppliers from different regions. Thus concentration alone is not enough. In this respect it is important to notice that for this sector the connectivity by air is more important than the connectivity by road and rail. This is different from most other sectors and is related to the importance of a good international network.

When we look at the performance we see that the three regions of inner London, Paris and Brussels all perform well if compared to their competitors. Inner London underperforms, however, in private knowledge. The reason is that firms generating private knowledge are typically not located in the City, but in outer London. Both regions of Brussels and Paris underperform in their share of foreign-owned companies. This may be due to the very large government sectors in both regions. The region of Warsaw mainly outperforms its competitors by the presence of a large number of foreign-owned companies. The strength of the financial and business services in this region seems therefore mainly driven by the local demand for these services.

7.3.4 The Manufacturing Sector in European Regions

We have seen in Chapter 2 that a smart specialization strategy for regional economic development should take the regional characteristics and network relations into account. It should be a 'smart' strategy for every region based on the specific regional circumstances and *not* a copy of a successful strategy in a completely different region. In Chapter 4 we have seen that many regions have a different economic profile and they are specialized and relatively 'good' in the production of different goods. Regional development strategies based on simply copying a 'new' Silicon Valley will therefore be mostly rejected within the context of a smart specialization strategy. Moreover, a focus on a low-tech or a medium-tech sector may be more appropriate for certain regions giving their specific locational and network characteristics. In this section we therefore discuss three types of manufacturing sectors separately. These sectors are based on a classification of industries by Eurostat in low-tech, medium-tech and high-tech manufacturing.[1]

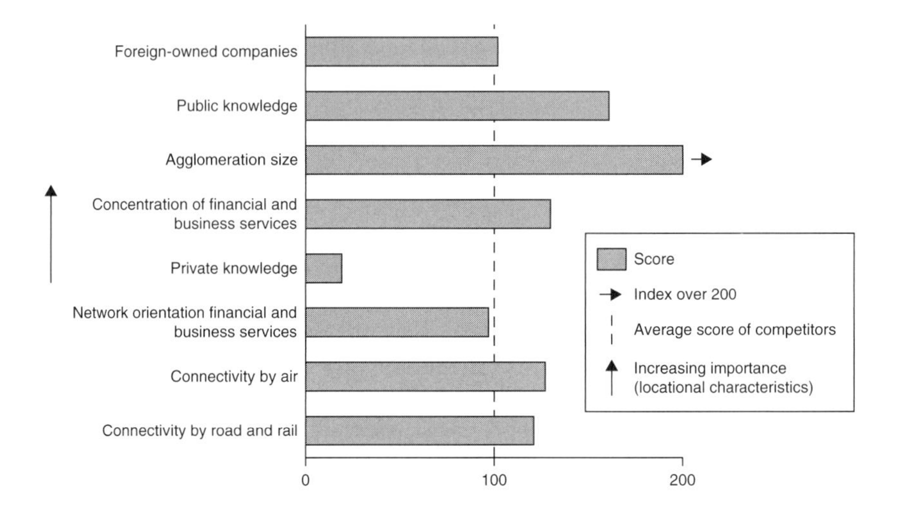

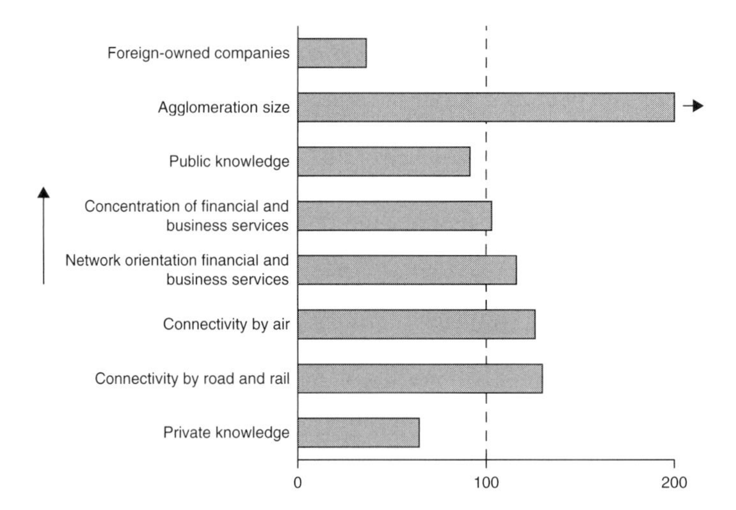

Figure 7.4 A benchmark for the financial and business services sector in the regions of inner London, Paris, Brussels and Warsaw

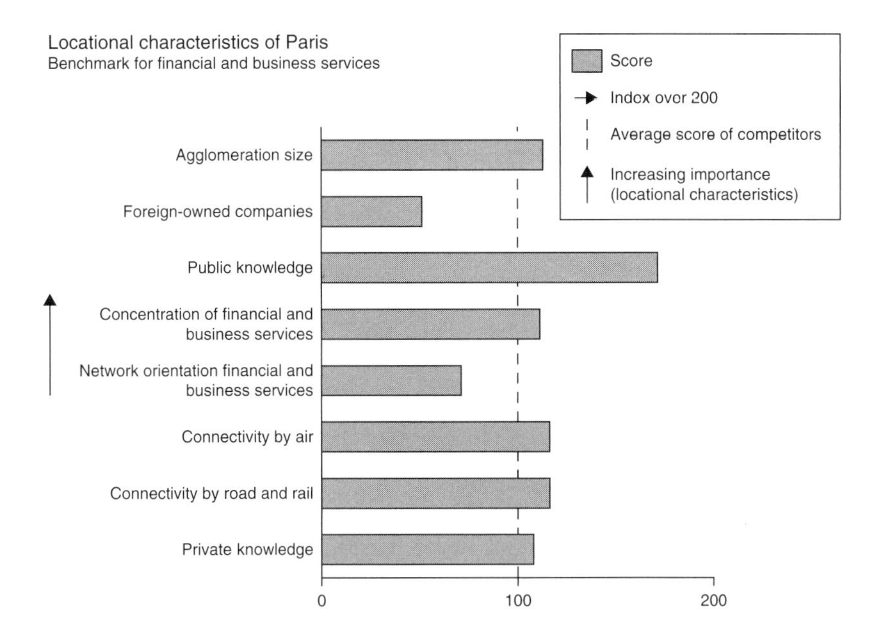

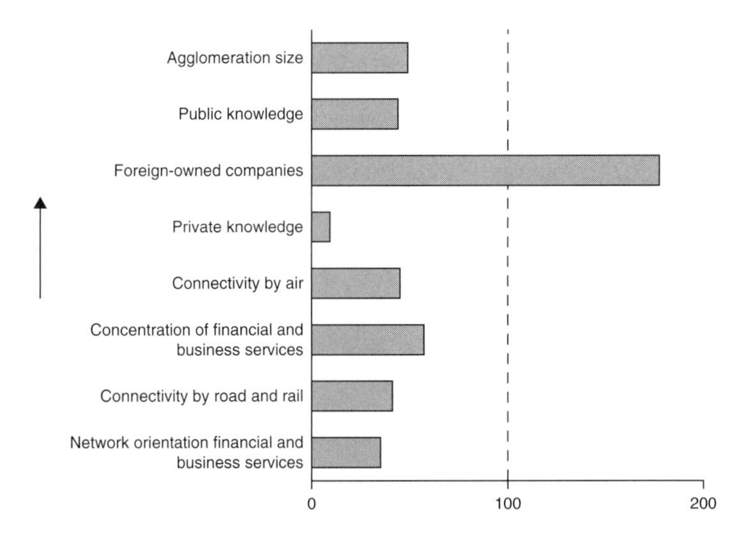

Figure 7.4 (continued)

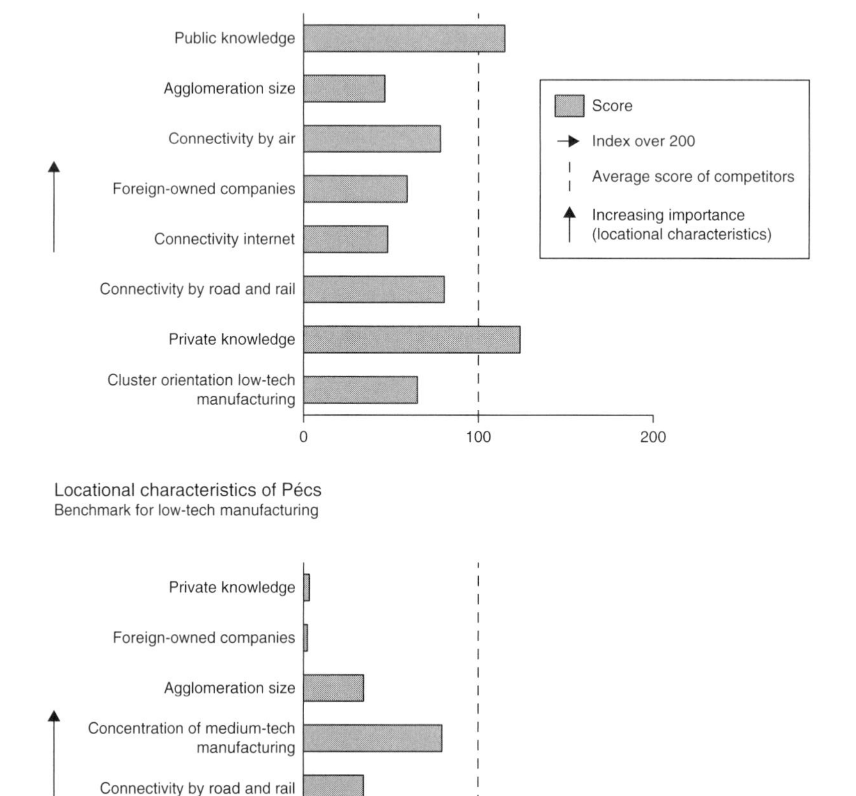

Figure 7.5 A benchmark for the low-tech manufacturing sector in the regions of Dresden and Pécs

Low-tech manufacturing sector

In Figure 7.5 we present a benchmark of the low-tech manufacturing sector in the regions of Dresden and Pécs. We observe in particular that the locational characteristics of Pécs underperform if compared to their competitors. In comparison to the agricultural benchmark in Figure 7.3 we may conclude that this region is stronger as an agricultural region than as a low-tech manufacturing region. Also both the sector concentration and clustering indicators are lower than in the competing regions, emphasizing the region's weakness with respect to this sector. The region of Dresden is different because it outperforms its competitors with respect to public and private knowledge creation. Although this may be a promising sign for this sector, it seems that these characteristics may be better for sectors where private knowledge is more important.

Medium-tech manufacturing sector

The medium-tech manufacturing sector is a typical sector where private knowledge is the most important locational characteristic. We can see this in the benchmark of this sector for the regions of Milan, Eindhoven and Budapest presented in Figure 7.6. Two of the top producing regions in medium-tech manufacturing are Milan and Eindhoven. It is remarkable that both regions have a different profile of underlying important locational characteristics. The region of Eindhoven is very strong in the most important locational private and public knowledge factors, while being slightly worse than their competitors on other factors. The region of Milan, on the other hand, is strong in the sector-specific cluster orientation and almost on a par with its competitors with respect to the concentration of the sector. Connectivity is also important for this sector where both Milan and Eindhoven perform slightly worse than their main competitors.

The large emerging economy of Budapest shows a comparable ranking of important locational characteristics than the other regions for this sector. Only the sector-specific concentration in the region is more important than for the other two regions. We see that the region underperforms on the top four most important locational factors. The regions of Milan and Eindhoven show that this sector can thrive with either a strong cluster or a strong knowledge base, but the lack of both locational characteristics in Budapest may be considered problematic for this industry.

High-tech manufacturing sector

Public knowledge is more important than private knowledge for the high-tech manufacturing sector. We observe this in the benchmark of three generally considered successful high-tech regions in the benchmarks in Figure 7.7. All three regions, Munich, Lyon and Helsinki, are stronger than their competitors in the most important locational public knowledge characteristic. Public knowledge seems to be very important for this sector

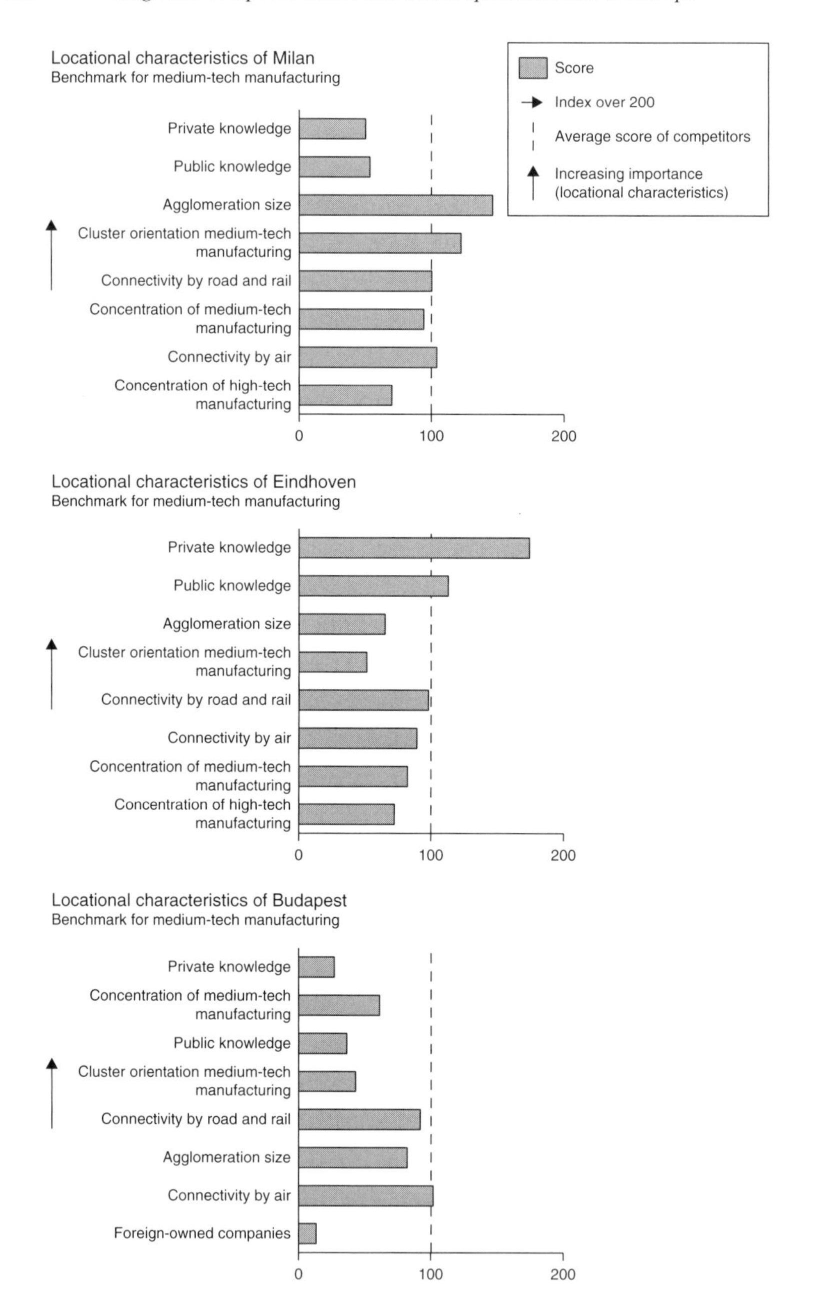

Figure 7.6 A benchmark for the medium-tech manufacturing sector in the regions of Milan, Eindhoven and Budapest

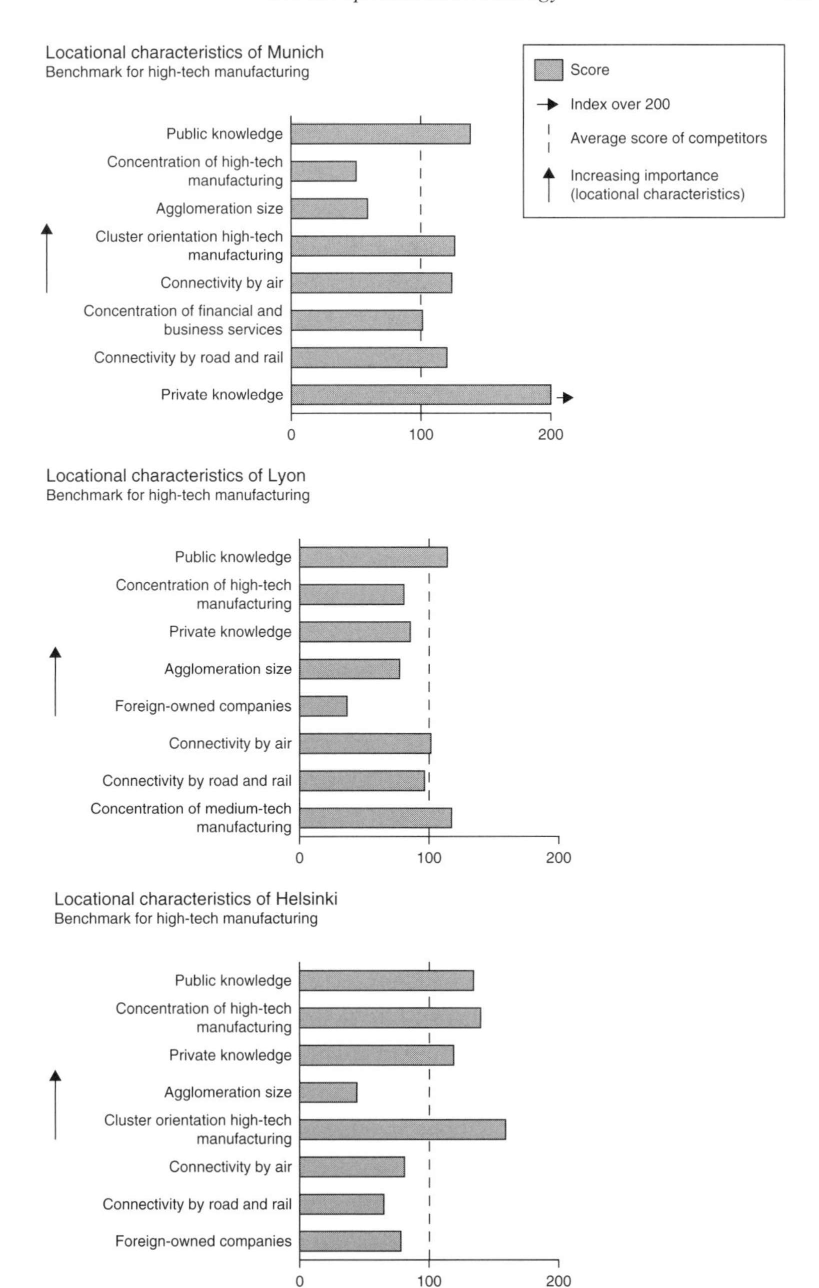

Figure 7.7 A benchmark for the high-tech manufacturing sector in the regions of Munich, Lyon and Helsinki

and more important than private knowledge. The connectivity by air is more important than the connectivity by road. This was also the case for the financial and business services, but not for other services. This suggests that there are not only local spillovers but also long-distance (knowledge) spillovers in this sector.

The second most important regional characteristic is the concentration of the high-tech manufacturing sector in the region. This indicates strong spillovers where firms profit from other firms in the neighbourhood and within the same sector. Among these three regions only Helsinki is stronger than its competitors in the concentration of high-tech manufacturing. Private knowledge is important on the markets where Lyon and Helsinki are active, but is only ranked in eighth place for the region of Munich. This may represent the weakness of the competitors of Munich who perform much worse on this indicator. Cluster orientation, on the other hand, is only of importance for Munich and Helsinki. Both regions perform relatively strongly with respect to this indicator.

7.3.5 A More Detailed Benchmark

In the benchmark analysis presented we have made use of several composite indicators as shown in Table 7.2. The reason for working with composite indicators is mainly to keep the analysis lucid and to group thematic information. The construction of the composite indicators may, however, affect the results of the benchmark analysis. The effect of the use of composite indicators is illustrated by an example of a more detailed benchmark in Figure 7.8. In these detailed benchmarks we present ten important characteristics instead of the eight characteristics used in the earlier benchmarks because the overall number of indicators has increased. We have chosen the benchmark of total regional production in Paris and the benchmark of medium-tech manufacturing in Milan as examples. These benchmarks were already presented with composite indicators in Figures 7.1 and 7.6.

The more detailed analysis gives additional insight into the underlying factors that may be influenced by policy-makers and that are driving factors in the earlier presented results. We see, for example, that the importance of the agglomeration size is mainly driven by density and to a lesser extent by population size. Moreover, while we earlier concluded that the Paris region is performing better than its competitors on agglomeration size (it is a bigger agglomeration), we now have to conclude that Paris is underperforming with respect to the density of the agglomeration if compared to its competitors. With respect to public R&D it seems to

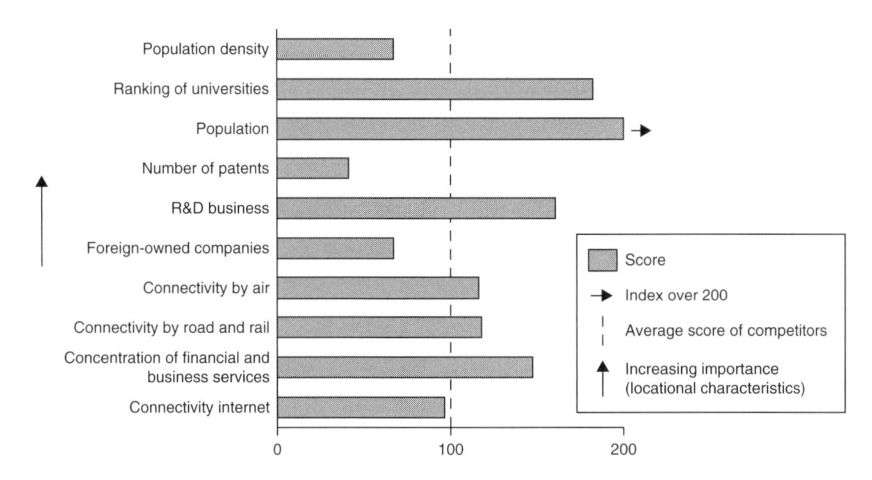

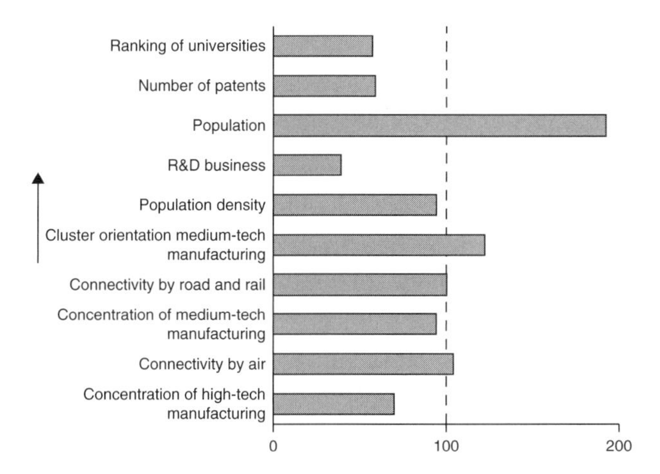

Figure 7.8 A detailed benchmark for regional production in Paris and medium-tech manufacturing in Milan

be that the quality of the university is the driving factor that determines the importance of this factor, and Paris still outperforms its competitors. With respect to private R&D we can again make an important split in the composite indicator. The Paris region performs well with respect to business R&D but underperforms with respect to the number of patents that are produced in the region. The main problem seems therefore to be the validation of research into patents.

The example of the benchmark for the medium-tech manufacturing sector in Milan shows that, in contrast to the benchmark of Paris, population size is more important than density. The ranking of the university is, just as in the case of Paris, the top indicator that determines the importance of public knowledge. The policy conclusions for Milan, however, are not affected: private and public knowledge are the main locational characteristics on which the Milan region underperforms if compared to its competitors in medium-tech manufacturing.

7.4 MAKING CHOICES: A SMART SPECIALIZATION SECTOR OR REGION STRATEGY

It is not always the case that a smart specialization sector strategy would coincide with a smart specialization region strategy. The reason is the importance of sector-specific locational characteristics that are not important across sectors, and the difference in importance of regional characteristics for different industries. For example, the importance of locational characteristics is more or less the same for the low-tech manufacturing sector and the total production in Dresden. The sector-specific cluster orientation is only ranked eighth in order of importance for the low-tech manufacturing industry. Also in the case of Milan one could argue that a focus on public and private knowledge creation is a wise strategy for both the medium-tech manufacturing sector and the region as a whole. However, according to the benchmark for the total production in the region there would be a higher preference for investment in public knowledge and less in private knowledge. Moreover, the sector-specific cluster orientation is especially important for medium-tech manufacturing in Milan.

The differences in strategies are greater with respect to the financial and business services sector in Paris and Warsaw if compared to the total regional economy in these regions. Foreign-owned companies are more important for the financial and business services sector in these regions while private knowledge is more important for the total production in the region. Moreover, sector-specific concentration and network orientation are generally found to be important for the financial and business services sector. Overall we conclude that there is no 'wonder cure' for regions, and a smart specialization strategy generally benefits some part of the economy but not necessarily the whole economy. Any smart specialization strategy therefore also involves making policy choices on the importance of sectors within the regional economy.

NOTE

1. See the Appendix for the industries that are classified as high, medium or low-tech.

8. Conclusion: one size fits only one in place-based regional policy

Important and large regions are increasingly considered to be one of the main contributors to the economic growth of nations (World Bank, 2009). This 'triumph of the city' (Glaeser, 2011) induces a discussion on regional economic development strategies in an attempt to create strong regions and stimulate development in lagging regions. The resulting place-based policies (Barca, 2009) evolved in the European context directly from the Lisbon Agenda in 2000, and accumulated into the current (smart, sustainable and inclusive) growth objectives of the Europe 2020 policy programme that are central in the envisioned cohesion policy reform after 2013. The policies take the form of a smart specialization development perspective based on a systems way of thinking about innovation and growth given the region's place in a complex regional system and local institutions (McCann and Ortega-Argilés, 2011).

Regional economic development policy is not helped by a 'one-size-fits-all' strategy but should be based on a 'one-size-fits-one' approach. Regional economic development is heavily dependent on place-based economic structures in a network of interregional relations. This important (but often rather neglected) importance of economic networks in a complex economic society suggests that custom-made regional policies are complex. The regional policies that set the conditions under which firms prosper should be custom-made with respect to region- and sector-specific networks describing the markets in which these firms actually operate. These place-based policies should specifically not be targeted at places per se, but at the specific regional needs for firms and people to accomplish economic growth and a higher welfare. This book confirms that the often presumed contradiction of place-based and place-neutral development strategies should be nuanced in a European context: place-based smart specialization and regional development can reinforce both place-neutral as well as place-specific economic processes. The simultaneous importance of location and network relations in regional economic development is emphasized by the wealth of heterogeneity in the specific trade relations of every region, the resulting region-specific geographical markets on which firms from different regions compete, and the various dynamic competitive relations that are analysed.

The optimal regional conditions for place-based development depend on the economic sector, the location and the position in the network. Place-based policies are therefore also 'place-neutral' in the definition of Glaeser (2011) since they are not attached to a specific place but targeted at the improvement of conditions such as regional education levels and accessibility to improve the needs of firms and people to enhance welfare and stimulate growth given the specific regional context. The crucial element in place-based regional policies is their foundation in the specific needs of people and firms, embedded in local circumstances of institutions, entrepreneurship and innovation capabilities, and not the general policies that often do not apply to specific cases ('a people and firm based policy in places').

In this book we have shown that different sectors in different regions are differently related to each other in dynamic competitive relations, which results in region-specific geographical markets. This finding stresses the importance of a place-based smart specialization approach to regional competitiveness where location and networks play an important role. European regional (cohesion) policy, which consumes a third of the EU budget, is aimed at improving the economic well-being of regions in the EU while avoiding regional disparities at the same time. The recent redirections of these policies towards place-based smart specialization policies is in line with this book to achieve the set targets and to make firms in regions more competitive and grow, thereby increasing European welfare.

In this book we provided an applied analytical framework to measure regional competition. The competitive position of regions could subsequently be identified by structural characteristics of cities and regions embedded in a theoretically informed analytical framework that uses actual networks of competing and economically valued relations between regions. This analytical framework allowed us to compare actual competitors and to take the specific characteristics of regional markets into account.

The theoretical framework based on network relations between regions trading in goods and services analysing actual revealed competition that was applied in this book is crucial to the understanding of the international competitiveness of European regions and is therefore essential for a smart specialization place-based development strategy. Competition is location-specific because it is determined by a network of regional trade-connections, and in order to improve the performance of firms these place-based conditions should be taken into account. Smart specialization policies should therefore be based on place-based circumstances embedded in interregional networks. The methodology proposed and illustrated in this book gives the economic rationale behind a smart specialization strategy which, as we have seen in Chapter 2, should be embedded in a governance structure with actor participation in the region itself.

The overlap in trade relations that defines the competition of firms from different regions gives information on what, and where, regions compete. The case studies based on the analyses of the actual European regional trade network showed a wealth of heterogeneity present in the relative competitiveness and showed the importance of a careful evaluation of regional place-based policies of regional, national and European governments in a smart specialization type of framework. There are many differences regarding with whom, where and on what firms from different regions compete. Regions with strong medium and high-tech production sectors do not have the same competitors and do not face mutual competition in the same degrees. This illustrates that these technological firms clearly operate in different geographical markets. We presented varying results for other sectors in our case studies. Geographical proximity for manufacturing goods and hierarchical functional proximities for (high-end) services coincide in practically all regional trade patterns analysed.

The need for custom-made regional place-based policies was also shown in Chapter 7 where we analysed important factors for different regions from different sector perspectives. The analyses clearly showed that a smart specialization strategy should be sector-specific where the policy-maker should make choices since different sectors need different optimal regional conditions to strengthen their competitive position. In other words, the same locational characteristics are not important across all sectors. These differences in place-based smart specialization strategies are, for instance, great with respect to the financial and business services sector in Paris and Warsaw when compared to the total regional economy in these regions. Foreign-owned companies are more important for the financial and business services sector in these regions while private knowledge is more important for the total production in the region. Moreover, sector-specific concentration and network orientation are generally found to be important for the financial and business services sector. The place-based benchmarking showed, however, that there is no 'wonder cure' for regions, and a smart specialization strategy may benefit parts of the economy, but in general not the whole economy. Any smart specialization strategy therefore involves policy choices on the importance of sectors within the regional economy.

We also argued in Chapter 4 that small regions are not sentenced to decline. Small regions may specialize and use sector-specific agglomeration economies while they 'borrow size' from other agglomerations via strong network relations. It may also prove to be profitable for small regions to specialize in a complete supply chain and to set up an industrial cluster. We showed that not all sectors and all regions should follow the same strategies and again we concluded that custom-made regional policies were required. The large regions in the core of Europe are often diversified and open. Their location in the centre of Europe provides them with ample supply of inputs from neighbouring regions while their size allows them to engage in a large range of activities. The small regions in the core are slightly more specialized but seem to follow a comparable strategy compensating their limited size by 'borrowing size' from large agglomerations in their vicinity.

Large peripheral regions showed fair diversification and clustering based on their internal mass. The location outside the core seems to be a crucial determinant of the clustered structure of production. Small, peripheral regions are specialized and clustered. In order to generate enough 'agglomeration economies' they cannot rely on their own or a neighbour's size but make use of the full extent of localization economies related to specialization in a cluster of a limited range of products. They focus on the trade of this final product and specialize in the complete supply chain including local suppliers on intermediate products.

During the first decade of the twenty-first century we observed that the large European agglomerations such as Madrid, Dublin, Paris, Barcelona and London have strengthened their international trade network position, possibly due to agglomeration economies, and dominate the market. However, we also observed a strong catching-up process of peripheral regions and emerging economies. This catch-up occurred for the large and small peripheral regions, emphasizing our case that small peripheral regions are not sentenced to future demise.

The analyses presented in this book form a building block in the emerging and burgeoning literature on smart specialization and place-based development ('a people and firm based policy in places' as we labelled it) in Europe. There obviously is a great need for the information and results presented, as each European region has to develop its smart specialization strategy. Analysis and conceptualizing do not stop with the network and competition analyses presented. Implications of the relations found to degrees of entrepreneurship, relatedness and related variety within the local economy, connectedness in other ways than trade (such as foreign direct investments, knowledge cooperation and knowledge workers' networks), and the differentiated knowledge bases and institutional embedding in various European regions (especially differing over West and Eastern European regions) are important to research in more detail the process of the long-lasting scale and network effects of regional economic development in Europe. Also the governance consequences of suggested policies in terms of appropriateness, bottlenecks, missing links, opportunism and accountability (as suggested in Chapter 2) need further elaboration, and insight can be gained from best policy practices. This book shows, however, that smart specialization strategies in European regions cannot be formulated without proper analysis and reference to international network positions.

Appendix: European regional trade flows

In this Appendix we introduce a unique dataset on bilateral trade between 256 European NUTS-2 regions for the year 2000 and an update of this dataset for the period 2000–10. Trade is divided into 59 product categories which cover both goods and services following the European Classification of Products by Activity (NACE 1.1 – CPA 2002). Regional import and export flows are constructed by bringing several sources together since there are no complete trade surveys at this detailed geographical level. The main sources used are: (1) the national accounts of the 25 selected countries in a supply and use format; (2) international trade data on goods from Feenstra et al. (2005) and on services from Eurostat (2009a); (3) regional information on production, investment and consumption made available in Cambridge Econometrics (2008); (4) information on freight transport among European regions from the Ministry of Infrastructure and the Environment (2007); and (5) first and business class airline ticket information from MIDT (2010). The 2000 trade matrix describes the most likely trade flows between European regions given all available information, and is consistent with the national accounts. Additional regional and national information is gathered from Eurostat to update this data for the period 2000–10. The final bi-regional panel trade dataset describes the most likely trade flows between European regions given all available information, and is consistent with the national accounts over the period 2000–10.

A.1 INTRODUCTION

We have seen in Chapters 2 and 3 that regional competitiveness is central in cohesion policy and the current smart specialization strategies of European regions. Place-based development policies (Barca, 2009) embedded in interregional networks are at the heart of these policies of innovation and growth. A smart specialization strategy uses the position of a region in its specific regional economic and institutional network to benefit optimally from its potential to address the challenges it faces. More traditional economic geography also puts the emphasis on a detailed geographical network approach towards regional development (see Porter, 1990; Saxenian, 1994; Florida, 2002). This tendency towards a rigorous regional network analysis strengthened after the seminal paper by Krugman (1991) which culminated in the new economic geography (NEG) literature.

The result of these recent developments is a growing demand for data at a more detailed geographical level in combination with network data on regional economic interactions. Although Eurostat publishes key regional statistics for the European Union (EU) and other important non-EU countries, crucial economic data on bilateral trade between regions are notably missing from European regional databases. There exists no dataset that describes complete interregional trade flows at a lower level of product detail. Some regional trade flows such as those for agriculture may be available for a specific region but there exists no comprehensive matrix of all trade between European regions.

The trade data presented here gives the possibility to develop a place-based smart specialization strategy underpinned by a regional trade network between European regions. We showed in different chapters how the data can be used to develop a strategy to strengthen a region's competitive position and how this position may develop over time. This trade dataset gives the most likely trade flows between European NUTS-2 regions inferred from all available information. The final result of our efforts is a trade matrix of bilateral flows for 59 product categories including services (European classification CPA 2002), between 256 NUTS-2 regions, belonging to 25 European countries, for the year 2000.

Our dataset is constructed to fit to the information available, but no structure has been imposed on the data. In other words, we did not use any specific model to estimate trade patterns. We have chosen a different approach because such an estimated dataset is of no further use in empirical research. For instance, research on the validity of the gravity model based on data generated by the gravity model will by definition result in the confirmation of the validity of the model. The dataset we document here is constructed following four main steps:

First, we build a consistent international trade matrix of flows in goods and services between all distinguished countries and with the rest of the world divided into several blocks. International trade in goods is based on the data collected by Feenstra et al. (2005). Services are based on Eurostat trade statistics taken from the balance of payments (Eurostat, 2009a). These two sources are the best available for international trade. However, they are not always consistent with the national accounts or the national use and supply tables, which give information on total imports and total exports by product. Since there are reasons to believe that national accounts are more accurate, our trade flows are constrained to the national accounts totals. The final country–country bilateral trade flows are obtained by determining the trade matrix, which stays the closest to Feenstra et al. (2005) and Eurostat (2009a), but are within the boundaries set by the national accounts. In this first step, corrections were applied for cost, insurance and freight (c.i.f.)/free-on-board (f.o.b.) inconsistencies, direct purchases abroad and re-exports.

In the second step the supply and use tables are regionalized for all 256 distinguished NUTS-2 regions. The disaggregation of the national accounts was carried out using non-survey techniques and data from Cambridge Econometrics (2008) on regional production, investment and consumption. Particular attention has been paid to solving the problem of cross-hauling, the simultaneous export and import of the same type of goods. The outcome of the regionalization is regional figures on imports and exports by product. These figures add up to the national accounts figures on exports and imports.

Third, approximations of regional trade flows have been determined using freight transport data from the Dutch Ministry of Infrastructure and the Environment (2007) and business flight ticket information from MIDT (2010). The former is used to estimate trade of goods, while the latter is used to estimate the trade in services. The existence of hubs or logistic centres in transport data is identified and explicitly accounted for. We obtained in this way two estimates for each of the 59 CPA goods and services. The first estimate was obtained by distributing regional export figures according to the outward transport pattern while the second estimate was obtained with the inverse procedure determining the origins of regional imports.

Fourth, in the final step, all the information available is combined to arrive at a final estimation of trade flows between 256 European NUTS-2 regions and the rest of the world for the 59 product and services aggregation level. The information gathered in the previous steps is present in two different estimates of the bilateral trade flows between European regions; we have regional total exports and total imports (by CPA), which are consistent with the national accounts (1); we have international trade flows, also consistent with the national accounts (2). The final trade matrix we document here is the one that, given the international trade flows – and constrained to regional total imports and exports – minimizes the distance between these two estimates made in the third step.

The update of the data from 2000 to 2010 is based on the extrapolation of the dataset for 2000. We used constrained non-linear optimization to update the trade matrix for 2000. The objective function in the non-linear optimization minimizes the quadratic distance between the coefficients of the new matrix in relation to the coefficients of the matrix of the previous year. These coefficients are defined as the element of the matrix divided by the respective row or column total. The quadratic distance between predicted and new national trade data, final demand, investment demand and supply and use tables are additional elements that are minimized in the objective function. The optimization is constrained by the regional accounts on gross value-added such that total national value-added is in line with the regional and national accounts. The resulting panel of trade data for the period 2000 to 2010 stays as close as possible to international trade statistics and the Eurostat supply and use tables and conforms with the national account statistics.

This Appendix is organized in three main sections. Section A.2 is dedicated to the description of the dataset with respect to the regional and product classification used. In Section A.3 we explain the construction of the trade dataset for the year 2000. In Section A.4 we present the extrapolation of the dataset to the years 2000–10.We conclude with a short discussion.

A.2 THE DATASET

The dataset documented here describes bilateral trade flows between 256 European regions. Export and import flows are measured in values (millions of euros) and they are divided into 59 product and service categories. These 256 regions are part of the EU25, with the exception of Cyprus and including Norway. This choice of regions has been determined by data availability. The regional classification follows the second level of Eurostat's Nomenclature of Statistical Territorial Units (NUTS-2), which in many cases in Europe is equivalent to a pre-existing countries' administrative division. In section A.2.1, we detail the regional units in which data are divided. We use the Classification of Products by Activity (NACE 1.1 – CPA 2002), the division that is also used by Eurostat for national accounts use and supply tables. Consistent with Eurostat's publications, we make use of the second level of this classification (2-digits), which distinguishes between 59 goods and services. This disaggregation of products is reported in section A.2.4 below.

It must be noted that the dataset not only gives information on international trade between regions, but also reports the trade between regions of the same country. Moreover, since for the whole research we put a great deal of emphasis on keeping all accounts consistent, the dataset also includes information on the regional production for their own use (the diagonal of the trade matrix).

Table A.1 The countries in the dataset

L1	Austria	L11	Hungary	L21	Portugal
L2	Belgium	L12	Ireland	L22	Sweden
L3	Czech Republic	L13	Italy	L23	Slovenia
L4	Germany	L14	Lithuania	L24	Slovakia
L5	Denmark	L15	Luxembourg	L25	United Kingdom
L6	Estonia	L16	Latvia		
L7	Spain	L17	Malta		
L8	Finland	L18	The Netherlands		
L9	France	L19	Norway		
L10	Greece	L20	Poland		

A.2.1 The European Regions

In the construction of the dataset, we included 256 NUTS-2 regions, which are part of 25 selected European countries. These are 24 EU countries, with the addition of Norway (see Table A.1).

The remainder of this section will be dedicated to a detailed list of all regions studied. For a more organic presentation of the information, regions will be grouped by country (see Figures A.1 to A.25). The first column refers to the code we used in the research presented in this book (from R1 to R256). The second column gives the corresponding NUTS-2 code, while the third and last column reports the name of the region.

A.2.2 Overview and the Rest of the World

The overview map in Figure A.26 shows that our data covers the trade flows in the largest part of Europe. The most prominent missing countries are Switzerland, Romania and Bulgaria. The reason for these missing regions is the lack of comparable data (supply and use tables) for Switzerland and the absence of any supply and use tables for Romania and Bulgaria at the start of the research presented in the book.

The dataset also covers the trade of the distinguished European regions with the rest of the world. The rest of the world has been split up into main economic countries and groups of less important countries. These extra-Europe trading partners are given in Table A.2.

A.2.3 The Regions Discussed in this Book

In this book we have focused on several representative regions and sectors in these regions. These region–sector combinations are presented

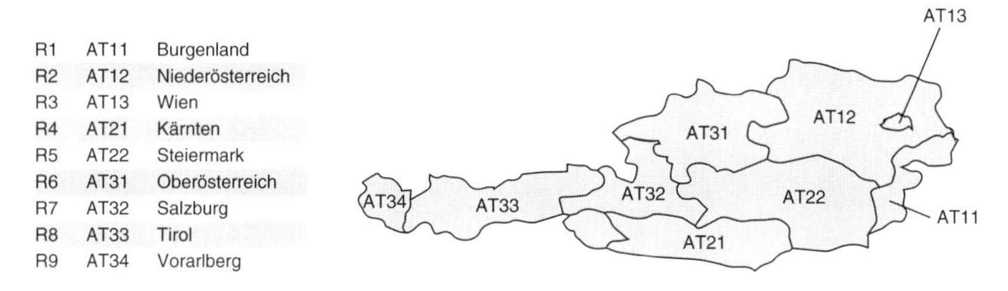

Figure A.1 *NUTS-2 regions in Austria (L1)*

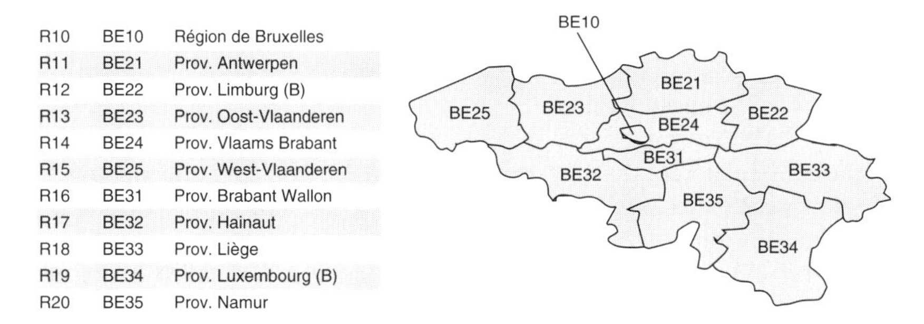

Figure A.2 *NUTS-2 regions in Belgium (L2)*

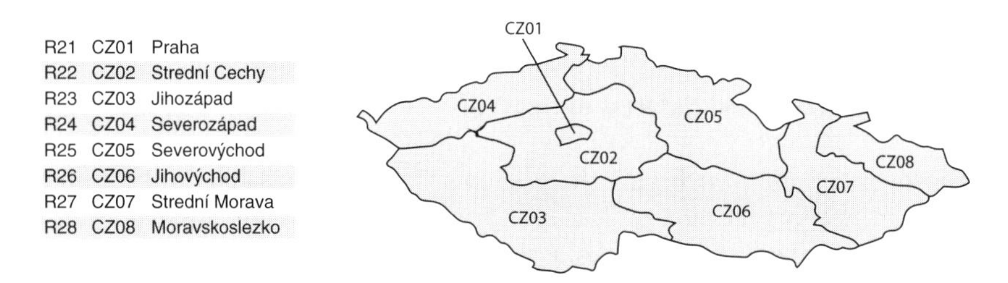

Figure A.3 *NUTS-2 regions in Czech Republic (L3)*

in Table A.3. We have chosen these regions according to their size, their sector orientation and their location in Europe. In this way we intend to cover the whole of Europe with respect to specific location and sector characteristics such that our book is representative for all types of regions in the European Union. In many cases we have chosen sectors in which a region is specialized. We describe the NUTS-2 regions using the name of the main city because the city names are better known than the regions' names. In Table A.3 we refer to both the city name and the Eurostat NUTS-2 code of the region to which the city belongs. We refer readers

R29	DE11	Stuttgart
R30	DE12	Karlsruhe
R31	DE13	Freiburg
R32	DE14	Tübingen
R33	DE21	Oberbayern
R34	DE22	Niederbayern
R35	DE23	Oberpfalz
R36	DE24	Oberfranken
R37	DE25	Mittelfranken
R38	DE26	Unterfranken
R39	DE27	Schwaben
R40	DE30	Berlin
R41	DE41	Brandenburg - NO
R42	DE42	Brandenburg - SW
R43	DE50	Bremen
R44	DE60	Hamburg
R45	DE71	Darmstadt
R46	DE72	Gießen
R47	DE73	Kassel
R48	DE80	Mecklen.-Vorpom.
R49	DE91	Braunschweig
R50	DE92	Hannover
R51	DE93	Lüneburg
R52	DE94	Weser-Ems
R53	DEA1	Düsseldorf
R54	DEA2	Köln
R55	DEA3	Münster
R56	DEA4	Detmold
R57	DEA5	Arnsberg
R58	DEB1	Koblenz
R59	DEB2	Trier
R60	DEB3	Rheinhessen-Pfalz
R61	DEC0	Saarland
R62	DED1	Chemnitz
R63	DED2	Dresden
R64	DED3	Leipzig
R65	DEE1	Dessau
R66	DEE2	Halle
R67	DEE3	Magdeburg
R68	DEF0	Schleswig-Holstein
R69	DEG0	Thüringen

Figure A.4 NUTS-2 regions in Germany (L4)

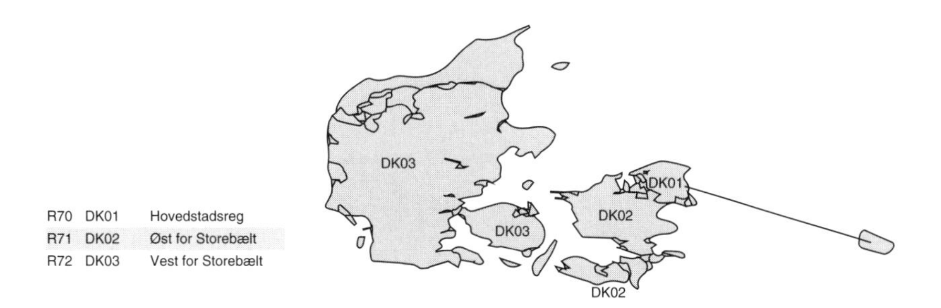

R70	DK01	Hovedstadsreg
R71	DK02	Øst for Storebælt
R72	DK03	Vest for Storebælt

Figure A.5 NUTS-2 regions in Denmark (L5)

to Chapter 4 for a more elaborate discussion on the specialization of European regions.

The first group of regions we distinguish are the large agglomerations of (inner-) London, Milan, Barcelona, Munich and Paris. These regions are

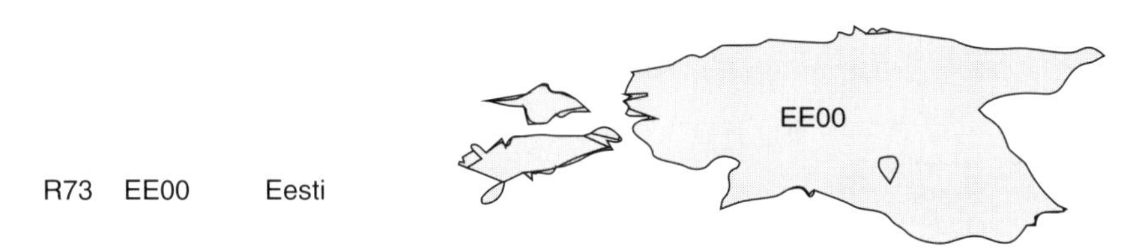

Figure A.6 NUTS-2 region in Estonia (L6)

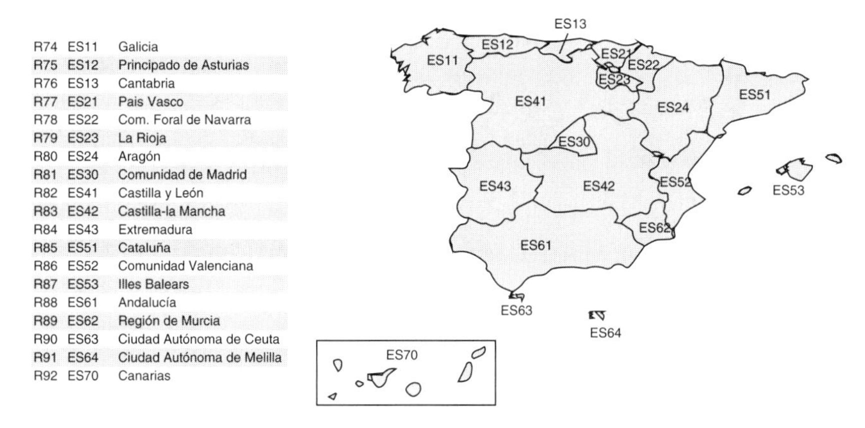

Figure A.7 NUTS-2 regions in Spain (L7)

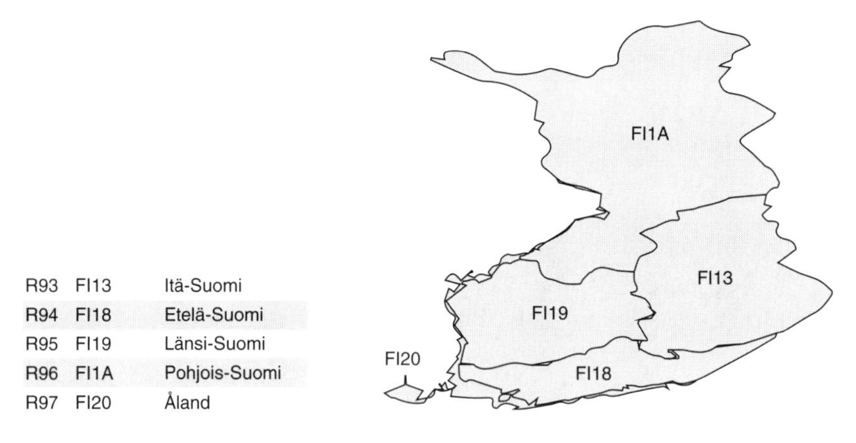

Figure A.8 NUTS-2 regions in Finland (L8)

large diverse economies. We therefore analyse the complex of all industries in Milan, Barcelona and Paris. London and Paris are both dominant players on the market for financial and business services and we therefore also focus on these sectors in these two regions. We discuss the medium-

R98	FR10	Île de France
R99	FR21	Champagne-Ardenne
R100	FR22	Picardie
R101	FR23	Haute-Normandie
R102	FR24	Centre
R103	FR25	Basse-Normandie
R104	FR26	Bourgogne
R105	FR30	Nord – Pas-de-Calais
R106	FR41	Lorraine
R107	FR42	Alsace
R108	FR43	Franche-Comté
R109	FR51	Pays de la Loire
R110	FR52	Bretagne
R111	FR53	Poitou-Charentes
R112	FR61	Aquitaine
R113	FR62	Midi-Pyrénées
R114	FR63	Limousin
R115	FR71	Rhône-Alpes
R116	FR72	Auvergne
R117	FR81	Languedoc-Roussillon
R118	FR82	Provence-Alpes-Côte d'Azur
R119	FR83	Corse

Figure A.9 NUTS-2 regions in France (L9)

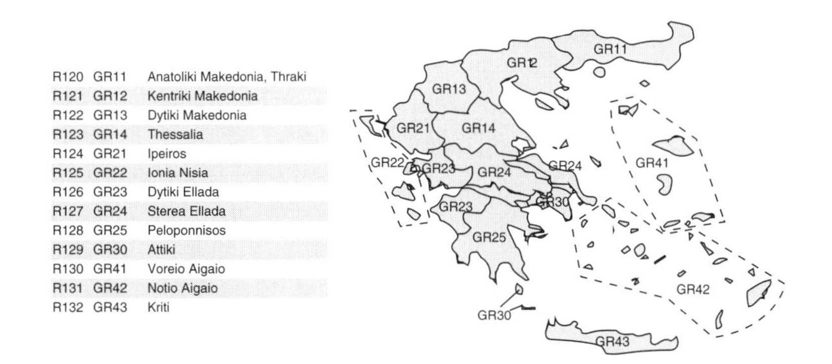

R120	GR11	Anatoliki Makedonia, Thraki
R121	GR12	Kentriki Makedonia
R122	GR13	Dytiki Makedonia
R123	GR14	Thessalia
R124	GR21	Ipeiros
R125	GR22	Ionia Nisia
R126	GR23	Dytiki Ellada
R127	GR24	Sterea Ellada
R128	GR25	Peloponnisos
R129	GR30	Attiki
R130	GR41	Voreio Aigaio
R131	GR42	Notio Aigaio
R132	GR43	Kriti

Figure A.10 NUTS-2 regions in Greece (L10)

technological industries in the region of Milan and the high-technological production in the region of Munich.

Recently, attention has shifted from large agglomerations towards strong, medium-sized regions as the main centres of economic growth (OECD, 2011c and 2012a). We have chosen Brussels, Eindhoven, Lyon, Helsinki and Rotterdam as typical examples of this group of medium-sized regions. Helsinki and Lyon are typical centres for high-technological producers while Eindhoven hosts a large number of medium-technological firms. In Brussels we focus on the financial and business services. The city

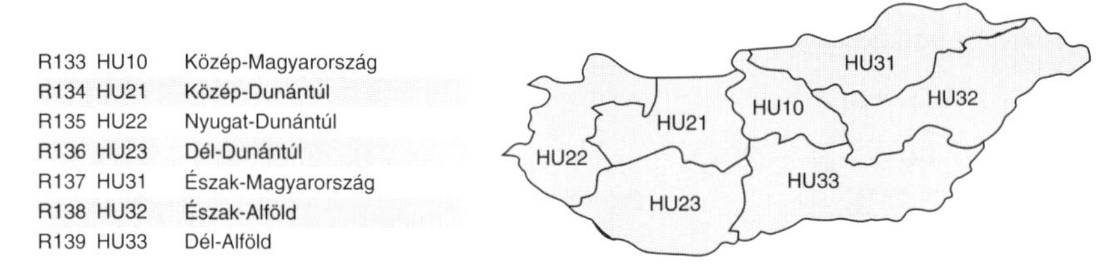

Figure A.11 NUTS-2 regions in Hungary (L11)

Figure A.12 NUTS-2 regions in Ireland (L12)

Figure A.13 NUTS-2 regions in Italy (L13)

of Rotterdam, which is mainly known for its harbour, has also one of the largest horticulture sectors in its vicinity. We therefore focus on the agricultural sector in the region of Rotterdam.

The last group of peripheral regions and emerging market economies

Figure A.14 NUTS-2 region in Lithuania (L14)

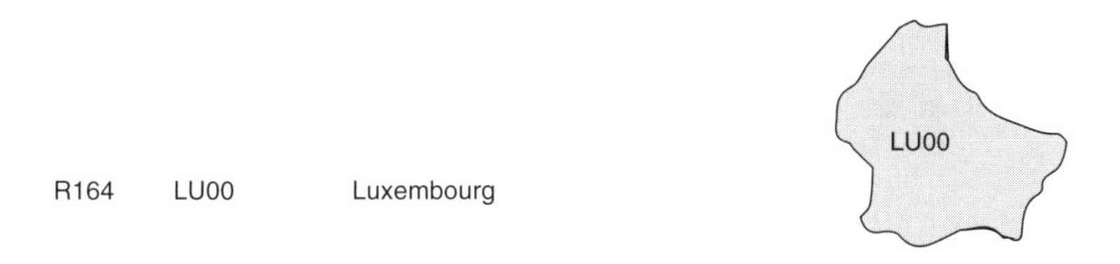

Figure A.15 NUTS-2 region in Luxembourg (L15)

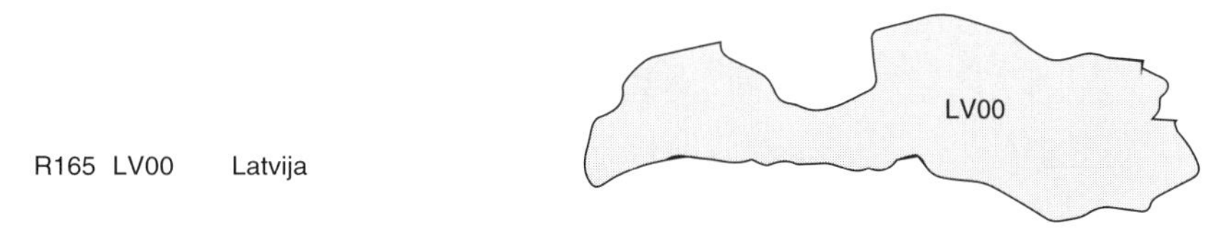

Figure A.16 NUTS-2 region in Latvia (L16)

Figure A.17 NUTS-2 region in Malta (L17)

may be especially important from a policy perspective. The Eastern European regions are characterized by low levels of income and are usually seen as highly problematic regions from an economic perspective. These regions do have potential and have higher growth rates than the Western regions. We have selected Budapest and Warsaw as typical large agglomerations in these emerging markets with specializations in the medium-technological industry and the financial and business services, respectively. Warsaw is also analysed from the perspective of a large and diverse economy. Dresden and Pécs have been chosen as medium to small

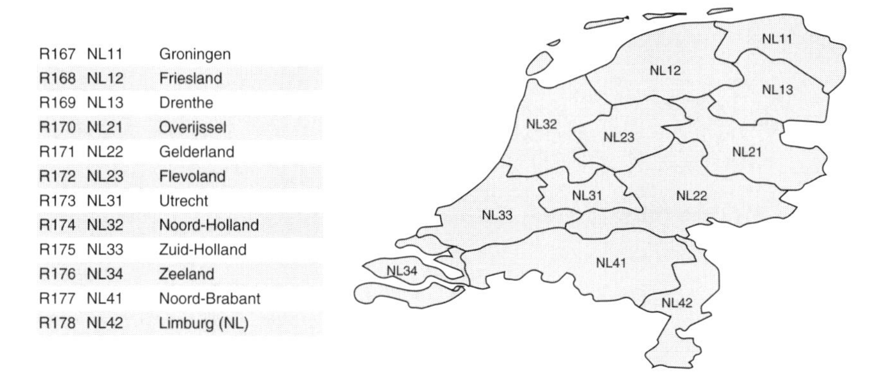

Figure A.18 NUTS-2 regions in The Netherlands (L18)

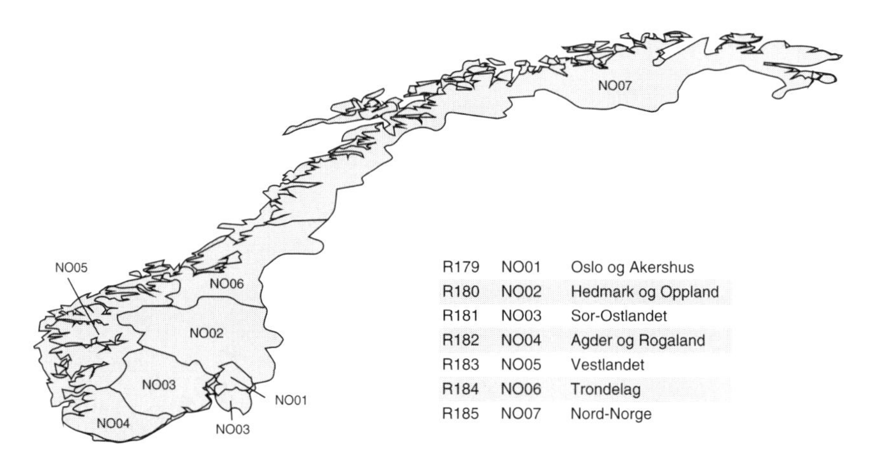

Figure A.19 NUTS-2 regions in Norway (L19)

sized emerging markets. We analyse the Pécs economy with respect to agriculture and low-technological industries, while we focus on the total economy and the low-technological industries in Dresden. Thessaloniki and Andalucía are both typical large peripheral regions. The total complex of production is central in our discussion of Thessaloniki's economy. Andalucía is analysed with respect to the large agricultural sector in this region.

We can see from Table A.3 that this selection of sector–region combinations covers the whole spectrum of possible combination in the economy. Therefore we primarily discuss regional competitiveness and smart specialization for these regions.

R186	PL11	Lódzkie
R187	PL12	Mazowieckie
R188	PL21	Malopolskie
R189	PL22	Slaskie
R190	PL31	Lubelskie
R191	PL32	Podkarpackie
R192	PL33	Swietokrzyskie
R193	PL34	Podlaskie
R194	PL41	Wielkopolskie
R195	PL42	Zachodniopomorskie
R196	PL43	Lubuskie
R197	PL51	Dolnoslaskie
R198	PL52	Opolskie
R199	PL61	Kujawsko-Pomorskie
R200	PL62	Warminsko-Mazurskie
R201	PL63	Pomorskie

Figure A.20 NUTS-2 regions in Poland (L20)

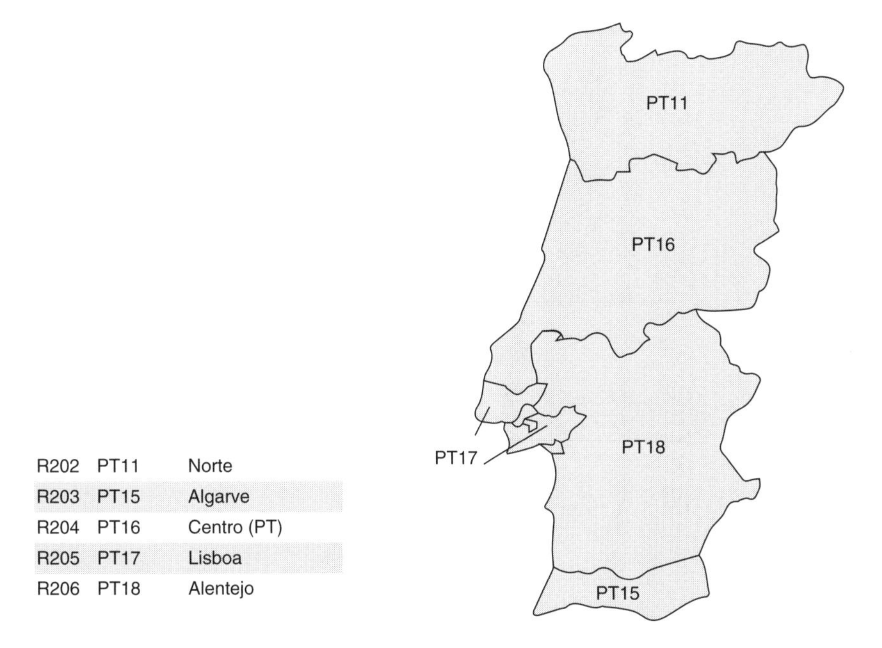

R202	PT11	Norte
R203	PT15	Algarve
R204	PT16	Centro (PT)
R205	PT17	Lisboa
R206	PT18	Alentejo

Figure A.21 NUTS-2 regions in Portugal (L21)

A.2.4 Product Categories

In our study, trade between European regions is detailed at the product level. Export and imports flows are divided according to the 2-digit Classification of Products by Activity (CPA 1996), which is the system

Figure A.22 NUTS-2 regions in Sweden (L22)

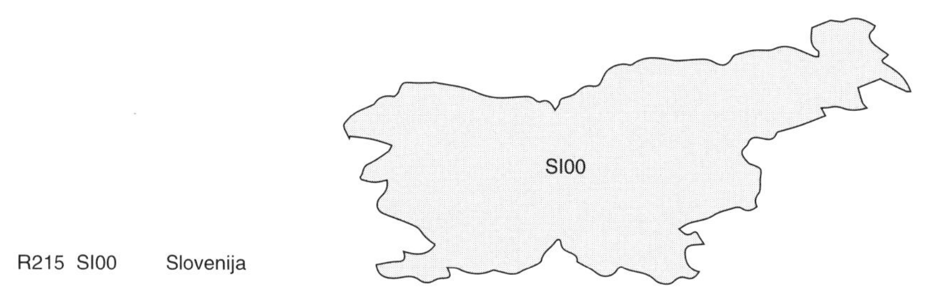

Figure A.23 NUTS-2 region in Slovenia (L23)

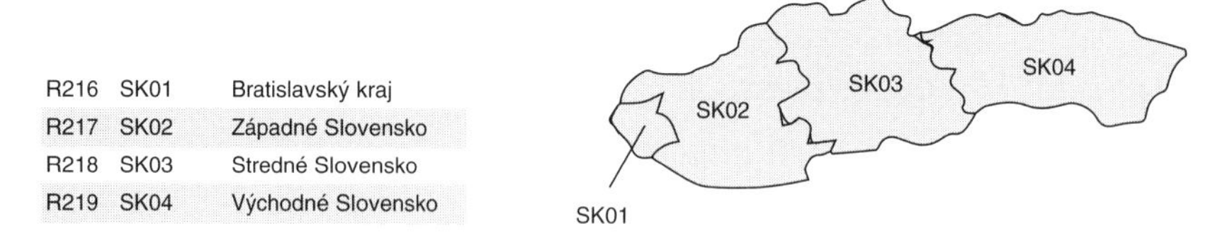

Figure A.24 NUTS-2 regions in Slovakia (L24)

Figure A.25 NUTS-2 regions in the United Kingdom (L25)

Table A.2 Extra-Europe trading partners

L26	Rest of Europe	L35	Cyprus
L27	Africa	L36	Canada
L28	Asia	L37	China
L29	Japan	L38	Hong Kong
L30	Middle and South America	L39	Korea
L31	Australia and Oceania	L40	Singapore
L32	Northern America	L41	Switzerland
L33	Russia	L42	Turkey
L34	Rest of the World	L43	United States

used by Eurostat to publish comparable national accounts of European countries. This organization of products was first implemented in 1993 under the authority of the Commission of the European Communities and it is legally binding in the European Union.

The classification has been revised since the 2002 version (CPA 2008). Nonetheless, to date, Eurostat publishes national accounts which are in line with the classification of 1996. There is a total of 62 goods and services in CPA 2002, but products with numbers 96, 97 and 99 (goods produced

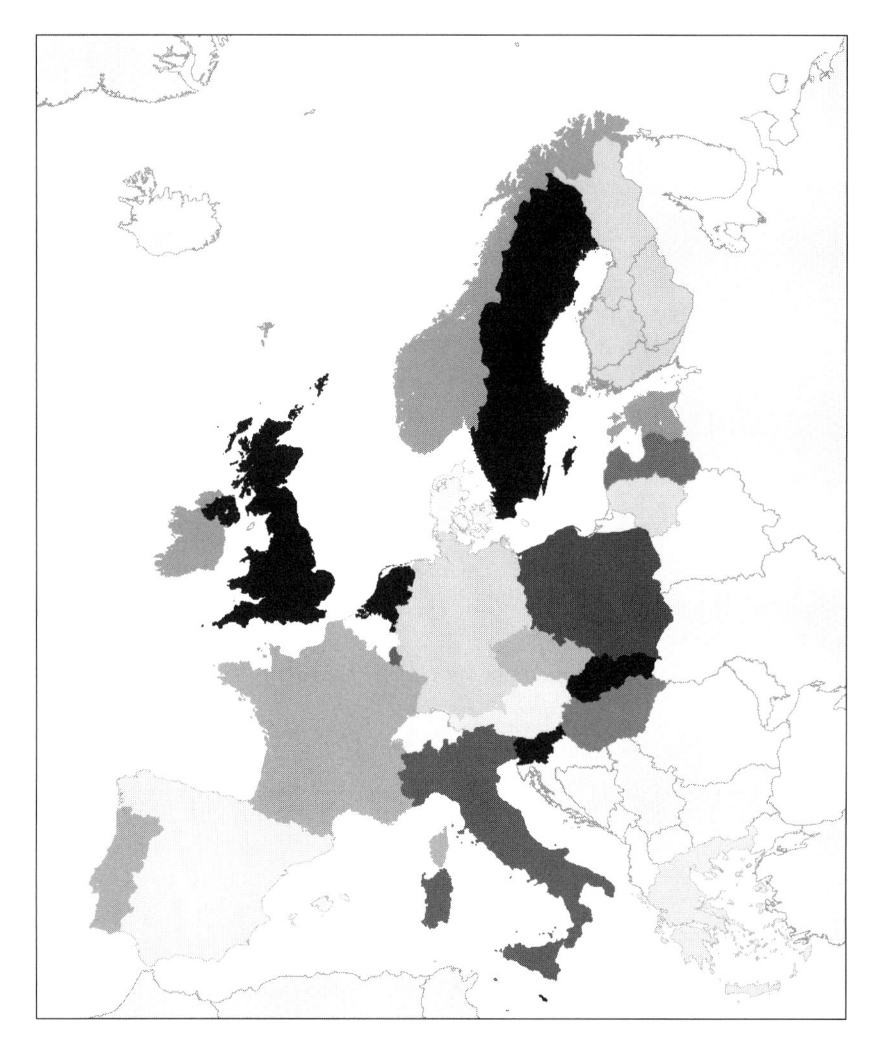

Figure A.26 Overview of NUTS-2 regions in Europe

by households for own use, services produced by households for own use and services provided by extra-territorial organizations and bodies) are not included in the supply and use system of accounts, reducing the total number of products to the 59 categories analysed in this book (see Table A.4).

Table A.3 Regions–sector combinations discussed in this book

	Code	Total	Agriculture	Financial & business services	Manufacturing		
					Low-tech	Medium-tech	High-tech
Large agglomerations							
London	UKI1						
Milan	ITC4						
Barcelona	ES51						
Munich	DE21						
Paris	FR10						
Strong medium-sized regions							
Brussels	BE10						
Eindhoven	NL41						
Lyon	FR71						
Helsinki	FI18						
Rotterdam	NL33						
Peripheral regions and emerging markets							
Budapest	HU10						
Warsaw	PL12						
Dresden	DED2						
Pécs	HU23						
Thessaloniki	GR12						
Andalucía	ES61						

A.2.5 Aggregate Product Groups

In the scope of this book it is not possible to analyse all the abovementioned product categories separately. We therefore group different product categories together into five main categories that are interesting from a policy perspective. We distinguish agricultural products, low, medium and high-technological manufacturing, and financial & business services. The precise definition of the product groups is based on Eurostat (2009c) and is given in Table A.5.

A.3 METHODOLOGY

The central principle in our methodology inferring European regional trade flows from different sources of information is increasing data reliability by imposing consistency with available statistics. Regional trade

Table A.4 2-digit Classification of Products by Activity (CPA 1996)

P1	AA01	Products of agriculture, hunting and related services
P2	AA02	Products of forestry, logging and related services
P3	BA05	Fish and other fishing products; services incidental to fishing
P4	CA10	Coal and lignite; peat
P5	CA11	Crude petroleum and natural gas; services incidental to oil and gas extraction excluding surveying
P6	CA12	Uranium and thorium ores
P7	CB13	Metal ores
P8	CB14	Other mining and quarrying products
P9	DA15	Food products and beverages
P10	DA16	Tobacco products
P11	DB17	Textiles
P12	DB18	Wearing apparel; furs
P13	DC19	Leather and leather products
P14	DD20	Wood and products of wood and cork (except furniture); articles of straw and plaiting materials
P15	DE21	Pulp, paper and paper products
P16	DE22	Printed matter and recorded media
P17	DF23	Coke, refined petroleum products and nuclear fuels
P18	DG24	Chemicals, chemical products and man-made fibres
P19	DH25	Rubber and plastic products
P20	DI26	Other non-metallic mineral products
P21	DJ27	Basic metals
P22	DJ28	Fabricated metal products, except machinery and equipment
P23	DK29	Machinery and equipment n.e.c.
P24	DK30	Office machinery and computers
P25	DL31	Electrical machinery and apparatus n.e.c.
P26	DL32	Radio, television and communication equipment and apparatus
P27	DL33	Medical, precision and optical instruments, watches and clocks
P28	DM34	Motor vehicles, trailers and semi-trailers
P29	DM35	Other transport equipment
P30	DN36	Furniture; other manufactured goods n.e.c.
P31	DN37	Secondary raw materials
P32	EA40	Electrical energy, gas, steam and hot water
P33	EA41	Collected and purified water, distribution services of water
P34	FA45	Construction work
P35	FA50	Trade, maintenance and repair services of motor vehicles and motorcycles; retail sale of automotive fuel
P36	GA51	Wholesale trade and commission trade services, except motor vehicles and motorcycles
P37	GA52	Retail trade services, except motor vehicles and motorcycles; repair services of personal and household goods
P38	HA55	Hotel and restaurant services

Table A.4 (continued)

P39	IA60	Land transport; transport via pipeline services
P40	IA61	Water transport services
P41	IA62	Air transport services
P42	IA63	Supporting and auxiliary transport services; travel agency services
P43	IA64	Post and telecommunication services
P44	JA65	Financial intermediation services, except insurance and pension funding services
P45	JA66	Insurance and pension funding services, except compulsory social security services
P46	JA67	Services auxiliary to financial intermediation
P47	KA70	Real estate services
P48	KA71	Renting services of machinery and equipment without operator and of personal and household goods
P49	KA72	Computer and related services
P50	KA73	Research and development services
P51	KA74	Other business services
P52	LA75	Public administration and defence services; compulsory social security services
P53	MA80	Education services
P54	NA85	Health and social work services
P55	OA90	Sewage and refuse disposal services, sanitation and similar services
P56	OA91	Membership organization services n.e.c.
P57	OA92	Recreational, cultural and sporting services
P58	OA93	Other services
P59	PA95	Private households with employed persons

flows need to be consistent with statistics on production and consumption by region, which, in turn, must be in line with the national figures of production and consumption. These regional flows must also be consistent with international trade statistics at the national level. Next, also international trade statistics must be consistent with national figures on production, consumption, imports and exports. Finally, trade statistics should be mutually consistent. That is, exports from a region or country A to a region or country B should equal the opposite flow of imports received by region or country B. All these consistency checks contain additional information and therefore add to the quality of the estimated trade flows.

Data we collected have been taken from various sources. International trade between countries has been taken from Feenstra et al. (2005) for goods and Eurostat (2009a) for services. The source for information on

Table A.5 Aggregated product groups analysed in this book

Agriculture		
Total	P1	Products of agriculture, hunting and related services
	P2	Products of forestry, logging and related services
	P3	Fish and other fishing products; services incidental to fishing
Manufacturing		
Low-tech	P9	Food products and beverages
	P10	Tobacco products
	P11	Textiles
	P12	Wearing apparel; furs
	P13	Leather and leather products
	P14	Wood and products of wood and cork (except furniture); articles of straw and plaiting materials
	P15	Pulp, paper and paper products
	P16	Printed matter and recorded media
	P17	Coke, refined petroleum products and nuclear fuels
	P19	Rubber and plastic products
	P20	Other non-metallic mineral products
	P21	Basic metals
	P22	Fabricated metal products, except machinery and equipment
	P30	Furniture; other manufactured goods n.e.c.
Medium-tech	P18	Chemicals, chemical products and man-made fibres
	P23	Machinery and equipment n.e.c.
	P25	Electrical machinery and apparatus n.e.c.
	P28	Motor vehicles, trailers and semi-trailers
	P29	Other transport equipment
High-tech	P24	Office machinery and computers
	P26	Radio, television and communication equipment and apparatus
	P27	Medical, precision and optical instruments, watches and clocks
Financial & business services		
Total	P44	Financial intermediation services, except insurance and pension funding services
	P45	Insurance and pension funding services, except compulsory social security services
	P46	Services auxiliary to financial intermediation
	P49	Computer and related services
	P50	Research and development services
	P51	Other business services

national production, consumption, imports and exports are the national accounts (Eurostat, 2009b). For two out of 25 considered countries (Latvia and Greece), national accounts were not available. Accounts from the year 1998 have therefore been updated using the commonly applied RAS method (or bi-proportional updating method). The necessary row and column sums for the supply and use tables for Latvia and Greece were taken from Eurostat. With respect to regional data, statistics on regional production, investment and consumption were taken from Cambridge Econometrics (2008). These different sources may have large discrepancies. For instance, the sum of regional statistics does not always match with the national totals or the sum of exports by country of destination does not match with the countries' export totals.

The national accounts are central in our analysis because they are the most reliable statistics of all sources available to us. A large amount of information is used in the construction of the national accounts being the result of the combination of many different data sources. We therefore constrain all other sources to be consistent with the national accounts. We start with section A.3.1, in which international trade is made consistent with figures on export and imports from the national accounts. In section A.3.2 we perform a regionalization of use and supply tables, using regional data from Cambridge Econometrics (2008). In this way, we make sure that we have reliable figures on regional imports and exports that are consistent with the national accounts. In section A.3.3, exports are distributed by country of destination and imports are distributed by country of origin. We use data on freight among European regions from the Ministry of Infrastructure and the Environment (2007) and first and business class flight data from MIDT (2010) to determine the origin and destination of the different trade flows. In this step we obtain two separate estimates of regional trade flows: one estimate from the export point of view and one from the import point of view. These two estimates are neither consistent with each other, nor with the other accounts. In the last step, explained in section A.3.4, we produce the final estimate of regional trade flows. This estimate stays as close as possible to the previous two estimates of section A.3.3, but it is constrained to be consistent with regional accounts, national accounts and international trade flows.

A.3.1 Consistent National Trade

In this section we present how the exports and imports from the national accounts statistics are divided over country of destination and country of origin using international trade statistics on goods (Feenstra et al., 2005) and services (Eurostat, 2009a). However, before we can compare imports and exports we have to deal with valuation differences and we have to take direct purchases abroad into account. The valuation differences occur because use and supply tables report exports valuated 'free-on-board' (f.o.b.: the value before transportation) while imports are valuated including 'cost, insurance and freight' (c.i.f.: inclusive of trade costs). We have chosen to value both exports and imports f.o.b. so they are comparable using the same prices. International trade statistics on the trade in goods also include the direct purchases abroad (both citizens abroad and non-citizens in domestic territory). We have therefore to include these separate items in the exports and imports of goods and services. Once again we need to make corrections to make different data sources comparable. We describe these corrections in detail in section A.3.1.2.

These trade data have also been made consistent internally. Thus, the statistics on export trade flows equal the same flow in the opposite direction registered as an import. Once these corrections are implemented, it is possible to make trade statistics from Feenstra et al. (2005) and Eurostat (2009a) consistent with national use and supply tables. First, we need to match the different product classifications. The maximum level of detail we can work on is the NACE 2-digit product classification because we take the national accounts supply and use tables as the starting point of our analyses. Trade in goods (Feenstra et al., 2005) is based on the 4-digit SITC and therefore requires a conversion and an aggregation. Trade in services, instead, is divided in only four macro-categories and requires a disaggregation. After this, we are left with two estimates (priors) of bilateral international trade for each of the 59 product categories. We then use linear programming to find a final estimate of bilateral trade. We want this final estimate to be the nearest possible to the two priors, but we also want it to be consistent with the (corrected) national accounts. The whole procedure is illustrated in section A.3.1.2.

Before moving to section A.3.2 and introducing regional data, section A.3.1 ends with a further correction. Total trade from national accounts and international trade data does not take re-exports into account. If a good is exported from country A to country B, via country C, in many cases the flow will be recorded twice (first A to C, then C to B). This generates two inconvenient results: one, it inflates the value of exported goods and, two, it misreports the true origin and destination of the flow of traded goods. An iterative procedure that tries to solve this problem is presented in section A.3.1.3.

A.3.1.1 Correction for c.i.f./f.o.b. valuation and direct purchases abroad

In this section we apply two corrections to the trade figures in the national account supply and use tables to make exports and import figures comparable. The first important correction concerns the valuation of exports with respect to trade costs, while the second deals with direct purchases abroad.

The problem of the valuation of trade costs arises from the fact that there are two ways used to record them. In the system of national accounts the exports of goods is generally recorded when the goods leave the producing country (at the customs of the origin country). The imports, however, are recorded when they enter the using country (at the customs of the destination country). The former way of registering exports is called 'free on board' (f.o.b.), while the latter way of registering imports is called 'cost, insurance and freight' (c.i.f.).

It is obvious that two trading countries will have a different value of the same trade flow if one of them uses f.o.b. and the other one uses c.i.f. The international guidelines for the construction of use and supply tables (the UN System of National Accounts SNA 1993 and European System of Accounts ESA95) recommend reporting the value of trade always f.o.b. for both imports and exports. However, for imports it is much easier to the have c.i.f. valuation, since imports are observed at the national customs. For this reason ESA95, the methodology used in Europe for national accounts (Eurostat, 2008), leaves some flexibility in this respect and prescribes to have only total imports in f.o.b. Therefore, many countries in Europe have their supply table reporting imports by product in c.i.f., together with an additional c.i.f./f.o.b. correction factor in the row so that the total imports are valued in f.o.b. To express imports in f.o.b. at product level, this correction factor on total imports has to be distributed over the different product categories.

The best information we have on how to distribute the correction factor among products is the column of trade and transport margins in the supply table of each nation. This column gives an indication on how much is spent in trade and transport costs by different product categories. Naturally these data refer to domestic transportation, but we can use them as a proxy for imported goods. Before applying the distribution, we notice that there is also a component of transport costs from the origin country (the exporter) to the destination (the importer) that is incurred by a foreign company and, hence, not accounted for in the correction factor. From transport statistics of the Netherlands, we know that 35 per cent of domestic transportation is operated by a foreign company. We use this figure for all countries and we increase the transport margin by an additional 35/65 = 0.53 per cent.

The following equations describe the adjustment. Let $TR_{c,g,d}$ be total transport costs for country c, in product g. Supply and use tables of many European countries distinguish, for year 2000, between products traded with EU15 partners and products traded with the rest of the world (ROW). We include the index d, area of destination, to keep this piece of information. We define $\tau_{c,g,d}$ as the share of transport costs by product:

$$\tau_{c,gnr,d} = \frac{TR_{c,gnr,d}}{\sum_{gnr',d'} TR_{c,gnr',d'}} \qquad (A.1)$$

where gnr stands for all products except trade and transport services gr. Let CF_c be the correction factor for the c.i.f./f.o.b. adjustment, κ the ratio between foreign and domestic transportation (≈53%) and $I_{c,g,d}$ imports. The correction on imports of products that are not transportation services is:

$$I_{c,gnr,d} = I_{c,gnr,d} - \tau_{c,gnr,d}(1+\kappa)CF_c \qquad (A.2)$$

We obtain imports valuated at f.o.b. using (A.2) to distribute the correction factors among different products. We must, however, still correct the accounts for transport services. The share of transport service, used from the different service categories gr (e.g. air transport, land transport) equals:

$$\tau_{c,gr,d} = \frac{TR_{c,gr,d}}{\sum_{gr',d'} TR_{c,gr',d'}} \qquad (A.3)$$

Imports of transport services are increased by the expected contribution of foreign companies in the transportation of imported goods, with respect to the correction factor. In fact, some of the value of CF, the correction factor which was subtracted from imports, is actually an import of transport services. The adjustment is carried out as follows:

$$I_{c,gr,d} = I_{c,gr,d} + \tau_{c,gr,d}(\kappa)\, CF_c \qquad (A.4)$$

The remaining component of CF is now evaluated as exports of transport services operated by domestic companies on the national territory. For this reason, we apply the last correction and remove this value of transport services from exports X:

$$X_{c,gr,d} = X_{c,gr,d} - \tau_{c,gr,d}\, CF_c \qquad (A.5)$$

The second issue we address in this section is the one of direct purchases abroad, which in some countries are a substantial part of exports and imports. In a comparable way as the c.i.f./f.o.b. valuation, supply and use tables report correction rows for purchases abroad by residents and domestic purchases by non-residents. These correction rows are adjustment for total exports and total imports, but do not report information on which product or service has been purchased. We need, therefore, to distribute the values in these rows to the different product categories.

Direct purchases abroad are likely to be in a large part attributable to tourism. Thus, we distribute the correction factor to those services that most probably have been consumed by tourism, namely hotels and restaurants, recreational, cultural and sporting services. In most countries the adjustment rows are distributed using the observed share of final demand in those service categories. Nevertheless, in Hungary and Luxembourg, purchases by non-residents are also distributed according to shares in food and real estate services. From the supply tables of these countries in 2000, it is clear that these two product categories are the only ones which have enough production to cover the total amount of the direct purchase correction.

We call Dp_c the direct purchases abroad by residents of country c, and Pd_c the purchases in the domestic territory of country c by non-residents. As previously in the text, X and I represent exports and imports and g different products. We also have tg, which stands for target product, those services the direct purchases will be distributed to. Lastly γ_{tg}, is the share of these services with respect to households' consumption $HC_{c,tg}$, and $\eta_{c,tg,d}$ the share on imports.

$$\gamma_{c,tg} = \frac{HC_{c,tg}}{\sum_{tg'} HC_{c,tg'}} \text{ and } \eta_{c,tg,d} = \frac{I_{c,tg,d}}{\sum_{tg'} I_{c,tg',d}} \tag{A.6}$$

Once again, imports in some countries are divided by destination, either within the EU15 or to the rest of the world (ROW). We apply the following adjustments:

$$X_{c,tg,d} = X_{c,tg,d} + \gamma_{c,g} \frac{X_{c,tg,d}}{X_{c,tg,eu15} + X_{c,tg,row}} Pd_c \tag{A.7}$$

and

$$I_{c,tg,d} = I_{c,tg,d} + \eta_{c,tg,d} Dp_{c,d} \tag{A.8}$$

In those countries whose tables do not distinguish between EU15 and ROW destination of trade, we simply use the total by destination to divide direct purchases abroad.

A.3.1.2 Estimation of consistent bilateral trade

The adjustments described in the previous section resulted in figures for exports and imports in 59 NACE 1.1 categories that are valued in the same prices. We can determine the origin and destination of trade flows and make them internally consistent using these comparable figures for exports and imports. We start with creating two estimates of trade flows. We call these estimates the priors. One prior is taken from the export point of view while the other prior is taken from the import point of view. Then we search for a final estimate that (1) stays as close as possible to the two priors, (2) satisfies the requirement that the export of a product from country A to country B matches with import of country B from country A, and (3) is consistent with total exports and imports as reported in the (corrected) national accounts.

The priors for goods and services are obtained from different sources. The prior of the trade in goods is obtained using Feenstra et al. (2005) data for the year 2000. First, this dataset is converted to the product classification used in this research, which implies an aggregation from 4-digit SITC classification to a 2-digit NACE 1.1. The conversion is achieved following the tables of the Eurostat RAMON website.[1] Then, Feenstra et al. (2005) data are used to create shares of exports by country of destination and shares of imports by country of origin. By multiplying the former shares by total exports and the latter by total imports, we obtain two priors for goods.

The origin and destination shares on a detailed product level are more difficult to obtain with respect to the trade in services. For the year 2000, only four broad categories of services are available: transportation, travel, other business services, and other services (Eurostat, 2009a). Moreover, data for the year 2000 has many missing values. We therefore pool data from 2000 to 2004 to obtain a full matrix of trade in services. This matrix is, subsequently, used to calculate the share of exports and imports by nation of destination and origin, respectively. We distributed imports and exports of 2-digit NACE 1.1 services, using the share of the Eurostat macro-sector to which these 2-digit services belong, to account for the difference in the classification detail of services.

After this distribution of exports and imports of goods and services over destinations and origins we have priors for both trade patterns. These are the export priors $X^{prior}_{i,g,j}$ from country i, to country j, in goods or services g and the import priors $I^{prior}_{i,g,j}$ of country i, from country j. These two priors are the starting point of the final estimate of the trade matrix

$T_{i,g,j}$. The values of T are found by use of constrained minimization. We minimize the absolute value of the relative distance between T and the two priors. The minimization is constrained to be consistent with total national exports and imports values, and totals for the EU15 are taken from the national accounts. We decide to give more weight to the error on imports, since – following the literature on constructing consistent international trade statistics (Feenstra et al., 2005; Oosterhaven et al., 2008; Bouwmeester and Oosterhaven, 2009) – import statistics are more reliable because they are used for tariff and registration purposes. In mathematics, the optimization is written as follows:

$$Min\, Z = \left| \frac{X_{i,g,j}^{prior} - T_{i,g,j}}{\frac{1}{4}X_{i,g,j}^{prior} + \frac{3}{4}I_{j,g,i}^{prior}} \right| + 3\left| \frac{I_{i,g,j}^{prior} - T_{j,g,i}}{\frac{1}{4}X_{j,g,i}^{prior} + \frac{3}{4}I_{i,g,j}^{prior}} \right| + \left| \frac{X_{i,g,eu15}^{prior} - T_{i,g,eu15}}{X_{i,g,eu15}^{prior}} \right| + 3\left| \frac{I_{i,g,eu15}^{prior} - T_{eu15,g,i}}{I_{i,g,eu15}^{prior}} \right|$$

$s.t.$

$$\begin{aligned} &1) \quad T_{i,g,eu15} = \textstyle\sum_{j=eu15} T_{i,g,j} \\ &2) \quad T_{eu15,g,i} = \textstyle\sum_{j=eu15} T_{j,g,i} \\ &3) \quad X_{i,g,total} = \textstyle\sum_{j=} T_{i,g,j} \\ &4) \quad I_{j,g,total} = \textstyle\sum_{i=} T_{i,g,j} \end{aligned} \tag{A.9}$$

A.3.1.3 Correction for re-exports

The matrix of international trade is consistent after the optimization. However, we want to further improve the quality of our dataset by removing re-exports. The existence and size of the re-exports problem is illustrated by the occurrence of exports that are larger than production in several typical product categories. In other words, according to the official statistics countries may export more than they produce. According to the definition of the main international guideline for the construction of national accounts (Commission of the European Communities, 2008): 'Re-exports are foreign goods (goods produced in other economies and previously imported with a change of economic ownership) that are exported with no substantial transformation from the state in which they were previously imported.' If a good goes from country A to B, making an intermediate transit in country C, the international guideline recommends recording the double trade flow (import from A to C, and export from C to B) if a resident of C acquires ownership of the good. It is clear that under the current system, countries that have no production of a certain good may export a positive quantity of it. In fact, in the SNA (Commission of the European Communities, 2008) the problem is acknowledged: 'because re-exported goods are not produced in the economy concerned, they have less connection to the economy than other exports'. In our view re-exports are problematic in at least two ways: first because national statistics over-report the total amount of trade and, second, they misreport the origin–destination pattern of products.

The data sources we use are based on the national accounts and are therefore inclusive of re-exports. Also the trade patterns are mostly inclusive of re-exports. Feenstra et al. (2005) dedicate a large amount of work to deal with the massive re-exports figures of Hong Kong, but they do not correct for other countries. The services trade has not been corrected for re-exports. It is therefore still necessary to correct the national trade for re-exports within Europe. Fortunately there is information about re-exports available in the import tables belonging to the national accounts. These tables were obtained from the statistical offices of most of the 25 countries studied.

In the rest of the section we outline the method we use to take re-exports out of the trade matrix T. The technique can be applied independently to different product categories. For this reason and to lighten the text, we leave out all reference to goods and service categories from the respective indices in the equations. We start defining the export destination shares e_{ij}^{c} from country i to country j:

$$e_{ij}^{c} = \frac{T_{ij}}{\sum_{j} T_{ij}}, j \neq c \tag{A.10}$$

While we define imports shares m_{ij} that country i receives from country j, so that:

$$m_{ij} = \frac{T_{ij}}{\sum_{i} T_{ij}} \tag{A.11}$$

The total re-exports (by product) RE_i, for country i, are taken from the input–output (import) tables. We used the minimum non-zero product re-export share observed among other countries for those countries where no information on re-exports was available. We estimate the pattern of re-exports R_{ij}^{c}, from i, to country j, via country c as:

$$R^c_{ij} = RE_c m_{ci} e^i_{cj} \quad \text{(A.12)}$$

When re-exports are identified in the intermediate country, they need to be redistributed to a different destination. The country of origin is excluded in equation (A.10) because it does not make sense to redistribute the trade flow back to the origin. We recall that re-exports do not receive any substantial re-elaboration in the intermediate country (they are at maximum repackaged) and can therefore be redistributed in this way.

Once the 'true' pattern has been identified we need to adjust the trade matrix accordingly. The trade flow between the origin i and the intermediate country c needs to be removed. The same is true for a flow of the same size from the intermediate country c to the destination country j. This trade flow (which is removed twice, from i to c and from c to j) is then added as an export from origin i to destination j. In mathematics:

$$T_{ij} = T_{ij} + \sum_c R^c_{ij} - \sum_c R^j_{ic} - \sum_c R^i_{cj} \quad \text{(A.13)}$$

The methodology has to take the following three issues into account to be successful:

1. The method produces results that are independent of the order of countries to which it is applied. This is certainly an advantage, but it comes with the disadvantage that adjusted export flows may incidentally become smaller than zero. An alternative methodology is available (doing it for every country separately), though this would have the opposite problem: it would not create negative flows, but it would be dependent on the order of the countries to which the methodology is applied. We find that the first methodology is to be preferred because the outcomes are easily reproducible and are not affected by the random choice of the order of countries to which the method is applied. The (small) negative export flows are corrected by changing them into positive imports.
2. It is possible that after the procedure, some countries have export flows which are still larger than production. We correct this by defining the excess of exports over production as re-exports (*RE*) and reapply the procedure.
3. Issues 1 and 2 may interact with each other. The correction in (1) may cause re-exports to become larger than production and the correction in (2) may cause some export flows to become negative. This can be solved by applying the procedure as many times as needed before both problems are solved.

A.3.2 Regionalization of Supply and Use Tables

The national supply and use tables with origins of imports and destination of the exports obtained in the previous section have to be regionalized in the next step. The main aim of this second step is to obtain, for every region, total exports and total imports, by product. This is achieved by constructing consistent regional use and supply tables.

These regionalized supply and use tables are consistent with the national supply and use tables. Thus, total use in the region matches total supply. It implies that the row totals of the use table equal the row totals of the supply table. This equality is nothing other than the regional versions of the macroeconomic condition that production is equal to consumption plus exports and minus imports. The column totals of the regional supply and use tables are also equal because total output of every (regional) industry equals this industry's total input and value-added. The regional supply and use tables give boundaries to the total regional exports and imports and are therefore crucial in order to infer the regional exports and import patterns.

In this section, we make use of available techniques to build the regional supply and use tables that we need to infer regional imports and exports, by product (CPA). More precisely, we employ the approach known as the Commodity Balance (CB) method, first suggested by Isard (1953). National supply and use tables are crossed with regional data from Cambridge Econometrics (2008) on total consumers' demand, sectoral added value and investment. These data provide relevant information on regional totals, without distinguishing among different products. All these pieces of information are used to obtain reliable column totals of the regional tables. To disaggregate these totals into different products (the rows), the national supply and use tables are used. It is assumed that the structure of the national supply and use tables gives a good approximation for the region tables. More formally, it is assumed that consumers have homogeneous preferences across the nation, there is homogeneous government spending over the regions and industries have the same homogeneous technology irrespective of their location in the nation. Under these assumptions regional household demand (*HHD*) by product (CPA, marked with index g) is obtained by the following equation:

$$HHD_g^r = \frac{HHD^r}{\sum_{k=1}^{R} HHD^k} HHD_g^N \tag{A.14}$$

Where N stands for nation and R for total number of regions in the nation. In a comparable way regional production is determined.

Since we do not have information on regional total exports and imports, we have to make use of one more assumption to obtain these key variables. We assume that exports originate from producing regions and imports are going to regions where these products are used. Exports and imports are therefore split according to production and consumption shares. To exemplify, exports would be:

$$X_g^r = \frac{Y_g^r}{\sum_{k=1}^{R} Y_g^k} X_g^N \tag{A.15}$$

where X is exports and Y is production by CPA region. The Commodity Balance (CB) approach has the advantage that it will automatically guarantee the national consistency, for every item of use and supply tables, so that if we sum the government demand of product g for every region, we obtain the national government demand of that product.

At the end of this operation, the regional macroeconomic condition that production equals consumption added with exports and reduced with imports no longer holds. This is not surprising because an important part of the puzzle is missing: intranational trade. While the obtained regional exports and imports refer to international trade, nothing has been done with intranational trade – trade among regions in the same nation. The regional intranational trade balance is the missing piece that will satisfy the regional macroeconomic condition.

Intranational trade is needed to construct fully consistent and reliable regional use and supply tables. We need information on cross hauling in order to determine the intranational trade. Cross-hauling is the simultaneous trade of the same product category (CPA in our case) among regions of the same country. Only recently was the existence and importance of cross-hauling recognized with respect to the regionalization of supply and use tables (see Kronenberg, 2009). Unfortunately, there were no procedures readily available to determine the cross-hauling for a consistent set of regions in a nation. We therefore introduce a new methodology in this section.

The remainder of the section on regionalization is organized as follows: paragraph A.3.2.1 explains how the supply and use tables are regionalized with respect to production and final demand. In Paragraph A.3.2.2 we explain the procedure used to construct regional exports and imports by product. In the concluding paragraph A.3.2.3, a methodology we developed to solve the cross-hauling problem will be presented.

Table A.6 Industry classification in 15 sectors

S1	Agriculture
S2	Mining, quarrying and energy supply
S3	Food, beverages and tobacco
S4	Textiles and leather etc.
S5	Coke, refined petroleum, nuclear fuel and chemicals etc.
S6	Electrical and optical equipment
S7	Transport equipment
S8	Other manufacturing
S9	Construction
S10	Distribution
S11	Hotels and restaurants
S12	Transport, storage and communications
S13	Financial intermediation
S14	Real estate, renting and business activities
S15	Non-market services

A.3.2.1 Production and consumption

In order to regionalize the national supply and use tables we first divide production and final demand over the regions. The regional demand in the use table is divided over intermediate demand (input by industry), household demand, government demand, demand from non-profit organizations, gross fixed capital formation, change in inventories, and change in valuables. With respect to the supply tables, it is necessary to determine regional output by industry, trade and transport margins and net taxes.

We start with industry production and intermediate demand. At the European NUTS-2 regional level there is no information on output, but there is data on value-added (VA) for 15 sectors made available by Cambridge Econometrics (2008).

Maintaining the index g for products and introducing the index s for sectors, regional output and input are constructed using information on value-added in the following way:

$$\text{input}_{gs}^{r} = \frac{VA_s^r}{\sum_{k=1}^{R} VA_s^k}\text{input}_{gs}^{N} \tag{A.16}$$

$$\text{output}_{gs}^{r} = \frac{VA_s^r}{\sum_{k=1}^{R} VA_s^k}\text{output}_{gs}^{N} \tag{A.17}$$

This approach depends on two main assumptions. First, the technology through which a sector transforms inputs into outputs is homogeneous across the national territory. Second, the value-added represents a good proxy for the magnitude of industries' inputs and outputs. It must be highlighted that this method maintains consistency not only by product, with the sum of output (or input) by regional product that equals the national output (input) by product, but also keeps consistency by industry, with the regional shares of VA fixed to the original proportions.

The second important assumption is that the preferences of final consumers in each region reflect the preferences at national level (homogeneous preferences across the territory). The formula employed for this part of the regionalization has been already presented in the introduction of this section and is repeated here:

$$HHD_g^r = \frac{HHD^r}{\sum_{k=1}^{R} HHD^k} HHD_g^N \tag{A.14}$$

Regional households' demand has been aggregated with demand by non-profit organizations because we have no information on non-profit organizations at the regional level. Non-profit organizations' demand is, on average, less than 2.5 per cent of household demand which therefore stays the main component. For simplicity, in the remainder of this Appendix we will therefore refer to this aggregated category as households' demand (HHD).

In order to regionalize the total government demand by region, we used data on value-added non-market services (sector 15). This sector includes typical government activities such as public administration, defence, education and health. It is reasonable to assume that this sector reflects how the government budget is allocated over the national territory. Assuming that the pattern of demand by product does not differ over regions, we have:

$$GOVD_g^r = \frac{VA_{S15}^r}{\sum_{k=1}^{R} VA_{S15}^k} GOVD_g^N \tag{A.18}$$

Gross capital formation is divided into three items: gross fixed capital formation, changes in inventories and changes in valuables. With respect to the first category, we proceed in a similar way to the government demand. Since we have information on investment by region we can write:

$$INV_g^r = \frac{INV^r}{\sum_{k=1}^{R} INV^k} INV_g^N \tag{A.19}$$

Changes in inventories and valuables require more effort. It is necessary to regionalize these two small fluctuating and unpredictable columns to keep full consistency between the regional and national accounts. The following observations are important in regionalizing these two accounts. First, Changes in inventories are a more common phenomenon than changes in valuables. Changes in valuables are often small and are even left blank in the accounts of some countries. Second, The two items have a similar pattern over the different goods, such that they are taken together in a subtotal under the name 'changes in inventories and valuables' in the ESA95 format. Given these observations, we decided to merge the two categories and to treat this new aggregated column as if it behaves like changes in inventories. Positive and negative changes in inventories reflect excess and shortage of supply over demand, respectively, within the time period of a year. If we assume that the demand of a certain product has the same kind of fluctuation across the nation, then producers in different regions are expected to face an excess or shortage of supply which is proportional to their production. Hence, changes in inventories and valuables (CIV) are defined as:

$$CIV_g^r = \frac{VA^r}{\sum_{k=1}^{R} VA^k} CIV_g^N \tag{A.20}$$

In a similar fashion, we can apply this last consideration to the two remaining columns in the supply table: trade and transport margins (TTM) and taxes and subsidies (TAX). Since their regional variation is also assumed to be proportional to the production, we can define them as:

$$TTM_g^r = \frac{VA^r}{\sum_{k=1}^{R} VA^k} TTM_g^N \text{ and } TAX_g^r = \frac{VA^r}{\sum_{k=1}^{R} VA^k} TAX_g^N \tag{A.21}$$

A.3.2.2 Exports and imports

In paragraph A.3.2.1, we defined all the variables of the use and the supply tables, with the exception of exports and imports. As mentioned, we do not possess information on regional exports and imports but we do have better information on regional production and consumption by product after the regionalization. We use this information to distribute exports proportionally to regional production, and imports proportionally to regional demand. A simple example may illustrate the rationale behind this operation. Imagine that in a country *N*, industry *s* is agglomerated in one region (region *r*). We also know, from the national supply table, that this industry is providing a certain mix of products *g* as output. If country *N* is an exporter of these products, then exports must be coming from the region where they are produced. This is region *r* in the example. Naturally, full agglomeration of one industry almost never happens. Nonetheless, the reasoning can be extended to less extreme cases. We may therefore safely assume that the largest share of exports (of a typical product) is produced in the largest producing region (of that product). A similar reasoning results in the following comparable conclusion with respect to imports. The largest share of imports (of a typical product) is used in the region that uses the most of this product in intermediate or final use.

Hence we determine for every product *g*, the regional production and consumption. These two figures are subsequently used to distribute national exports and imports in different regions. Defining regional production and consumption is not as straightforward as it looks. The general rule is that consumption (*D* henceforth) equals use minus exports (*X*), and production (*Y*) is supply minus imports (*I*). Hence:

$$D_g^r = Use_g^r - X_g^r = \sum_s Input_{gs}^r + HHD_g^r + GOVD_g^r + INV_g^r + CIV_g^r$$

and (A.22)

$$Y_g^r = Supply_g^r - I_g^r = \sum_s Output_{gs}^r + TTM_g^r + TAX_g^r$$

However, there are some minor, but important, corrections that must be taken into account. A change in inventories should be added to the production (in this period) although it is only demanded in the next period. Hence negative entries under 'changes in inventories and valuables' are part of the supply and not a negative correction on the demand. In the same way, negative entries in trade and transport margins, as well as negative values of taxes (thus, subsidies), are a positive demand instead of a negative supply. Once these corrections have been applied, we can finally define regional exports and imports:

$$X_g^r = \frac{Y_g^r}{\sum_{k=1}^{R} Y_g^k} X_g^N \quad \text{and} \quad I_g^r = \frac{D_g^r}{\sum_{k=1}^{R} D_g^k} I_g^N \qquad \text{(A.23)}$$

It must be emphasized that the exports and imports in equation (A.23) refer to international trade, that is goods and services going to and coming from a foreign country. Products that are sold outside the producing region but in the same country are also exports from the perspective of a region. We refer to this type of exports as intranational exports (IX) to avoid possible confusion. Similarly, we use intranational imports (II) and, more generally, intranational trade. The following subsection is dedicated to intranational exports and intranational imports.

A.3.2.3 Cross-hauling and intranational trade

At the national level we have information about the share of production consumed in the national territory since re-exports have been removed from use and supply tables (see section A.3.1.3). If we call *own production* (OY) the national production supplied to the own national market and *own consumption* (OD) the national consumption of nationally produced products, we can write:

$$OY_g^N = Y_g^N - X_g^N = D_g^N - I_g^N = OD_g^N \qquad \text{(A.24)}$$

Own production or own consumption can be derived in two ways: either production minus exports or consumption minus imports. These two values are, of course, the same.[2]

At the regional level exports do not include intranational exports and we have therefore the following slightly different relationship

$$IY_g^r = OY_g^r + IX_g^r = Y_g^r - X_g^r \quad \text{and} \quad ID_g^r = OD_g^r + II_g^r = D_g^r - I_g^r \qquad \text{(A.25)}$$

with IY being intranational production and ID being intranational demand. Thus, IY is the production in a region, which is either sold in the same region (OY) or is sold in the other regions of the same country (intranational exports, IX). ID is the demand in a region, which is either satisfied by the production in the same region (OD) or is satisfied by the production in other regions of the same country (intranational imports,

II). In equation (A.25) it is shown that *IY* and *ID* can be derived by subtracting exports (*X*) from production (*Y*) and imports (*I*) from consumption (*D*), respectively. While internal production and internal demand are known, we do not know how much stays in the own region. Hence, we are unable to split *IY* into its components: own production (*OY*) and internal exports (*IX*). Equivalently, we cannot directly split *ID* into own consumption (*OD*) and internal imports (*II*).

Although by definition own production equals own consumption ($OY = OD$) it is likely that intranational exports will deviate from intranational imports. We therefore define the internal trade balance (*IZ*) as follows:

$$IZ_g^r = ID_g^r - IY_g^r \tag{A.26}$$

which is also equal to the difference between intranational imports (*II*) and intranational exports (*IX*). A full regionalization of supply and use tables may be obtained assuming that there is no cross-hauling, and trade between regions is appropriately described by the internal trade balance (*IZ*). However, cross-hauling is an important and sizeable empirical phenomenon that invalidates this type of regionalization (see Kronenberg, 2009). We therefore present a theoretical model that allows for cross-hauling and use constraint non-linear optimization techniques to estimate the size of cross-hauling in the 256 distinguished NUTS-2 regions.

The Krugman (1991b) model is the only theoretical international macro model derived from microeconomic behaviour that allows for cross-hauling. This approach is to be preferred[3] because if it is applied to all regions in a country it (1) guarantees consistency with the national accounts and (2) is rigorously derived from microeconomic theory. For a more extensive explanation of the model we refer to Diodato and Thissen (2011). However, below we provide a concise description of the approach.

The core of the model is built around the assumption that consumers have a 'love for variety' and the demand for varieties of goods can be described by a Dixit–Stiglitz–Krugman demand function. This demand function is a CES function (constant elasticity of substitution) including (iceberg) transport costs to deal with the demand from different locations. This function describes that consumers perceive a difference among varieties of each product category, which are imperfect substitutes. Even though producers in every region have the same technology, the model differs from perfect competition, because consumers identify every variety as unique and, consequently, each producer possesses a certain degree of monopolistic power. The basic Dixit–Stiglitz monopolistic competition (Dixit and Stiglitz, 1977) has been extended by Krugman (1991b) with iceberg-type transport costs (Samuelson, 1954) to build a spatial two-region model. We use this basic theoretical model to derive cross-hauling.

It is important to emphasize that we use a two-region model because we only want to determine the size of cross-hauling in every region. We do *not* use the model to determine trade patterns. It was explained before that using a model to estimate the trade patterns would make the dataset useless for any further data analysis. The use of the Krugman model to determine only the size of cross-hauling and not the trade patterns is therefore crucial in the presented approach.

The two-region model used consists of the region under investigation (the focus region r) and the rest of the country h (the second region). The second region is the aggregation of all regions in the country except the focus region. This second region will therefore be different for every focus region. Producers of product g are distributed over both regions. When consumers buy a product they have to pay either transport costs for products from the own region or interregional transport costs if the products come from other regions in the rest of the country.[4] Given the theoretical model we therefore have intranational exports from region r to the rest of the country h equal to:

$$IX^r = \frac{(P^r T_{rh})^{1-\sigma}}{n^h (P^h T_{hh})^{1-\sigma} + n^r (P^r T_{rh})^{1-\sigma}} ID^h n^r \tag{A.27}$$

And intranational imports of region r from the rest of the country h are:

$$II^r = \frac{(P^h T_{hr})^{1-\sigma}}{n^r (P^r T_{rr})^{1-\sigma} + n^h (P^h T_{hr})^{1-\sigma}} ID^r n^h \tag{A.28}$$

where P is price, n is number of firms, σ is elasticity of substitution and T are iceberg transport costs. The index g for the product category was omitted to simplify the equations.

With homogeneous technology we have that:

$$n^r = \frac{IY^r}{\alpha P^r} \tag{A.29}$$

where α equals optimal output per variety, which in the model is the same for every producer, regardless of its location. Substitution of the number of varieties (A.29) in both equations (A.28) and (A.27) leads to a simplification of the intranational exports and imports. Combining (A.28) and (A.27) results in two expressions which, after rearranging, results in expressions for intranational exports and internal imports expressed as a function of values and not of prices or quantities.

$$IX^{r} = f(T,\sigma,ID^{r},ID^{h},IZ^{r}) \equiv II^{h}$$

and (A.30)

$$II^{r} = f(T,\sigma,ID^{r},ID^{h},IZ^{h}) \equiv IX^{h}$$

Internal imports (*II*) and exports (*IX*) are now functions of only two unknown quantities: transport costs and the elasticity of substitution.[5] We could compute internal trade if we knew these two parameters. Since we do not, the problem must be approached in a different way. The elasticity of substitution σ is taken from the literature, where it is commonly assumed to be equal to 1.5 (McKitrick, 1998). Transport costs are estimated (together with internal trade) using non-linear programming.

Given the theoretical model described by (A.30) we determine the optimal values for transportation costs t_{rh} between regions r and h in the non-linear optimization such that the national transport costs by product are as close as possible to the national accounts' data on trade and transport margins (TTM). In the optimization we assume a common transport costs function which is declining in transported distance according to a logarithmic relationship. The cross-hauling or the total intranational trade of a region is endogenously determined in the procedure.

Unfortunately the data on trade and transport by product is limited to the national level and is not always of a very high quality. We therefore extended the methodology with a second objective in the non-linear optimization procedure based on cross-hauling derived from freight data from the Dutch Ministry of Infrastructure and the Environment (2007). The cross-hauling derived by freight data is described by the share *ChS* of the total of goods staying within regional borders over the goods sold to other regions. The services need a correction since cross-hauling is expected to be less important than in the case of goods. The share for services is calculated as follows

$$ChS_{r}^{services} = ChS_{r}^{goods} \frac{\sum_{g \in services} Supply_{g}^{N} \Big/ \sum_{g \in services} (X_{g}^{N} + Supply_{g}^{N})}{\sum_{g \in goods} Supply_{g}^{N} \Big/ \sum_{g \in goods} (X_{g}^{N} + Supply_{g}^{N})} \qquad (A.31)$$

The correction is based on a division that describes the relative propensity of exporting services in comparison to goods.

All described elements taken together lead to the following non-linear minimization problem that is solved to determine the degree of cross-hauling or, in other words, the share of production that is used within the own region.

$$Min\ Objective = Z_1 + Z_2$$

$$s.t.$$

$$Z_1 = \sum_c \left[TTM_c - \sum_{r \in c} (T_{rh} - 1) IX^r - \sum_{r \in c} (T_{rr} - 1)(IY^r - IX^r) \right]^2$$

$$Z_2 = \sum_r [ChS_r IY_r - (IY^r - IX^r)]^2$$

$$t_{rh} = (1 + \ln[\beta + \gamma dist_{rh}])^{1-\sigma}$$

$$(t_{rr}t_{hh} - t_{rh}^2)IX_r^2 + (IZ_r t_{rr} t_{hh} + ID_h t_{rh}^2 - IZ_r t_{rh}^2 + ID_r t_{rh}^2)IX_r$$
$$+ (ID_h IZ_r t_{rh}^2 - ID_h ID_r t_{rh}^2) = 0 \qquad (A.32)$$

In (A.32) there are seven free variables, which need to be determined: the objective variables (Z_1 and Z_2), the transportation variables (β, γ, t and T) and intranational exports (IX). All other elements are fixed parameters, whose value has been taken from the available data sources. We used the CONOPT3 solver of the GAMS software to solve the problem described by (A.32).

A.3.3 The Origin and Destination of Regional Trade Flows

In this section we describe how the origin and destination of regional trade is determined. The main sources for the origin and destination of trade in goods and services are data on freight transport and airline ticket information on first class and business class travel. The procedure used to determine the trade flows distributes the trade over the regions given the amount produced and consumed in every region.

The amounts of goods and services that are produced and consumed in the same region have been determined in the previous section. Thus, the diagonal of the trade matrix is known. The amount of produce and services leaving a region and the amount of produce and services entering a region are therefore also determined in the regionalized supply and use tables. These regional 'exports' are divided into international exports (those which leave the country) and intranational exports (those that go to different regions in the same country).

In this section we determine the complete trade network between all distinguished NUTS-2 regions given the intranational and international exports of the different regions. To determine the destination of exports we use a simplified transport model based on the probabilities of trade flows between different regions. These probabilities are derived from data on airline business trips (compare Derudder and Witlox, 2005), while the probabilities of goods transport destinations are based on data on freight transport.

A.3.3.1 Logistics centres and the estimation of trade from transport data

The existence of logistics centres (or hubs) makes the derivation of trade from transport data a complex procedure. The consequence of logistics centres is that transported goods may be going to a logistics centre instead of going to their final destination. Therefore there is a large difference between transport and trade data. We found that only 40 per cent of *all* goods traded do not make use of any logistics centre and reach their final destination being directly transported between the origin and destination. The rest of the goods will use at least one logistics centre before they reach their final destination. In particular in the case of international trade we expect more than one hub: one logistics centre in the country of origin and another logistics centre in the country of destination.

The methodology used is based on a combination of two estimates for international trade between NUTS-2 regions. The first estimate is based on the export of goods (the destination), while the second is based on the imports of goods (the origin). We give both estimates a weight of a half and minimize the quadratic difference between the final trade matrix and the two estimates. Below we will first describe the methodology for the destination (exports) of goods and services. Subsequently we describe the methodology to determine the trade based on the origin (imports) of goods. This is a similar method where the destination probabilities are replaced by origin probabilities and consumption is distributed over regions of origin instead of production being distributed over regions of destination.

The methodology to determine the two estimates consists of three steps. In the first step the direct flows are determined. These are the traded goods and services that are directly transported from the region of origin to the region of destination without the use of any logistics centre. In the second step the indirect flows are determined. These indirect trade flows are goods and services that use at least one logistics centre when being transported from the producer to the consumer. In the third step the higher order indirect flows are determined. Higher order trade flows are traded goods or services that are transported via one or more logistics centre before they reach their final destination. These three steps are described below before we present the last step to determine the final trade matrix.

A.3.3.2 The estimation of intra- and international export trade flows

The first estimate distributes the production of every region over the destination regions. In this trade flow estimation the distribution of intra- and international export trade flows are not predetermined with respect to their destination regions. Only the overall international flows are predetermined.

Step 1 – Direct trade flows: export perspective The direct trade flows are goods and services that are directly transported from the production location (origin) to the consumption location (destination) without being reloaded in a logistics centre. In order to determine these direct flows we need the direct probability $P^0_{i,k}$ of goods being exported from a region i to a region k. This probability can be described as follows.

$$P^0_{i,k} = \frac{T_{i,k}}{\sum_k T_{i,k}} \tag{A.33}$$

where $P^0_{i,k}$ is equal to the probability that a good is transported from i to k without using a hub and $T_{i,k}$ is the data on the amount of goods (or number of trips) transported from origin i to destination k. Given the (intranational and international) exports X_j that are exported from region j we can describe the direct flows of exports X^0_{ik} from origin i to destination k in the following way:

$$X^0_{ik} = \lambda P^0_{i,k} X_i \tag{A.34}$$

where λ is a fraction of the goods which on average are transported directly (this is 40 per cent of the goods). However, in some regions and especially in hubs there will not be enough goods imported (I_k) if compared to the amount of goods exported to these regions. We therefore introduce the following parameter Z^0_k.

$$Z_k^0 = \max\left(- I_k + \lambda \sum_i P_{i,k}^0 X_i, 0\right) \tag{A.35}$$

The exports to an area k are larger than the imports in this area if Z_k is positive. In those cases we have to adjust our equation (A.34) to determine the trade flows as follows:

$$X_{ik}^0 = \lambda P_{i,k}^0 X_i - \frac{Z_k^0}{\lambda \sum_i P_{i,k}^0 X_i} \lambda P_{i,k}^0 X_i \tag{A.36}$$

The two equations (A.36) and (A.35) are sufficient to determine the direct trade flows between all regions.

Step 2 – Indirect trade flows using a hub: export perspective In the next step we determine the indirect trade flows that are reloaded in a logistics centre when transported from the production to the consumption location. The probability $P_{i,k}^1$ that a good is transported from i to k using a hub, the export amount X_j^1 which still has to be distributed over the regions of destination and the import amount I_k^1 that has still to be imported in the region are calculated as follows:

$$P_{i,k}^1 = \sum_j P_{i,j}^0 P_{j,k|k \neq i}^0 \tag{A.37}$$

$$X_i^1 = X_i - \sum_j X_{ij}^0 \tag{A.38}$$

$$I_k^1 = I_k - \sum_i X_{ik}^0 \tag{A.39}$$

where a condition is imposed such that goods cannot be transported back to a region where they have been produced or reloaded. Analogous to the direct trade flows we determine whether the estimate of the exports using a hub will generate more exports to regions than imports available in that region.

$$Z_k^1 = \max\left(-I_k^1 + \sum_i P_{i,k}^1 X_i^1, 0\right) \tag{A.40}$$

The exports to an area k are larger than the imports in this area if Z_k is positive. In those cases we adjust the exports such that the exports to a region are always smaller or equal to the imports in that region. Our indirect trade flows are therefore determined by the following equation:

$$X^1_{ik} = P^1_{i,k}X^1_i - \frac{Z^1_k}{\sum_i P^1_{i,k}X^1_i} P^1_{i,k}X^1_i \tag{A.41}$$

Step 3 – Higher order indirect trade flows using multiple hubs: export perspective Higher order indirect trade flows use multiple logistics centres transporting goods from the production to the consumption location. We use the same methodology as described with the indirect flows and we can therefore describe the higher order probabilities and trade flows by the following set of equations:

$$P^2_{i,k} = \sum_{j,l|l \neq i} P^0_{i,j} P^0_{j,l} P^0_{l,k|k \neq i,k \neq j} \tag{A.42}$$

$$X^2_i = X_i - \sum_j X^1_{ij} - \sum_j X^0_{ij} \tag{A.43}$$

$$I^2_k = I_k - \sum_i X^1_{ik} - \sum_i X^0_{ik} \tag{A.44}$$

$$Z^2_k = \max\left(-I^2_k + \sum_i P^2_{i,k}X^2_i, 0\right) \tag{A.45}$$

$$X^2_{ik} = P^2_{i,k}X^2_i - \frac{Z^2_k}{\sum_i P^2_{i,k}X^2_i} P^2_{i,k}X^2_i \tag{A.46}$$

Any subsequent hub is treated in the same way. The procedure is continued including more hubs up to a maximum of five hubs. The remaining X^n_k is bi-proportionally distributed such that all exports match with all imports. Total trade between the regions will be the aggregate over all subsets of trade using n different numbers of hubs. Thus we have the following equations describing total exports between regions:

$$X^{prior}_{ik} = \sum_n X^n_{i,k} \tag{A.47}$$

A.3.3.3 The estimation of intra- and international import trade flows

After estimating the export trade flows we can perform a similar procedure and get the estimated trade flows from the imports perspective. Thus, we try to find the origin of product consumed in a region instead of finding the destination of product produced in a region. The procedure for the imports is mostly the same as for the exports and we will therefore only give a concise description below.

Step 1 – Direct trade flows: import perspective The main difference between the export estimation is that we now use the probability $Q^0_{i,k}$ that a good is imported in region k from region i without using a hub to distribute the imports over the exporting regions of origin. We use the following equation to determine the probability $Q^0_{i,k}$

$$Q^0_{i,k} = \frac{T_{i,k}}{\sum_i T_{i,k}} \quad \text{(A.48)}$$

Using this probability we can determine the flow of goods between destination region j and origin region i with the following set of equations:

$$I^0_{k,i} = \lambda Q^0_{k,i} I_i - \frac{ZZ^0_k}{\lambda \sum_i Q^0_{k,i} I_i} \lambda Q^0_{k,i} I_i \quad \text{(A.49)}$$

$$ZZ^0_k = \max\left(-X_k + \lambda \sum_i Q^0_{k,i} I_i, 0\right) \quad \text{(A.50)}$$

where the adjustment parameter ZZ_k is positive if the imports coming from a region k are larger than the exports leaving this region.

Steps 2 and 3 – Indirect trade flows using a hub: import perspective In the next steps we have to determine the trade flows which use one or more hubs. Analogous to the export trade flows we can determine the flows using one hub with the following set of equations:

$$Q^1_{i,k} = \sum_j Q^0_{i,j} Q^0_{j,k} \quad \text{(A.51)}$$

$$I^1_i = I_i - \sum_j I^0_{ji} \quad \text{(A.52)}$$

$$X^1_k = X_k - \sum_i I^0_{k,i} \quad \text{(A.53)}$$

$$I^1_{k,i} = \lambda Q^1_{k,i} I^1_i - \frac{ZZ^1_k}{\lambda \sum_i Q^1_{k,i} I^1_i} \lambda Q^1_{k,i} I^1_i \quad \text{(A.54)}$$

$$ZZ^1_k = \max\left(- X^1_k + \lambda \sum_i Q^1_{k,i} I^1_i, 0\right) \quad \text{(A.55)}$$

where $Q^1_{i,k}$ is the probability that a good is transported from i to k using one hub, and the amount I^1_j and X^1_j still has to be imported and exported from other regions, respectively.

Also step 3 is completely analogous to the methodology used to estimate the export flows and is therefore not presented here. The total import flows imported in region k from region i are simply the following sum of all the direct and indirect flows:

$$I^{prior}_{i,k} = \sum_n I^n_{i,k} \tag{A.56}$$

A.3.4 Final Estimation

In the previous section exports and imports were distributed to regions of destination and origin by use of a logistic trade model. This resulted in two estimates of bilateral interregional trade. The first estimate, $X^{prior}_{i,j,g}$, was introduced in equation (A.47) and is the trade matrix from region i, to region j, of product g from the export point of view. The second estimate, $I^{prior}_{i,j,g}$, was introduced in equation (A.56) and is the trade matrix from region i, to region j, of product g from the import point of view. In the used estimation methodology both the international as well as the intranational trade were distributed simultaneously. This implies that both 'compete' for a destination in the estimation procedure. The international and the intranational quantities are therefore not predetermined. They are endogenously determined in the process based on the probabilities of trade flows between regions. The resulting priors from the export point of view are therefore consistent with international exports from the regionalized use and supply tables but inconsistent with the international imports. Vice versa, import priors are consistent with international imports from the regionalized use and supply tables but inconsistent with the international exports. In addition, export and import priors are not entirely consistent with data on bilateral international trade at the country level.[6] The total international and intranational exports and imports are consistent with the regionalized supply and use tables in both estimates.

The purpose of this last step is bring to consistency to our two estimates of regional bilateral trade. The methodology applied is that of constrained optimization, the same that we use in section 3.1.2 to estimate consistent trade flows at the country level. The final estimate of the regional trade matrix $T_{i,j,g}$ is determined as the trade matrix $T_{i,j,g}$, which is as near as possible to both priors ($X^{prior}_{i,j,g}$ and $I^{prior}_{i,j,g}$), while satisfying the conditions on total exports, total imports and national bilateral trade.

The objective function we minimize, Z, is the sum between the errors (absolute value of relative error) with respect to the two priors $X^{prior}_{i,j,g}$ and $I^{prior}_{i,j,g}$. This can be described in mathematics as follows:

$$\min Z = \sum_{i,j,g} \left(\frac{|X^{prior}_{i,j,g} - T_{i,j,g}| + |I^{prior}_{j,i,g} - T_{i,j,g}|}{X^{prior}_{i,j,g} + I^{prior}_{j,i,g}} \right)$$

s.t.

$$\begin{aligned} &1) \quad X^{total}_{i,g} = \sum_{j} T_{i,j,g} \\ &2) \quad I^{total}_{j,g} = \sum_{i} T_{i,j,g} \\ &3) \quad T^{country}_{o,d,g} = \sum_{i \in o} \sum_{j \in d} T_{i,j,g} \end{aligned} \tag{A.57}$$

We observe that, since all product categories are independent of each other, one can achieve the same results by solving the minimization in (A.57) for every product separately.

A.4 UPDATE OF TRADE FLOWS TO 2010

The update of the data from 2000 to 2010 is based on the extrapolation of the dataset for 2000. We use constrained non-linear optimization to update the data. The objective function in the non-linear optimization minimizes a quadratic error. This error is defined as the distance between the structure of the new matrix in relation to the structure of the matrix of the previous year. The quadratic distance between predicted and new national trade data, final demand, investment demand and supply and use tables are additional elements that are minimized in the objective function. Total national value-added is consistent with the regional and national accounts because the optimization is constrained by the regional accounts on gross value-added. New information was not always available for all years. A constraint or an element in the objective function was skipped when no information was available for a specific year. The updating methodology resulted in a panel of trade data that is consistent with the national account statistics for the period 2000 to 2010.

The updating procedure is applied in two steps. A first step determines regional intranational trade within the country and international trade between regions and other countries. In a second step the international trade between regions and European countries is subdivided into multi-regional international trade. In the next subsection we present the first updating step where intraregional and multi-country trade is extrapolated. In the subsequent subsection we continue with step 2 and present the methodology to determine the full multiregional trade table. We discuss the used data sources in the separate subsection A.4.3.

A.4.1 Intranational Regional and International Country Trade

In this first updating step we determine the intranational regional trade between regions of the same country and the international trade of these regions with countries in the rest of the world using constraint non-linear optimization. The non-linear minimization function gives us the most likely trade matrix given the information available. We will first discuss the non-linear optimization function and subsequently turn to the constraints that describe additional information and consistency rules.

The quadratic objective function (A.58) that is minimized in our non-linear optimization problem is central in the updating procedure. It describes how new information is used to update matrices given the growth in production and demand that is given in the national and regional accounts. In general we minimize the change in the structure of the demand, supply and regional trade pattern given new information on, for instance, regional production and international trade. The complete minimization problem can be described as follows:

$$
\begin{aligned}
Min\, Z = {} & s_m \sum_c [(\hat{a}_t^c - a_{t-1}^c)^2 + (\hat{a}_t^c - a_{t-1}^r)^2] \\
& + s_c \sum_c [(\hat{f} - f)^2 + (\hat{u} - u)^2 + (\hat{m} - m)^2 + (\hat{t}_c - t_c)^2] \\
& + s_r \sum_r [(\hat{q} - q)^2 + (\hat{e}_r - e_r)^2 + (\hat{i}_r - i_r)^2 + (\hat{d}_r - d_r)^2] \\
& + s_l \sum_r [(\hat{v} - v)^2] \\
& s.t. \quad Constraints
\end{aligned} \tag{A.58}
$$

where a_t^c is the shares in production and trade in period t determined as the value divided by total demand, a_t^r is the shares in production and trade in period t determined as the value divided by total supply. These two variables represent the structure of the matrix because they are presented in shares of the totals. The vectors of national final demand (household consumption, government consumption and investment) are represented by f. National use and supply tables are represented by u and m, respectively. The other parameters in the equation are: country's trade pattern of good or service is given by t_c, regional household income divided by national household income q, the share of goods that are produced and consumed in the same region d_r, the change in inventories v, and the share of good or service in the region's exports or imports by e_r and i_r, respectively. The indices for goods and services are left out of the equation to keep the equation lucid. In the objective function the variable Z is minimized. In this way the quadratic error between the estimated and the old structure of the matrix and the error between estimated and observed additional information is minimized. The circumflex accent on a variable represents its estimated value.

All variables are rescaled with factors s_m, s_c or s_r such that all deviations are with respect to an expected value of 1 and the weight for country information is comparable to the weight for region information. Thus, s_m has a value of 65 because a row or column of the SAM matrix has on average 65 non-zero elements and the expected value for a^c is therefore equal to 0.01538 (1 divided by 65). The country scaling factor s_c gets a value of 30 to correct for the multiple regions that are available in every country and the higher reliability of country information if compared to region information. This scaling of the elements in the objective function is important because it makes the quadratic errors for the different variables comparable. Inventory changes are weighted with a large scaling factor s_I.[7] We have no information on inventories except that they are on average equal to zero over a long time period. It is therefore the most logical approach to minimize the inventory changes and keep them close to zero.

Table A.7 provides a summary of the variables included in the objective function. The system is constrained to generate outcomes conforming with the regional and national accounts and to use additional information. This additional information is partly derived from economic theory. The most common additional information derived from theory is the non-negativity of trade flows. The limitation to only have positive trade values guarantees that all goods have a positive price and are therefore valued with a positive

Table A.7 Variables in the objective function

$\tau_{i,j}^{ex}$	The prior for the export from region *i* to region *j*.
$\tau_{i,j}^{im}$	The prior for the import in region *j* from region *i*.
$Ex_{i,c}$	The exports of region *i* destined for country *c*. Result of the first step, exogenous in the second step of the updating procedure.
$Im_{j,c}$	The imports in region *j* coming from country *c*. Result of the first step, exogenous in the second step of the updating procedure.
Z, Z'	Objective variables
RE	Quadratic relative error
AE	Quadratic absolute error

number in the SAM. We discuss below all used constraints with respect to the information they contain.

1. We know that all products sold by an economic agent are received and paid for by another economic agent.
2. We have information on the regional value-added for the NACE main categories[8] and national value added for all NACE categories. The second and third constraints therefore enforce the consistency of the tables with the national and regional accounts. Labour and capital income is required to sum over the 59 NACE subcategories to the regional value-added in the regional accounts.[9] The sum of capital and labour income over the regions in a country is enforced to be equal to their respective national account totals.
3. Finally, there is a no re-export constraint that guarantees that the production always exceeds the exports for every region and product.

The combination of these constraints with the objective function gives the update of the regional trade tables over a period of 10 years with intranational trade between regions and international trade to the European countries and groups of countries in the rest of the world.

A.4.2 International Regional Trade

The international trade flows have to subdivide over regions of destination and regions of origin to get a full regional origin–destination matrix. We have no additional information on these trade patterns except the new regional supply to countries and the regional demand by country. We use constrained non-linear optimization to combine this information with the existing trade pattern to determine the final panel trade data between NUTS-2 regions for the period 2000–10. We propose a mixed objective function where a quadratic absolute and a quadratic relative error are minimized simultaneously. We also take two priors into account. One prior is the estimate of trade from the export perspective while the other estimate is from the import perspective. This gives the following objective function:

$$Min\, Z' = RE + AE$$

$$s.t.$$

$$RE = \sum_{i,j} \frac{1}{\tau_{i,j}^{ex}} (\hat{\tau}_{i,j}^{ex} - \tau_{i,j}^{ex})^2 + \sum_{i,j} \frac{1}{\tau_{i,j}^{im}} (\hat{\tau}_{i,j}^{im} - \tau_{i,j}^{im})^2$$

$$AE = \sum_{i,j} \frac{1}{\overline{\tau}_i^{ex}} (\hat{\tau}_{i,j}^{ex} - \tau_{i,j}^{ex})^2 + \sum_{i,j} \frac{1}{\overline{\tau}_j^{im}} (\hat{\tau}_{i,j}^{im} - \tau_{i,j}^{im})^2$$

$$Ex_{i,c} = \sum_{j \in c} \hat{\tau}_{i,j}^{ex}$$

$$Im_{j,c} = \sum_{i \in c} \hat{\tau}_{i,j}^{ex} \tag{A.59}$$

where Z' is the objective function variable, RE and AE are the relative and absolute errors, $\tau_{i,j}^{ex}$ and $\tau_{i,j}^{im}$ are priors for the export from region i to region j and for the import in region j from region i, respectively.

The exports of region i destined for country c is given by $Ex_{i,c}$, while the imports in region j coming from country c is given by $Im_{j,c}$. The line over a variable represents its average value.

The priors of exports (imports) are determined by the regional trade pattern of exports (imports) from the previous year proportionally increased to the level determined in the first step of the updating procedure. Please note that we define the quadratic relative error slightly differently than with percentages.[10] The reason is related to the weight of both errors in the objective function. In the above specification both weights are exactly the same because the sum over all regions of trade $\tau_{i,j}^{ex}$ is equal to the sum over all regions of the average value of the trade $\overline{\tau}_i^{ex}$.

A.4.3 The Data Sources

The data needed for the update is collected from Eurostat and several individual bureaux of statistics. Thus, all data is obtained from public sources. Data on national GDP, gross value-added in 33 branches, final demand, investment demand, total country trade, services and goods trade were all for the period 2000–10.[11] The national accounts supply and use tables were obtained from Eurostat, while the import tables were obtained from the different bureaux of statistics. For all countries tables were available for different years with the latest available year being 2007. The regional gross value-added and the compensation for employees at NUTS-2 level for NACE main categories was obtained from Eurostat for the period 2000–2008. We have corrected the national exports and imports for the re-exports using the information from the import tables. We did not have import tables for all countries and for all years. We therefore estimated the re-exports for those countries where more than one table was available by use of a simple OLS regression. With respect to those countries where no import tables

Table A.8 Data used in updating the bilateral trade for the period 2000–10

Data on	Time-period	Data source	Version date	Extraction date	Source
National GDP	2000–2010	GDP and main components: current prices	14-7-11	15-7-11	Eurostat
Gross value-added in 33 branches	2000–2010	National accounts by 60 branches: aggregates at current prices	14-7-11	15-7-11	Eurostat
Final demand	2000–2010	Final consumption aggregates: current prices	14-7-11	21-7-11	Eurostat
Investment demand	2000–2010	Gross fixed capital formation by 6 asset types: current prices	14-7-11	21-7-11	Eurostat
Total country trade	2000–2010	Exports and imports by Member States of the EU/third countries: current prices	16-7-11	17-7-11	Eurostat
Services trade A	2000–2003	International trade in services (from 1985 to 2003)	30-6-11	9-7-11	Eurostat
Services trade B	2004–2010	International trade in services (since 2004)	17-5-11	11-7-11	Eurostat
Goods trade	2000-2010	EU27 trade since 1988 by HS2–HS4	n.a.	17-7-11	Eurostat
Goods trade Norway	2000-2010	Norway trade by HS1988	n.a.	20-7-11	Statistics Norway
National accounts, supply and use tables	2000–2007 if available	National accounts, supply and use tables	various	23-9-10	Eurostat
National accounts, import tables	2000–2007 if available	National accounts, import tables	various	September 2010	Various bureaux of statistics
Regional GVA, NUTS-2, NACE main industries	2000–2008	Gross value added at basic prices at NUTS level 3	30-6-11	8-7-11	Eurostat
Wage sum, NUTS-2, NACE main industries	2000–2008	Compensation of employees at NUTS level 2	7-7-11	8-7-11	Eurostat

were available we used the minimum of the re-export figures from the other countries.

The estimated trade data for 2000 differs slightly in the panel dataset 2000–10 if compared to the base year 2000 dataset. The reason is the change in data sources and the construction of a completely consistent dataset. Thus, contrary to the 2000 tables, the panel regional trade data are no longer dependent on the Cambridge Econometrics (2008) dataset and the Feenstra et al. (2005) trade data. A complete list of the data used is presented in Table A.8.

A.5 DISCUSSION

The trade data presented represent the most likely trade between European NUTS-2 regions given all the information available to us. This information not only comes from all the data sources used, but also from simple economic consistency and bookkeeping rules applied in the methodology. The most simple economic consistency rule was that if a product is exported to a region it should also be used in that region, and the export to a country coincides with the imports from that country. Consistency and bookkeeping improved the quality of the data, but one has to keep in mind that the presented trade data are inferred from other data sources. The data is not measured as a flow from one region to the other region. Small errors on the trade flows between regions will therefore remain at the CPA 2-digit product level. The data should therefore preferably be used as network data without putting too much focus on every single individual trade flow.

NOTES

1. http://ec.europa.eu/eurostat/ramon/.
2. This happens automatically due to the way use and supply tables are built. In fact, as can be seen from the equation (A.22), Y = Supply − I and D = Use − X. In combination with equation (A.24), we have that OY = Supply − I − X and OD = Use − X − I. Since Supply = Use, it is verified that $OY = OD$. The corrections we applied in the previous paragraph (on negative changes in inventories, negative trade and transport margins and subsidies) do not interfere with this line of reasoning.
3. See Kronenberg (2009) for a discussion of different approaches.
4. This is known in the literature as the common assumption of mill pricing.
5. The explicit functional form is:

$$IX_r = \frac{-(IZ_r t_{rr} t_{hh} + ID_h t_{rh}^2 - IZ_r t_{rh}^2 + ID_r t_{rh}^2) + \sqrt{\begin{array}{l}[IZ_r t_{rr} t_{hh} + ID_h t_{rh}^2 - IZ_r t_{rh}^2 + ID_r t_{rh}^2]^2 + \\ -4[t_{rr} t_{hh} - t_{rh}^2][ID_h IZ_r t_{rh}^2 - ID_h ID_r t_{rh}^2]\end{array}}}{2(t_{rr} t_{hh} - t_{rh}^2)} \equiv I_h$$

where $t_{ij} = T_{ij}^{1-\sigma}$. Refer to Diodato and Thissen (2011) for more details.

6. In fact, the following equivalence must hold: the sum of exports from all regions *i* belonging to country *o*, to all regions *j* belonging to country *d* needs to be equal to exports occurring between country *o* and country *d*.
7. This weight has been set to 625. Increasing the weight any further does not affect the outcome of the extrapolation.
8. These NACE main categories are A–B Agriculture and fishing; C–E Industry (except construction); F Construction; G–I Wholesale and retail trade; hotels and restaurants; transport; J–K Financial intermediation; real estate; and L–P public administration and community services; activities of households.
9. Please note that within every country one region and sector combination can be skipped from the constraints because it is automatically satisfied by the constraint that all value-added adds up to the national totals.
10. A relative error based on percentage would have been as follows:

$$RE = \sum_{i,j}\left(\frac{1}{\tau_{i,j}^{ex}}\right)^2(\hat{\tau}_{i,j}^{ex} - \tau_{i,j}^{ex})^2 + \sum_{i,j}\left(\frac{1}{\tau_{i,j}^{im}}\right)^2(\hat{\tau}_{i,j}^{im} - \tau_{i,j}^{im})^2$$

11. They were obtained from the following Eurostat statistics: GDP and main components – current prices; national accounts by 60 branches – aggregates at current prices; final consumption aggregates – current prices; gross fixed capital formation by 6 asset types – current prices; exports and imports by member states of the EU/third countries – current prices; international trade in services (from 1985 to 2003), international trade in services (since 2004), EU27 trade since 1988 by HS2–HS4. Norway trade by HS1988 was obtained from Statistics Norway.

Bibliography

Acs, Z.J. (2002), *Innovation and the Growth of Cities*, Cheltenham, UK and Northampton, MA, USA: Edward Elgar Publishing.

Almeida, P. and B. Kogut (1999), 'Localization of knowledge and the mobility of engineers in regional networks', *Management Science*, **45**, 905–17.

Alonso, W. (1973), 'Urban zero population growth', *Daedalus*, **102**(4), 191–206.

Anderson, J.E. and E. van Wincoop (2004), 'Trade costs', *Journal of Economic Literature*, **43**(3), 691–751.

Annoni, P. and K. Kozovska (2010), *EU Regional Competitiveness Index 2010*, Ispra: European Commission.

Ark, B. van, M. O'Mahony and M.P. Timmer (2008), 'The productivity gap between Europe and the United States: trends and causes', *Journal of Economic Perspectives*, **22**, 25–44.

Asheim, B., P. Cooke and R. Martin (eds) (2006), *Clusters and Regional Development: Critical Reflections and Explorations*, London: Routledge.

Atzema, O.A.L.C. (2007), 'Philips: a global electronics firm restructuring its home base', in P.H. Pellenbarg and E. Wever (eds), *International Business Geography: Case Studies of Corporate Firms*, London: Routledge, pp. 186–215.

Balassa, B. (1965), 'Trade liberalization and "revealed" comparative advantage', *The Manchester School of Economic and Social Studies*, **33**, 92–123.

Baldwin, R. and C. Wyplosz (2009), *The Economics of European Integration*, London: McGraw-Hill.

Baldwin, R., R. Forslid, P. Martin, G. Ottaviano and F. Robert-Nicoud (2003), *Economic Geography and Public Policy*, Princeton and Oxford: Princeton University Press.

Barca, F. (2009), 'An agenda for a reformed cohesion policy: a place-based approach to meeting European Union challenges and expectations', independent report prepared at the request of Danuta Hubner, Commissioner for Regional Policy.

Barca, F., P. McCann and A. Rodriguez-Pose (2012), 'The case for regional development intervention: place-based versus place-neutral approaches', *Journal of Regional Science*, **52**(1), 134–52.

Barry, F. (2004), 'Export-platform foreign direct investment: the Irish experience', *EIB Papers*, **9**(2), pp. 8–37, available at http://hdl.handle.net/10419/44837.

Bartik, T.J. (2005), 'Solving the problems of economic development incentives', *Growth & Change*, **36**, 139–66.

Basile, R., D. Castellani and A. Zanfei (2008), 'Location choices of multinational firms in Europe: the role of EU cohesion policy', *Journal of International Economics*, **74**, 238–340.

Basile, R., R. Capello and A. Caragliu (2012), 'Technological interdependence and regional growth in Europe: proximity and synergy in knowledge spillovers', *Papers in Regional Science*, **91**, 697–722.

Begg, I. (1999), 'Cities and competitiveness', *Urban Studies*, **36**, 795–810.

Bijleveld, P. and C. Geerdink (2010), 'Twente index 2010: een vergelijkend economisch jaarbeeld van Twente', Stichting Twente Index [in Dutch].

Blázquez-Lidoy, J., J. Rodriquez and Javier Santiso (2006), 'Angel or devil? China's trade impact on Latin American emerging markets', *OECD Working Paper*, no. 252, Paris: OECD.

Bloom, N., R. Sadun and J. van Reenen (2005a), 'It ain't what you do, it's the way that you do I.T.: testing explanations of productivity growth using US affiliates', Centre for Economic Performance, London School of Economics, mimeo.

Bloom, N., S. Dorgan, J. Dowdy, J. van Reenen and T. Rippin (2005b), 'Management practices across firms and nations', Centre for Economic Performance, London School of Economics, mimeo.

Bontje, M., S. Musterd and P. Pelzer (2011), *Inventive City-Regions: Path Dependence and Creative Knowledge Strategies*, Aldershot: Ashgate.

Borras, S. and D. Tsagdis (2008), *Cluster Policies in Europe: Firms, Institutions and Governance*, Cheltenham, UK and Northampton, MA, USA: Edward Elgar Publishing.

Boschma, R.A. (2005), 'Proximity and innovation: a critical assessment', *Regional Studies*, **39**, 61–74.

Boschma, R.A. and K. Frenken (2003), 'Evolutionary economics and industry location', *Review for Regional Research*, **23**, 183–200.

Boschma, R.A. and K. Frenken (2011), 'Technological relatedness and regional branching', in H. Bathelt, M.P. Feldman and D.F. Kogler (eds), *Dynamic Geographies of Knowledge Creation and Innovation*, London: Taylor and Francis, Routledge.

Boschma, R.A. and S. Iammarino (2009), 'Related variety, trade linkages and regional growth', *Economic Geography*, **85**(3), 289–311.

Boschma, R.A., A. Minondo and M. Navarro (2012), 'Related variety and regional growth in Spain', *Papers in Regional Science*, **91**(2), 241–56.

Bouwmeester, M.C. and J. Oosterhaven (2009), 'Methodology for the construction of an international supply-use table', working paper, University of Groningen.

Brakman, S., H. Garretsen and C. van Marrewijk (2009), *The New Introduction to Geographical Economics*, Cambridge: Cambridge University Press, revised edn of *An Introduction to Geographical Economics* (2001), Cambridge: Cambridge University Press.

Brenner, T. (2004), *Local Industrial Clusters: Existence, Emergence and Evolution*, London and New York: Routledge.

Breschi, S. and F. Lissoni (2009), 'Mobility of skilled workers and co-invention networks: an anatomy of localized knowledge flows', *Journal of Economic Geography*, **9**(4), 439–68.

Bristow, G. (2005), 'Everyone's a "winner": problematising the discourse of regional competitiveness', *Journal of Economic Geography*, **5**, 285–304.

Bristow, G. (2010a), 'Resilient regions: re-'place'ing regional competitiveness', *Cambridge Journal of Regions, Economy and Society*, **3**, 153–67.

Bristow, G. (2010b), *Critical Reflections in Regional Competitiveness: Theory, Policy, Practice*, London: Routledge.

Bröcker, J. (1998), 'Operational spatial computable general equilibrium modelling', *Annals of Regional Science*, **32**, 367–87.

Bröcker, J. and N. Schneekloth (2006), 'European transport policy and cohesion: an assessment by CGE analysis', *Italian Journal of Regional Science* (*Scienze Regionali*), **5**, 47–70.

Bröcker, J., A. Korzhenevych and C. Schürmann (2009), 'Assessing spatial equity and efficiency impacts of transport infrastructure projects', *Transportation Research B*, **44**, 795–811.

Bröcker, J., R. Meyer, N. Schneekloth, C. Schürmann, K. Spiekermann and M. Wegener (2004), 'Modelling the socio-economic and spatial impacts of EU transport policy', IASON (Integrated Appraisal of Spatial economic and Network effects of transport investments and policies), deliverable 6, funded by the 5th Framework RTD Programme, Kiel/Dortmund: Christian-Albrechts-Universität Kiel/Institut für Raumplaning, Universität Dortmund.

Brülhart, M. and N.A. Mathys (2008), 'Sectoral agglomeration economies in a panel of European regions', *Regional Science and Urban Economics*, **38**, 1045–68.

Brülhart, M. and R. Traeger (2005), 'An account of geographic concentration patterns in Europe', *Regional Science and Urban Economics*, **35**, 597–624.

Buckley, P.J. and F. Ruane (2006), 'Foreign direct investment in Ireland: policy implications for emerging economies', *The World Economy*, **29**, 1611–28.

Burger, M.J., G.A. Van der Knaap and R.S. Wall (2013), 'Revealed competition for greenfield investments between European regions', *Journal of Economic Geography*, **13**(4), 619–48.

Camagni, R. (2002), 'On the concept of territorial competitiveness: sound or misleading?', *Urban Studies*, **39**, 2395–411.

Cambridge Econometrics (2008), 'Regional production, investment and consumption in Europe for year 2000', data acquired in 2008.

CBS (2010), 'StatLine', The Hague: Statistics Netherlands, Centraal Bureau voor de Statistiek.

Chapelle, K., A. Markusen, G. Schrok, D. Yamamoto and P. Yu (2004), 'Gauging metropolitan "high-tech" and "i-tech" activity', *Economic Development Quarterly*, **18**, 10–29.

Cheshire, P. (1999), 'Cities in competition: articulating gains from integration', *Regional Studies*, **5**, 843–64.

Christaller, W. (1933), *Central Places in Southern Germany*, Englewood Cliffs, NJ: Prentice Hall.

Combes, P.P. and H. Overman (2004), 'The spatial distribution of economic activities in the European Union', in J.V. Henderson and J.F. Thisse (eds), *Handbook of Regional and Urban Economics: Cities and Geography*, Amsterdam: Elsevier, pp. 2845–909.

Combes, P.P., T. Mayer and J.F. Thisse (2009), *Economic Geography*, Princeton, NJ: Princeton University Press.

Commission of the European Communities, International Monetary Fund, Organisation for Economic Co-operation and Development, United Nations and World Bank (1993), 'System of National Accounts 1993', Brussels/Luxembourg, New York, Paris, Washington, DC, available at United Nations Website, http://unstats.un.org/unsd/nationalaccount/sna.asp.

Commission of the European Communities, International Monetary Fund, Organisation for Economic Co-operation and Development, United Nations and World Bank (2008), 'System of National Accounts, 2008', Brussels/Luxembourg, New York, Paris, Washington, DC, available at United Nations Website, http://unstats.un.org/unsd/nationalaccount/sna.asp.

Cortright, J. and H. Mayer (2004), 'Increasingly rank: the use and misuse of rankings in economic development', *Economic Development Quarterly*, **18**, p. 34–9.

Crescenzi, R. and A. Rodríguez-Pose (2012), 'An "integrated" framework for the comparative analysis of the territorial innovation dynamics of developed and emerging countries', *Journal of Economic Surveys*, **26**(3), 517–33.

Crespi, G., C. Criscuolo and J. Haskel (2007), 'Information technology, organizational change and productivity', *CEPR Discussion Paper*, no. 6105.

David, P., D. Foray and B. Hall (2009), 'Measuring smart specialisation: the concept and the need for indicators', Knowledge for Growth Expert Group, available at http://cemi.epfl.ch/files/content/sites/cemi/files/users/178044/public/Measuring%20smart%20specialisation.doc.

De la Dehesa, G. (2006), *Europe at the Crossroads: Will the EU Ever be Able to Compete with the United States as an Economic Power?*, New York: McGraw-Hill.

Delgado, M., M.E. Porter and S. Stern (2010), 'Clusters and entrepreneurship', *Journal of Economic Geography*, **10**, 495–518.

Derudder, B. and F. Witlox (2005), 'An appraisal of the use of airline data in assessing the world city network: a research note on data', *Urban Studies*, **42**(13), 2371–88.

Diodato, D. and M. Thissen (2011), 'Towards a new economic geography based estimate of trade elasticity and transport costs', Working Paper.

Diodato, D. and A. Weterings (2012), 'The resilience of Dutch regions to economic shocks: measuring the relevance of interactions among firms and workers', Papers in Evolutionary Economic Geography, Utrecht University.

Dixit, A.K. and J.E. Stiglitz (1977), 'Monopolistic competition and optimum product diversity', *The American Economic Review*, **67**, 297–308.

Dogaru, T., F. van Oort and M. Thissen (2011), 'Agglomeration economies in European regions: perspectives for objective-1 regions', *Tijdschrift voor Economische and Sociale Geografie*, **102**, 486–94.

Draca, M., R. Sadun and J. van Reenen (2006), 'Productivity and ICTs: a review of the evidence', in R. Mansell, C. Avgerou, D. Quah and R. Silverstone (eds), *The Oxford Handbook of Information and Communication Technologies*, Oxford: Oxford University Press.

Duboz, M.L. and J. Le Gallo (2011), 'Are EU15 and CEEC agricultural exports in competition? Evidence for 1995–2005', *Economic Bulletin*, **31**, 146–54.

Dühr, S., C. Colomb and V. Nadin (2010), *European Spatial Planning and Territorial Cooperation*, London: Routledge.

Dumais, G., G. Ellison and E.L. Glaeser (2002), 'Geographic concentration as a dynamic process', *The Review of Economics and Statistics*, **84**, 193–204.

Duranton, G. and H.G. Overman (2005), 'Testing for location using microgeographic data', *Review of Economic Studies*, **72**, 1077–106.

Duranton, G. and D. Puga (2005), 'From sectoral to functional urban specialization', *Journal of Urban Economics*, **57**(2), 343–70.

Ellison, G. and E.L. Glaeser (1997), 'Geographic concentration in US manufacturing industries: a dartboard approach', *Journal of Political Economy*, **105**(5), 889–927.

Erken, H., and F. van Es (2007), 'Disentangling the R&D shortfall of the EU vis-à-vis the US', *Jena Economic Research Papers*, 2007107.

European Commission (2004), 'A new partnership for cohesion convergence competitiveness cooperation', Third report on economic and social cohesion, Luxembourg: Office for Official Publications of the European Communities.

European Commission (2010), *Investing in Europe: Fifth Cohesion Report on Economic, Social and Territorial Cohesion*, Brussels: European Commission.

Eurostat (2008), 'Eurostat manual of supply, use and input–output tables', Eurostat Methodologies and Working Papers, Luxembourg: office for Official Publications of the European Communities.

Eurostat (2009a), 'International trade in services', data for years from 2000 to 2004, available at Eurostat website, downloaded in 2009.

Eurostat (2009b), 'National use and supply tables', data from year 2000 for Austria, Belgium, Czech Republic, Germany, Denmark, Estonia, Spain, Finland, France, Hungary, Ireland, Italy, Lithuania, Luxemburg, Malta, the Netherlands, Norway, Poland, Portugal, Sweden, Slovenia, Slovakia, United Kingdom; data from year 1998 for Greece and Latvia, available at Eurostat website, downloaded in 2009.

Eurostat (2009c), 'High-technology and knowledge based services aggregations based on NACE Rev. 2', available at http://epp.eurostat.ec.europa.eu/cache/ITY_SDDS/Annexes/htec_esms_an3.pdf.

Farole,T., A. Rodriguez-Pose and M. Storper (2009), 'Cohesion policy in the European Union: growth, geography, institutions', London: London School of Economics.

Faulconbridge, J., E. Engelen, M. Hoyler and J. Beaverstock (2007), 'Analysing the changing landscape of European financial centres: the role of financial products and the case of Amsterdam', *Growth and Change*, **38**, 279–303.

Feenstra, R.C., R.E. Lipsey, H. Deng, A.C. Ma and H. Mo (2005), 'World Trade Flows: 1962–2000', Cambridge, MA: National Bureau of Economic Research.

Finger, J.M. and E. Kreinin (1979), 'A measure of export similarity and its possible uses', *The Economic Journal*, **78**, 905–12.

Florida, R. (2002), *The Rise of the Creative Class*, New York: Basic Books.

Florida, R. (2008), *Who's your City?*, New York: Basic Books.

Florida, R. and G. Gates (2001), 'Technology and tolerance: the importance of diversity to high-tech growth', Washington, DC: Brookings Institution.

Foray, D., P. David and B. Hall (2009), 'Smart specialisation – the concept', *Knowledge Economists Policy Brief*, no. 9, June.

Foray, D., P. David and B. Hall (2011), 'Smart specialization: from academic idea to political instrument, the surprising career of a concept and the difficulties involved in its implementation', MTEI Working Paper, École Polytechnique Fédérale de Lausanne.

Foray, D., J. Goddard, X. Goenaga, M. Landabuso, P. McCann, K. Morgan, C. Nauwelaers and R. Ortega-Argilés (2012), 'Guide to research and innovation strategies for smart specialization (RIS3), Smart Specialization Platform', Regional Policy, European Commission, available at http://s3platform.jrc.ec.europa.eu/s3pguide.

Frenken, K. and J. Hoekman (2006), 'Convergence in an enlarged Europe: the role of network cities', *Tijdschrift voor Economische & Sociale Geografie*, **97**, 321–6.

Frenken, K. and R.A. Boschma (2007), 'A theoretical framework for evolutionary economic geography: industrial dynamics and urban growth as a branching process', *Journal of Economic Geography*, **7**(5), 635–49.

Frenken, K., F.G. van Oort and T. Verburg (2007), 'Related variety, unrelated variety and regional economic growth', *Regional Studies*, **41**, 685–97.

Fritsch, M. and. V. Slavtchev (2007), 'Universities and innovation in space', *Industry and Innovation*, **14**, 201–18.

Fujita, M. and J.-F. Thisse (2002), *Economics of Agglomeration: Cities, Industrial Location, and Regional Growth*, Cambridge: Cambridge University Press.

Fujita, M., P. Krugman and A. Venables (1999), *The Spatial Economy: Cities, Regions and International Trade*, Cambridge, MA: The MIT Press.

Gardiner, B., R. Martin and P. Tyler (2004), 'Competitiveness, productivity and economic growth across the European regions', *Regional Studies*, **38**, 1045–67.

Geerdink, C. (2010), 'Economic development: games of competition and cooperation', PhD thesis, University of Twente.

Gill, I. (2010), *Regional Development Policies: Place-based or People-centred?*, Paris: OECD Regional Development Policy Division.

Glaeser, E.L. (1999), 'Learning in cities', *Journal of Urban Economics*, **46**, 254–77.

Glaeser, E.L. (2001), 'The economics of location-based tax incentives', *Harvard Institute of Economic Research Discussion Paper*, no. 1932.

Glaeser, E.L. (2008), *Cities, Agglomeration and Spatial Equilibrium*, Oxford: Oxford University Press.

Glaeser, E.L. (2011), *Triumph of the City*, London: Macmillan.

Glaeser, E.L., H.D. Kallal, J.A. Scheinkman and A. Schleifer (1992), 'Growth in cities', *Journal of Political Economy*, **100**, 1126–52.

Gomez-Salvador, R., A. Musso, M. Stocker and J. Turunen (2006), 'Labour productivity developments in the Euro Area', *European Central Bank Occasional Paper*, no. 53.

Gordon, R.J. (2004), 'Five puzzles in the behavior of productivity, investment and innovation', *NBER Working Paper*, no. 10660.

Gordon, R.J. and I. Dew-Becker (2005), 'Why did Europe's productivity catch-up sputter out? A tale of tigers and tortoises', paper presented at Federal Research Bank of San Francisco Conference 'Productivity Growth: Causes and Consequences', 18 November.

Groot, H.L.F. de, J. Poot and M. Smit (2007), 'Agglomeration, innovation and regional development: theoretical perspectives and meta-analysis', *Tinbergen Institute Discussion Paper*, no. 07-079/3.

Gu, W. and W. Wang (2004), 'Information technology and productivity growth: evidence from Canadian industries', in D. Jorgenson (ed.), *Economic Growth in Canada and the United States in the Information Age*, Industry Canada Research Monograph Series, Ottawa: Industry Canada, pp. 51–81.

Gu, W., M. Kaci, J.P. Maynard and M.A. Sillamaa (2002), 'The changing composition of the Canadian workforce and its impact on productivity growth', in J.R. Baldwin and T.M. Harchaoui (eds), *Productivity Growth in Canada*, Ottawa: Statistics Canada, pp. 69–75.

Heckscher, E. (1919), 'The effect of foreign trade on the distribution of income', *Ekonomisk Tidskrift*, 21, 497–512, trans. in *Readings in the Theory of International Trade* (1949), Philadelphia: American Economic Association.

Henderson, J.V. (2009), 'Urbanization in China: policy issues and options', China Economic Research and Advisory Programme, Brown University.

Henderson, J.V. (2010), 'Cities and development', *Journal of Regional Science*, **50**, 515–40.

Henderson, J.V., A. Kuncoro and M. Turner (1995), 'Industrial development in cities', *Journal of Political Economy*, **103**, 1067–85.

Hessels, M. (1992), 'Locational dynamics of business services: an intrametropolitan study on the Randstad Holland', Netherlands Geographical Studies, **147**, University of Utrecht.

Hoover, E.M. (1948), *The Location of Economic Activity*, New York: McGraw-Hill.

Huggins, R. (2010), 'Regional competitive intelligence: benchmarking and policy-making', *Regional Studies*, **44**, 639–58.
Huggins, R. and H. Izushi (eds) (2012), *Competition, Competitive Advantage, and Clusters: The Ideas of Michael Porter*, Oxford: Oxford University Press.
Isard, W. (1953), 'Regional commodity balances and interregional commodity flows', *American Economic Review*, **43**, 167–80.
Isard, W. (1960), *Methods of Regional Science*, Cambridge, MA: MIT Press.
Jacobs, J. (1969), *The Economy of Cities*, New York: Vintage.
Jenkins, R. (2008), 'Measuring the competitive threat from China for other southern exporters', *The World Economy*, **31**, 1351–66.
Jensen-Butler, C. (1996), 'Competition between cities: urban performance and the role of urban policy: a theoretical framework', in C. Jensen-Butler, A. Schacher and J. van Weesep (eds), *European Cities in Competition*, Aldershot: Avebury, pp. 3–42.
Jorgenson, D.W. (2001), 'Information technology and the US economy', *American Economic Review*, **90**(1), 1–32.
Jorgenson, D.W., M.S. Ho and K.J. Stiroh (2005), *Information Technology and the American Growth Resurgence*, Cambridge, MA: MIT Press.
Jorgenson, D.W., M.S. Ho and K.J. Stiroh (2008), 'A retrospective look at the US productivity growth resurgence', *Journal of Economic Perspectives*, **22**(1), 3–24.
Keeble, D. and L. Nachum (2002), 'Why do business service firms cluster? Small consultancies, clustering and decentralization in London and southern England', *Transactions of the Institute of British Geographers*, **27**(1), 67–90.
Kessel, H. van, J. van Ee, B. McCarthy and A. Middelburg (2009), 'Greenports gewogen: op zoek naar de afwegingen bij vragen naar ruimte in en nabij de greenports vanuit ondernemersperspectief', NovioConsult, Nijmegen [in Dutch].
Kitson, M., R. Martin and P. Tyler (2004), 'Regional competitiveness: an elusive yet key concept?', *Regional Studies*, **38**, 991–1000.
Klepper, S. (2007), 'Disagreements, spinoffs, and the evolution of Detroit as the capital of the US automobile industry', *Management Science*, **53**(4), 616–31.
Kronenberg, T. (2009), 'Construction of regional input–output tables using nonsurvey methods: the role of cross-hauling', *International Regional Science Review*, **32**, 40–64.
Krugman, P.R. (1991a), *Geography and Trade*, Cambridge, MA: MIT Press.

Krugman, P.R. (1991b), 'Increasing returns and economic geography', *Journal of Political Economy*, **99**, 483–99.

Krugman, P.R. (1996a), *Pop Internationalism*, Cambridge, MA: MIT Press.

Krugman, P. (1996b), 'Making sense of the competitiveness debate', *Oxford Review of Economic Policy*, **12**, 17–25.

Krugman, P.R. and M. Obstfeld (2000), *International Economics: Theory and Policy*, 5th edn, Upper Saddle River, NJ: Addison-Wesley.

Krugman, P.R. and A.J. Venables (1995), 'Globalization and the inequality of nations', *The Quarterly Journal of Economics*, **110**(4), 857–80.

Lengyel, I. (2003), 'The pyramid model: enhancing regional competitiveness in Hungary', *Acta Oeconomica*, **54**(3), 323–42.

Levelt, M. (2010), 'Global trade and the Dutch hub: understanding variegated forms of embeddedness of international trade in the Netherlands: Clothing, flowers and high-tech products', dissertation, University of Amsterdam.

Lissoni, F. (2001), 'Knowledge codification and the geography of innovation: the case of Brescia mechanical cluster', *Research Policy*, **30**(9), 1479–500.

LNV (2004), 'Het Nederlandse agrocluster in kaart', The Hague: Ministerie van Landbouw en Visserij [in Dutch].

Lovering, J. (1999), 'Theory led by policy: the inadequacies of the "New Regionalism"', *International Journal of Urban and Regional Research*, **23**, 379–96.

Lucas, R.E. (1988), 'On the mechanics of economic development', *Journal of Monetary Economics*, **22**(1), 3–42.

Lundvall, B.A. and M. Tomlinson (2002), 'International benchmarking as a policy learning tool', in M.K. Rodrigues (ed.), *The New Knowledge Economy in Europe: A Strategy for International Competitiveness and Social Cohesion*, Cheltenham, UK and Northampton, MA, USA: Edward Elgar Publishing.

Maas, J.H. (1994), *De Nederlandse Agrosector*, Assen: van Gorcum [in Dutch].

Malecki, E.J. (2002), 'Hard and soft networks for urban competitiveness', *Urban Studies*, **39**, 929–45.

Malecki, E.J. (2007), 'Cities and regions competing in the global economy: knowledge and local development policies', *Environment & Planning C*, **25**, 638–54.

Manshanden, W. (1996), 'Zakelijke diensten en regionaal-economische ontwikkeling: de economie van nabijheid', Nederlands Geographical Studies 205, Amsterdam University [in Dutch].

Markusen, A. (1994), 'Studying regions by studying firms', *Professional Geographer*, **46**, 477–90.
Marrocu, E., R. Paci and S. Usai (2012), 'Productivity growth in the old and new Europe: the role of agglomeration externalities', *Journal of Regional Science* (early view).
Marshall, A. (1890), *Principles of Economics*, New York: Prometheus Books.
Martin, R. (2005), 'A study on the factors of regional competitiveness', draft final report for The European Commission, Directorate-General Regional Policy, Cambridge: University of Cambridge.
Martin, R. (2012), 'Regional economic resilience, hysteresis and recessionary shocks', *Journal of Economic Geography*, **12**, 1–32.
Martin, R. and P. Sunley (1996), 'Paul Krugman's geographical economics and its implications for regional development theory: a critical assessment', *Economic Geography*, **72**, 259–92.
Mathieu, A. and B. van Pottelsberghe de la Potterie (2008), 'A note on the drivers of R&D intensity', *CEPR Discussion Paper*, 6684.
McCann, P. and Z.J. Acs (2011), 'Globalization: countries, cities and multinationals', *Regional Studies*, **45**, 17–32.
McCann, P. and R. Ortega-Argilés (2011), 'Smart specialisation, regional growth and applications to EU cohesion policy', available at DGRegio Website, http://ec.europa.eu/regional_policy/cooperate/regions_for_economic_change/index_en.cfm#4 and http://ipts.jrc.ec.europa.eu/docs/s3_mccann_ortega.pdf.
McCann, P. and R. Ortega-Argilés (2013), 'Smart specialisation, regional growth, and applications to EU cohesion policy', *Regional Studies*, forthcoming.
McKitrick, R. (1998), 'The econometric critique of computable general equilibrium modeling: the role of functional forms', *Economic Modelling*, **15**, 543–74.
Melo, P.C., D.J. Graham and R.B. Noland (2009), 'A meta-analysis of estimates of urban agglomeration economies', *Regional Science and Urban Economics*, **39**, 332–42.
MIDT (2010), Regional flights, business and first class, data for November 2000.
Miller, R.E. and P.D. Blair (2009), *Input–Output Analysis: Foundations and Extensions*, Cambridge: Cambridge University Press.
Ministry of Infrastructure and the Environment (2007), Interregional freight, data for years from 2000–04.
Moreno, R., R. Paci and S. Usai (2005), 'Spatial spillovers and innovation activity in European regions', *Environment & Planning A*, **37**, 1793–812.

Muller, E. and D. Doloreux (2009), 'What we should know about knowledge-intensive business services', *Technology in Society*, **31**, 64–72.
Neffke, F. and M. Henning (2012), 'Skill-relatedness and firm diversification', *Strategic Management Journal*, **34**(3), 297–316.
Neffke, F., M. Henning and R. Boschma, (2011), 'How do regions diversify over time? Industry relatedness and the development of new growth paths in regions', *Economic Geography*, **87**(3), 237–65.
Ni, P. and P.K. Kresl (2010), *The Global Urban Competitiveness Report 2010*, Cheltenham, UK and Northampton, MA, USA: Edward Elgar Publishing.
OECD (1992), *Technology and the Economy: the Key Relationships*, Paris: OECD.
OECD (2005), 'Growth in services: fostering employment, productivity and innovation', Paris: OECD.
OECD (2006), *OECD Territorial Reviews; Competitive Cities in the Global Economy*, Paris: OECD.
OECD (2009a), 'How regions grow', Paris: OECD.
OECD (2009b), *Regions Matter: Economic Recovery, Innovation and Sustainable Growth*, Paris: OECD.
OECD (2011a), *Regions and Innovation Policy*, Paris: OECD.
OECD (2011b), *OECD Regional Outlook 2011*, Paris: OECD.
OECD (2011c), *Regions at a glance 2011*, Paris: OECD.
OECD (2011d), *OECD Regional Outlook: Building Resilient Regions for Stronger Economies*, Paris: OECD.
OECD (2012a), 'Promoting growth in all regions', Paris: OECD.
OECD (2012b), *Redefining 'Urban': A New Way to Measure Metropolitan Areas*, Paris: OECD.
Ohlin, B. (1933), *Interregional and International Trade*, Cambridge, MA: Harvard University Press.
Oliner, S. and D. Sichel (2000), 'The resurgence of growth in the late 1990s: is information technology the story?', *Journal of Economic Perspectives*, **14**, 3–22.
O'Mahony, M. and B. van Ark (eds) (2003), *EU Productivity and Competitiveness: An Industry Perspective. Can Europe Resume the Catching-up Process?* Luxembourg: European Commission.
Oosterhaven, J., D. Stelder and S. Inomata (2008), 'Estimating international interindustry linkages: non-survey simulations of the Asian-Pacific Economy', *Economic Systems Research*, **20**, 395–414.
Ortega-Argilés, R. (2012), 'The transatlantic productivity gap: a survey of the main causes', *Journal of Economic Surveys*, **26**(3), 395–419.
Ottaviano, G.I.P. and J.-F. Thisse (2002), 'Integration, agglomeration and

the political economics of factor mobility', *Journal of Public Economics*, **83**, 429–56.

Peters, A. and P. Fischer (2004), 'The failures of economic development initiatives', *Journal of the American Planning Association*, **70**, 27–37.

Ponds, R., F. van Oort and K. Frenken (2010), 'Innovation, spillovers and university–industry collaboration: an extended knowledge production function approach', *Journal of Economic Geography*, **10**(2), 231–55.

Porter, M. (1990), *The Competitive Advantage of Nations*, London: Macmillan.

Porter, M. (1995), 'The competitive advantage of the inner city', *Harvard Business Review*, May–June, 55–71.

Porter, M. (1998), 'Competing across locations', in: M. Porter (ed.), *On competition*, Boston, MA: Harvard Business Review Books, pp. 309–48.

Porter, M. (2000), 'Location, competition, and economic development: local clusters in a global economy', *Economic Development Quarterly*, **14**, 15–34.

Puga, D. (1999), 'The rise and fall of regional inequalities', *European Economic Review*, **43**(2), 303–34.

Puga, D. (2002), 'European regional policies in light of recent location theories', *Journal of Economic Geography*, **2**, 373–406.

Quah, D.T. (1996), 'Empirics for economic growth and convergence', *European Economic Review*, **40**, 1353–75.

Raspe, O. and M. van den Berge (2010), *De Ruimtelijke Structuur van Clusters van Nationaal Belang*, The Hague: The PBL Netherlands Environmental Assessment Agency [in Dutch].

Raspe, O., A. Weterings and M. Thissen (2012a), *De Internationale Concurrentiepositie van de Topsectoren*, The Hague: The PBL Netherlands Environmental Assessment Agency [in Dutch].

Raspe, O., A. Weterings, M. Thissen and D. Diodato (2012b), *De Concurrentiepositie van de Topsectoren in Noord-Brabant*, The Hague: The PBL Netherlands Environmental Assessment Agency [in Dutch].

Ricardo, David (1821), *On the Principles of Political Economy and Taxation*, London: John Murray.

Rodriguez-Pose, A. (2011), 'Economists as geographers and geographers as something else: on the changing conception of distance in geography and economics', *Journal of Economic Geography*, **11**, 347–56.

Romer, P.M. (1986), 'Increasing returns and long-run growth', *Journal of Political Economy*, **94**(5), 1002–37.

Rose, R. (1993), *Lesson-drawing in Public Policy*, Chatham, NJ: Chatham House.

Rosenthal, S.S. and W.C. Strange (2004), 'Evidence on the nature and sources of agglomeration economies', in J.V. Henderson and J.F. Thisse (eds), *Handbook of Regional and Urban Economics*, Amsterdam: Elsevier, pp. 2119–71.

Rosenthal, S.S. and W.C. Strange (2008), 'The attenuation of human capital spillovers', *Journal of Urban Economics*, **64**, 373–89.

Ross, C. (2008), *Megaregions: Planning for Global Competitiveness*, Washington, DC: Island Press.

Sabel, C. (1996), 'Learning-by-monitoring: the dilemmas of regional economic policy in Europe', in OECD, *Networks of Enterprises and Local Development: Competing and Co-operating in Local Productive Systems*, Paris: OECD.

Salet, W. and S. Majoor (eds) (2005), *Amsterdam Zuidas: European Space*, Rotterdam: 010-Publishers.

Sampson, G. and R. Snape (1985), 'Identifying the issues in trade in services', *The World Economy*, **8**, 171–81.

Samuelson, P.A. (1948), 'International trade and the equalisation of factor prices', *Economic Journal*, **58**(230), 163–84.

Samuelson, P.A. (1954), 'The transfer problem and transport costs, II: analysis of effects of trade impediments', *Economic Journal*, **LXIV**, 264–89.

Sassen, S. (ed.) (2002), *Global Networks: Linked Cities*, London: Routledge.

Sassen, S. (2010), 'Global inter-city networks and commodity chains: any intersections?', *Global Networks*, **10**(1), 150–63.

Saxenian, A. (1994), *Regional Advantage: Culture and Competition in Silicon Valley and Route 128*, Cambridge, MA: Harvard University Press.

Schoenberger, E. (1998), 'Discourse and practice in human geography', *Progress in Human Geography*, **22**, 1–14.

Sheppard, E. (2000), 'Competition in space and between places', in E. Sheppard and T. Barnes (eds), *A Companion to Economic Geography*, Oxford: Blackwell.

Solow, R.M. (1956), 'A contribution to the theory of economic growth', *Quarterly Journal of Economics*, **70**, 65–94.

Spender, J.C. (1998), 'The geographies of strategic competence: borrowing from social and educational psychology to sketch an activity and knowledge-based theory', in A.D. Chandler, P. Hagstrom and O. Solvell (eds), *The Dynamic Firm: The Role of Technology, Strategy, Organization and Regions*, Oxford: Oxford University Press.

Stelder, D. (2005), 'Where do cities form? A geographical agglomeration model for Europe', *Journal of Regional Science*, **45**, 657–79.

Stiroh, K.J. (2002a), 'Information technology and the US productivity revival: what do the industry data say?', *American Economic Review*, **92**, 1559–76.

Stiroh, K.J. (2002b), 'Reassessing the role of IT in the production function: a meta-analysis', mimeo, Federal Reserve Bank of New York.
Storper, M. (1997), *The Regional World*, New York: Guilford Press.
Storper, M. and A.J. Venables (2004), 'Buzz: face-to-face contact and the urban economy', *Journal of Economic Geography*, **4**, 351–70.
Strijker, D. (2000), 'Ruimtelijke verschuivingen in de EU-landbouw 1950–1992', thesis, Rijksuniversiteit Groningen [in Dutch].
Taylor, P.J. (2004), *World City Network: A Global Urban Analysis*, London: Routledge.
Terluin, I.J. (2001), 'Rural regions in the EU: exploring differences in economic development', Netherlands Geographical Studies, 289, University of Groningen.
Thissen, M.J.P.M. (2005), 'RAEM: regional applied general equilibrium model for the Netherlands', in Frank van Oort, Mark Thissen and Leo van Wissen (eds), *A Survey of Spatial-economic Planning Models in the Netherlands: Theory, Application and Evaluation*, Rotterdam/The Hague: NAi Uitgevers/RPB, pp. 63–86.
Thissen, M. and D. Diodato (2011), 'European regional trade flows: an update for 2000–2010', The Hague: The PBL Netherlands Environmental Assessment Agency.
Thissen, M.J.P.M. and D. Diodato (2013a), 'Trade between European NUTS2 regions in 2000', working paper, The Hague: The PBL Netherlands Environmental Assessment Agency.
Thissen, M.J.P.M. and D. Diodato (2013b), 'Trade between European NUTS2 regions from 2000 to 2010: an update of trade data for 2000', working paper, The Hague: The PBL Netherlands Environmental Assessment Agency.
Thissen, M.J.P.M. and F.G. van Oort (2010), 'European place-based development policy and sustainable economic agglomeration', *Tijdschrift voor Economische en Sociale Geografie*, **101**, 473–80.
Thissen, M., H. Hilbers and P. Van de Coevering (2009), 'The difference between bi-regional and full networks when analysing agglomeration effects', *Tijdschrift voor Economische en Sociale Geografie*, **100**(2), 171–82.
Thissen, M., N. Limtanakool and H. Hilbers (2011), 'Road pricing and agglomeration economies: a new methodology to estimate indirect effects applied to the Netherlands', *The Annals of Regional Science*, **47**(3), 543–67.
Thissen, M., A. Ruijs, F.G. van Oort and D. Diodato (2011), 'De concurrentiepositie van Nederlandse regio's: regionaal-economische samenhang in Europa', The Hague: The PBL Netherlands Environmental Assessment Agency [in Dutch].

Timmer, M.P. and B. van Ark (2005), 'Does information and communication technology drive EU–US productivity growth differentials?', *Oxford Economic Papers*, **57**, 693–716.

Tracey, P. and G. Clark (2003), 'Alliances, networks and competitive strategy: rethinking clusters of innovation', *Growth and Change*, **34**, 1–16.

Vaal, A. de and J.J. Stibora (1995), *Services and Services Trade: a Theoretical Inquiry*, Rotterdam: Thesis Publishers.

Van Oort, F.G. (2004), *Urban Growth and Innovation: Analysis of Spatially Bounded Externalities in the Netherlands*, Aldershot: Ashgate.

Varga, A., D. Pontikakis and G. Chorafakis (2012), 'Metropolitan Edison and cosmopolitan Pasteur? Agglomeration and interregional research network effects on European R&D productivity', *Journal of Economic Geography*, (advance access, doi:10.1093/jeg/lbs041).

Venables, A. (1996), 'Equilibrium locations of vertically linked industries', *International Economic Review*, **37**(2): 341–59.

Venables, A.J. (2006), 'Shifts in economic geography and their causes', proceedings, Federal Reserve Bank of Kansas City, pp. 15–39.

Vinciguerra, S., K. Frenken, J. Hoekman and F. van Oort (2011), 'European infrastructure networks and regional innovation in science-based technologies', *Economics of Innovation and New Technology*, **20**, 517–37.

Von Thünen, J.H. (1842), 'Der isolierte Staat', in P. Hall (ed.), *Von Thünen's Isolated State*, (1966), London: Pergamon Press.

Von Tunzelmann, N. (2009), 'Regional capabilities', in M. Farshchi, O.E.M. Janne and P. McCann (eds), *Technological Change and Mature Industrial Regions: Firms, Knowledge, and Policy*, Cheltenham, UK and Northampton, MA, USA: Edward Elgar Publishing.

Wall, R. (2009), *Netscape: cities and global corporate networks*, dissertation, Erasmus University Rotterdam.

Weber, A. (1909), *Theory of the Location of Industries*, Chicago, IL: University of Chicago Press.

Wilson, D.J. (2009), 'IT and beyond: the contribution of heterogeneous capital to productivity', *Journal of Business and Economic Statistics*, **27**(1), 52–70.

Wood, P. (2009), 'Service competitiveness and urban innovation policies in the UK: the implications of the "London Paradox"', *Regional Studies*, **43**(8), 1047–59.

World Bank (2009), 'World development report 2009: reshaping economic geography', Washington, DC: World Bank.

Index